He has the jersey, he has the jersey

The gold button jersey, the yellow jersey

He has the jersey, the crowd cries bravo

And sings its praise

For its champion

He has the jersey, he has the jersey

The gold button jersey, the yellow jersey

He has the jersey, and is heading quickly for home

To watch his victory on television

HE HAS THE YELLOW JERSEY *Marcel Amont 1960*

Il a le maillot, il a le maillot

Le maillot bouton d'or, le maillot jaune

Il a le maillot, la foule crie bravo

Et chante sur l'air des lampions

Pour son champion

Il a le maillot, il a le maillot

Le maillot bouton d'or, le maillot jaune

Il a le maillot, vite à la maison

Pour voir son triomphe à la télévision

IL A LE MAILLOT JAUNE *Marcel Amont 1960*

THE YELLOW JERSEY

Le Maillot Jaune

THE YELLOW JERSEY

Le Maillot Jaune

PETER COSSINS

YELLOW JERSEY PRESS
LONDON

1 3 5 7 9 10 8 6 4 2

Yellow Jersey Press, an imprint of Vintage
20 Vauxhall Bridge Road
London SW1V 2SA

Yellow Jersey Press is part of the Penguin Random House group
of companies whose addresses can be found at
global.penguinrandomhouse.com.

Penguin
Random House
UK

First published by Yellow Jersey Press in 2019

www.vintage-books.co.uk

A CIP catalogue record for this book is available from the British Library

ISBN 9781787290389

Printed and bound by L.E.G.O. SpA, Italy

Penguin Random House is committed to a sustainable future for our
business, our readers and our planet. This book is made from Forest
Stewardship Council® certified paper.

MIX
Paper from
Responsible Sources
FSC   FSC® C018179

Cover photography © Seamus Masters
Yellow jersey's: Front – Antonin Magne 1934 and Geraint Thomas 2018
Back and spine – Antonin Magne 1934

YELLOW JERSEY PRESS
LONDON

'It takes me back to summer holidays when I was a kid.
Yellow is the colour of the fields blasted by the sun around
the village of Meensel-Kiezegem where our grandparents
farmed. The harvested wheat and faded hay at Hesbaye,
the scent of which I used to love to breathe in and where
I used to play for day after day with the local children.
Then, every afternoon, we would rerun the Tour de France
stage on our little bikes. Whoever finished at the front
earned the right to wear a yellow T-shirt, which would
be handed around between us. I can't remember now
whether anyone washed it in between races...
in the village I earned the nickname "Tour de France".'
EDDY MERCKX *Secrets de Maillots Jaunes*

TARNISHING THE JERSEY

BEACON AND TARGET

IN THE BEGINNING

L'Auto - 10th July 1919

1

ORIGINS OF THE YELLOW JERSEY
Le Maillot Jaune

Antonin Magne 1934

THE OLDEST YELLOW JERSEY AT THE
MUSÉE NATIONAL DU SPORT IN NICE. THE CRAB BADGE
WAS THE SYMBOL OF HIS HOME CLUB IN ARCACHON

Louis.

DUNKERQUE. — Café des Arcades, place Jean-Bart.
PARIS. — Vélodrome du Parc des Princes, à Boulogne-sur-Seine.

AUTOUR DU TOUR

Pour reconnaître le leader

Une heureuse idée de notre rédacteur en chef !
Afin de permettre aux sportsmen de reconnaître du premier coup d'œil dans le peloton des Tours de France le leader de notre grande randonnée, notre rédacteur en chef, Henri Desgrange, vient de décider qu'à l'avenir le routier figurant à la première place du classement général sera porteur d'un maillot spécial.

Ce maillot est aujourd'hui commandé. Il est probable que dès Marseille le leader du Tour en sera détenteur.

Une réclamation

Une réclamation nous est parvenue hier contre un coureur du Tour de France qui, affirme-t-on, aurait emprunté le chemin de fer dans l'étape Le Havre-Cherbourg.

Comme il n'entre pas dans les habitudes de nos commissaires du Tour de France de sabrer d'office un coureur sur une dénonciation quelconque et sans avoir au préalable procédé à une enquête sérieuse, aucune sanction n'a encore été prise. Mais justice sera rendue, sainement, nous prions nos lecteurs de le croire !...

Pourquoi Perrin n'est pas parti

Georges Perrin n'est pas parti dans notre grande randonnée parce qu'il est malade depuis un mois. Il a, en effet, attrapé froid dans Paris-Tours.

Perrin va s'établir marchand de cycles à Saumur et, en nous annonçant son intention de se consacrer désormais au commerce, il nous certifie qu'il fera tout son possible pour encourager les jeunes régionaux. Bravo Perrin pour

TO RECOGNISE THE RACE LEADER

'A nice idea from our editor-in-chief.

In order to enable sportsmen to recognise the leader of our great trek without hesitation when he's within the Tour de France peloton, our editor-in-chief, Henri Desgrange, has decided that in future the rider holding first place in the general classification will wear a special jersey.

An order has been put in for this jersey today. It is probable that the Tour leader will be wearing it when the race leaves Marseille.'

L'Auto - 10th July 1919

A great idea from our editor-in-chief!

This first mention of a distinctive jersey for the leader of the world's greatest race appeared in the 10 July 1919 edition of *L'Auto*, the Tour de France's organising newspaper.

Heralding the imminent arrival of what is arguably sport's most iconic prize and lauding the man behind both the race and the newspaper for his latest innovation, the article evokes a sense of anticipation, of a prophetic moment, fitting with the narrative of the *maillot* *jaune* as cycling's grail.

This is a misapprehension, for this announcement appeared not on the front of the sports daily's yellow paper, but amid the news in brief on the second of the paper's four pages. It was hidden halfway down the third of six narrow columns filled with tiny and tightly packed text broken up with adverts for Hotchkiss and De Dion-Bouton automobiles, Sclaverand valves and a viciously jagged profile of the seventh stage between Luchon and Perpignan.

Given the yellow jersey's long-standing embodiment as the universally recognised emblem of the Tour de France, its positioning in between an article telling fans where to address letters to their favourites over the race's remaining stages, and news that the organisation had received an allegation that a competitor had taken a train during the stage from Le Havre

| Henri Desgrange, creator of the Tour de France

to Cherbourg, could hardly have been less auspicious. It doesn't even mention its colour.

It was a footnote in a Tour of momentous landmarks: theb first to take place following the devastation of the Great War, the first to enter the very recently re-annexed province of Alsace and, at 5,560 kilometres, the longest hitherto organised, a race that many argued should not even have started. Writing in the illustrated sports weekly *La Vie au Grand Air*, Jacques-Charles Sels was blunt in his appraisal of its prospects. 'It wasn't the best choice of time for it. There was a lack of equipment, the riders were short of training, the manufacturers were shying away from publicity because they couldn't fulfil orders, the means of transport were disorganised, the cost of living was expensive – everything, in short, seemed to be conspiring against the successful running of the Tour de France.' However, Desgrange, who had himself only recently been demobilised after volunteering for service in 1917 at the age of fifty-two, was determined that the hiatus since the 1914 edition wouldn't be extended for another year. He argued that the Tour would assist France's return to normality by providing a distraction from the many privations still affecting the population, while at the same time acting as a tribute to those

Three Tour de France winners killed in WW1
(left to right) François Faber, Octave Lapize, Lucien Petit-Breton

who had died in the conflict, including three Tour winners, François Faber, Octave Lapize and Lucien Petit-Breton. He urged the French public to come: 'more in pilgrimage than in the search for spectacle, that they come to look at those who have taken the places of the cherished souls that the Boche have snatched from our tender embrace... Certain stages, Metz–Dunkirk for instance, will be terrible calvaries to endure: this is still war and, more than ever, the riders will have to look after their equipment, equipment that is, unfortunately, very rare. In short, the task ahead is frightening.'

Initial registrations pointed towards a talented, multinational field, with strong representation from Belgium, headed by Philippe Thys, victorious at the two pre-war Tours, and Italy, who announced a strong line-up put together by sporting daily *La Gazzetta dello Sport*, supported by Bianchi and led by Costante Girardengo, winner of seven stages and the overall crown at the Giro d'Italia just three weeks before the Tour began in Paris on 29 June.

France's hopes rested on the Pélissier brothers, Françis and Henri, precocious climber Honoré Barthélémy and veterans Jean Alavoine and Eugène Christophe, best known for the legendary incident that cost him victory in the 1913 Tour when he carried his bike for ten kilometres down the Col du Tourmalet to the forge at Sainte-Marie-de-Campan, where he fixed his broken forks.

The logistical weakness of their teams undermined the French racers' prospects of competing with their foreign rivals. Supply lines had been affected by a fall in the value of the French franc, which had in turn raised the cost of importing rubber and cloth. Manufacturing had been hit by strikes called to support demands for higher wages, as well as the impact of the war, with factories damaged, destroyed or, in the case of some bicycle companies, still focused on turning out goods vital to the war effort. Inevitably, the quality as well as the quantity of what was produced were well below pre-war levels. This didn't bode well, given the extent of the deterioration of the roads during the conflict, which had been highlighted two months earlier at the Tour of the Battlefields, a seven-stage race based on the Western Front where only twenty-one of the eighty-seven starters finished.

Fearing they wouldn't be able to compete as individual entities, the manufacturers responded by pooling their resources, creating a coalition comprising almost twenty companies including most of the major French marques, notably Peugeot, Alcyon, Automoto, La Française, Hutchinson, Michelin and Wolber. Known as La Sportive, the consortium was managed by highly experienced Peugeot team boss Alphonse Baugé and quickly dubbed 'la marque grise', thanks to its light-grey jerseys with a blue horizontal band. In all, close to two-thirds of the field that began the race in Paris were wearing the consortium's colours, including the top thirteen finishers from that season's Paris–Roubaix and Paris–Brussels one-day Classics. The prospect of competing against a line-up that effectively was made up of all of the best Belgian and French riders persuaded La Gazzetta and Bianchi to withdraw their backing and only two Italians started.

La Sportive's 'essence was more commercial than sporting', according to Sels, and he was far from alone in criticising this combine of resources. Desgrange and, of course, L'Auto defended the move, indicating that they wanted to prevent a situation where companies that had the means to buy or get access to a lot of equipment could gain a significant edge over those still engulfed by post-conflict hardship. The Tour director, who consistently focused on implementing measures designed to reduce the control teams had over the race, depicted La Sportive as a means of setting rider against rider. By underpinning this with rigorous implementation of a rule prohibiting riders from offering each other any assistance, he argued that the grouping of most of the favourites under the same banner meant they were more likely to ride as individuals than as a team.

Yet, rather than the influence of La Sportive or even the appalling state of the roads, the sub-standard equipment and the riders' lack of physical condition had a far greater influence on the race. By the time the second stage finished in Cherbourg, forty-two of the sixty-seven starters had abandoned, including defending champion Thys. Many soon exhausted their bodily reserves, but most simply ran out of tubes after sustaining multiple punctures. By the time Desgrange implemented a new rule prior to the third stage allowing the occupants of official cars to carry spare tubes and hand them out to stricken riders, the journalists covering the event were already devoting a considerable amount of their editorial focus to the question of how many riders would reach Paris. At the halfway point in Luchon, where Barthélémy announced his arrival as the new king of the mountains with a supreme solo victory, a mere sixteen remained. Thanks to Baugé's pre-race stockpiling of a thousand tubes, most of the riders still racing were in La Sportive's grey colours.

Even in a peloton this small, spectators would still have found it difficult to pick out their favourites, particularly in the early hours of stages that mostly began between midnight and three in the

*Punctures were the dominant theme through the early stages of the
1919 Tour de France as riders battled on roads destroyed by the Great War*

morning. Riding at thirty kilometres per hour, wearing aviator goggles and cloth caps, the racers were quickly cloaked by dust or caked in mud. Following the trend that had started in the United States, the fashion for moustaches was also ending, so racers such as Christophe had shaved off their distinctive whiskers, in his case a bountiful handlebar moustache with carefully waxed and upturned ends that had been his pre-war trademark and had earned him the respectful nickname 'The Old Gaul'.

To help spectators pick out his riders, Baugé had assigned jerseys knitted with bands of a different colour around the elbow – sky blue for Alavoine, dark green for Christophe, violet for Lambot. Nevertheless, only the most eagle-eyed would have been able to discern them. At every start, finish and control point in between, riders and officials could hear fans puzzling over the identity of the racers. Baugé, most sources agree, reacted to this by suggesting a solution to Desgrange that led to *L'Auto's* announcement of the new jersey for the race leader on 10 July, during the rest day in Luchon.

In his captivating biography of Eugène Christophe, Le Damné de la Route, Jean-Paul Rey suggests that the seed for this article had been planted a few days earlier and recounts a discussion between Baugé, Desgrange and L'Auto's correspondent Robert Desmarets that took place in Les Sables d'Olonne prior to the start of the fifth stage, which Christophe was set to start as the new race leader. Rey describes the La Sportive team director as chiding Desgrange for the worried look on his face, instead the Tour director should be

exultant at the performance being produced by '*Le Vieux Gaulois*', rather than concerned by the introverted personality of the Tour leader and the effect his ordinariness might have on *L'Auto's* sales.

'In your position, I would make him the star,' Baugé says in Rey's account. 'In their grey jerseys that blend in with the buildings behind them, the riders are passing through towns incognito, nobody recognises anyone. I've already had epaulettes of different colours sewn into their jerseys so that they can be picked out a bit more... but that hasn't changed a thing... Listen to the people at the control points: "Who's the leader? Do you recognise that one?" They all look like each other "Cézig" [as Baugé dubbed those he was familiar with]. Why don't you get the rider leading the general classification to wear a jersey that's a different colour?'

'And where would I find this jersey?' Desgrange grumbles.

'You would have it made, of course.'

'By the time it's knitted our Tour would be a long way from Les Sables d'Olonne.'

'What does that matter? Give the riders the news at the start tonight,' Desmarets suggests to him. 'Then tell the journalists tomorrow: you know them better than me, they'll spend their time speculating and getting rumours started. That would help to ensure that everyone remains patient until the day, when it finally arrives, that you can present this jersey to the leader of your Tour de France.'

'Good heavens, perhaps it is a good idea,' says Desgrange, coming around to it. 'But what colour should this jersey be?'

'I don't know,' replies Baugé. 'I don't know anything about knitting. But, off the top of my head, if I were in your position, I would ensure that it's a big publicity coup by having a jersey that's the same colour as the paper in your newspaper.'

'Yellow? You mean to say yellow?'

'Exactly, a yellow jersey. But I don't care as long as it's not grey,' says Baugé.

It's a beautiful tale, drawn from conversations the writer had with Christophe's family and through access to the rider's racing and training diaries.

However, a note at the beginning of Rey's book states: 'Nothing has been imagined by the author. At most he has modified or in rare cases imagined some dialogue, while taking care to respect the meaning of the original remarks.' Is this one of those instances? Unfortunately, Rey is no longer with us to confirm. But even if it is an example of the tendency among French cycling journalists to be inventive when it comes to moments of historical significance and isn't entirely exact, it does tally with an account given by Christophe to cycling journalist Jock Wadley in the May 1959 edition of *Sporting Cyclist*, which confirms that it was indeed Baugé who came up with the idea.

'So soon after the war the cycle industry was not yet in action again, and the only *marque* supplying material was "La Sportive", and there

'There's yellow and there's yellow. They're yellow enough to make you want to scream. You can see them from 500 metres away; from that distance they look like sunbeams'

L'Auto

was little difference between any of the jerseys they supplied. One day... Monsieur Baugé, an official, remarked to Henri Desgrange that it was difficult enough for him to pick out the various riders, and the public must find it impossible. Couldn't the race leader wear a special jersey? Monsieur Desgrange thought it a grand idea. They decided on the spot to make it a yellow one, that being the colour of the pages of *L'Auto*... Desgrange telegraphed that night to Paris for them to be made and rushed to the race.'

While, according to Rey, Baugé may not have cared greatly about the colour of the new jersey and it is accepted that it was chosen because of the publicity boost it could give to the organising newspaper, La Sportive's manager did already have plenty of form when it came to yellow. Before taking over at Peugeot, Baugé had overseen the Labor and Alcyon teams and insisted at each of them that the jersey feature a substantial amount of yellow because it made his riders easier to pick out, noticing perhaps how clearly the soigneurs at his then rival team Peugeot stood out when they waited for their riders at race control points. Their jerseys were so bright that *L'Auto* said of them: 'There's yellow and there's yellow. They're yellow enough to make you want to scream. You can see them from 500 metres away; from that distance they look like sunbeams.'

For Christophe to reach Marseille in the lead and claim this new prize, he first needed to negotiate the many perils within the Pyrenees and the windswept roads of Roussillon and Languedoc. He achieved this by implementing a strategy that has long been associated with the yellow

jersey. 'Thinking only of the general classification, I held myself back as much as possible, riding a race focusing on consistency, and I was always among the first few finishers,' he explained in *Le Miroir des Sports*' serialisation of his life and career. His approach would certainly receive critical condemnation now for its lack of panache and would perhaps be branded 'Sky-like' by sections of the French media that have been dismissive of the British team's attitude towards the yellow jersey. However, as with Sky and most other Tour contenders, thirty-four-year-old Christophe had good reason to set aside flamboyance and entertainment for the sake of consistency. He wanted to win the overall title in Paris but knew that this was a gamble that hinged on the extent of his physical resources after participating in just a handful of races over the previous five years.

Mobilised within days of finishing eleventh overall in the 1914 Tour, Christophe raced on just half a dozen occasions over the next four-and-a-half years. A locksmith and mechanic by trade, his remarkable ability as a skilled craftsman had already been famously illustrated by his fork-fettling heroics during the 1913 Tour. The French army took note and he was assigned the rank of corporal-mechanic within the 1st Group of Chasseurs Cyclistes based at the Noisy-le-Sec fort in the eastern suburbs of Paris. Although automation had a significant impact on how the war was waged, lots of troops relied on bicycles to move around and Christophe was one of the mechanics who maintained them.

In December 1915, he was re-reassigned as a mechanic and welder, soldering aluminium parts on Peugeot-built planes, before joining the 1st Aviation Group at Dijon, where he joined a fellow soldier on evening sorties to 'chase away the blues'. During the war's final year, he slowly regained his competitive edge by sprinting for village signs, and returned to full-time training following his demobilisation in March 1919.

'I had no idea at all how good I would be after four years without any sporting activity... My first race was Paris–Roubaix on 20 April. I finished ninth, fifteen minutes behind Henri Pélissier, Thys and Barthélémy. I wasn't unhappy with this result as I had dropped riders from neutral countries who hadn't been mobilised,' he explained in *Le Miroir des Sports*. He subsequently won a tandem race at the Parc des Princes track on 27 April, finished sixth in Bordeaux–Paris, eighth in Paris–Tours, and then signed up for the Tour. 'Suspecting that my rivals would be in the same boat, I took the slightly mad decision to register to race. That's why, on the 29 June 1919, the day after the signing of the Treaty of Versailles, I lined up for the start of my eighth Tour de France, with the ambition of targeting overall victory once again.'

Second in Perpignan on the heels of Jean Alavoine, with whom he shared a room in the third-rate hotels where the race lodged the racers, he was fifth into Marseille in the lead group, once again led in by his roommate. Thirty minutes ahead of second-placed Belgian Firmin Lambot in the general classification, 'the Old Gaul', a lifelong smoker who would roll a cigarette as soon as he dismounted from his bike, should have left the port city resplendent in one of Desgrange's freshly knitted yellow jerseys, which, historian Serge Laget

suggests was most likely to have been commissioned from the former champion racer Elims Pierre, whose workshop was in the same building as *L'Auto* at 10 rue du Faubourg-Montmartre in Paris. However, these hadn't yet arrived from the capital. Just as significantly for the riders, their civvies hadn't arrived from Perpignan either and, after a bath and a massage, they had to go down to dinner that evening in dressing gowns provided by the hotel.

Christophe, who had the same burning desire to beat rivals that Bernard Hinault would later become renowned for, but with, says Rey, a 'sad, absent expression similar to that of [2011 Tour champion] Cadel Evans', raced on in La Sportive grey to Nice, where he lost four minutes to Lambot and sustained a deep cut to a knee after being knocked to the ground just beyond the finish line by a policeman attempting to control exuberant spectators. Here there was a delivery, but not of the yellow jersey. Instead, the race leader received a letter from his wife in Paris, which included the news that his son Albert had taken top prize in a beautiful baby contest.

Unable to sleep soundly due to his injury and hampered by it when back on his bike, Christophe lost another three minutes to his Belgian rival on the stage over the Allos and Bayard passes into Grenoble, but still held the overall lead. Here, finally, the yellow jersey was waiting and ready for its first presentation. On Monday 18 July, a rest day in between the Tour's two major Alpine stages, Desgrange sent *L'Auto*'s François Mercier to Christophe at the riders' hotel with a package. The journalist was always a welcome sight for the race

An August 1919 cover of La Vie au Grand Air offered the first depiction of the yellow jersey,
the illustration showing the leader riding through the recently returned province of Alsace

survivors because he updated each of them on the running total of their prize money before going on to collect snippets of gossip for his '*La Journée des Coureurs*' column that offered insight into what was going on away from the race. According to Rey, Baugé hailed Mercier's arrival by calling out, 'Gentlemen, the jam cupboard is open.'

Christophe's hands were trembling as he opened the package. 'I guessed its contents, something much more enticing than jam. I started to shake even more when I saw five jerseys knitted with pale yellow wool.'

'My dear "Old Gaul", from tomorrow you will wear one of these jerseys that Henri Desgrange will formally hand over to you at the start as you hold first place in the general classification,' Mercier tells him. 'You will have one for each day if you achieve the feat of maintaining this position to Paris, as I believe you will, and I'm not the only one, believe you me! If that's the case, you lucky devil, you won't have to do any more washing! Even better, there's one left for your lap of honour at the Parc des Princes! Assuming you don't find a way of breaking your forks between here and there.'

'Don't kid around like that, François, you don't want to jinx me!' the race leader replies, not finding Mercier's joke the least bit funny.

The official presentation of the new jersey took place in Grenoble's impressive Café de l'Ascenseur immediately prior to the early morning start of the stage to Geneva. The report of the brief ceremony that appeared in the following day's edition of *L'Auto* featured the very first mention of the '*maillot jaune*':

The phrasing of the uncredited article suggests

L'Auto's jersey goes to Christophe

This morning I handed over to the valiant Christophe a superb yellow jersey. You already know that our director has decided that the man at the top of the general classification should wear a jersey in L'Auto's colours. The battle for possession of the jersey is going to be passionate!

Alavoine and especially Lambot would really like to wear it.

Mercier or another of *L'Auto*'s special correspondents wrote the piece, but Christophe's later confirmation that he received the jersey from Desgrange confirms that this a common instance of the Tour director writing about himself in the third person. This is all the newspaper has to say about what has become an iconic moment in the race's history, but in Rey's book Christophe recalls that the Tour director, 'just handed it to me at the corner of the bar without any kind of ceremony. It was in front of that great Grenoble establishment on the corner of Cours Gambetta and Rue Béranger that the start was taking place at 1.15am with Geneva the destination.' According to cycling historian Serge Laget and other sources, Desgrange told the Frenchman:

'You're the first one to wear it. I hope you'll wear it till the end of the race.'

As the other ten riders left in the race gathered at the Café de l'Ascenseur, the new jersey inspired mirth rather than respect. 'Everyone was making fun of me,' Christophe recalled. 'Look at the beautiful canary. What's Madame Cri-Cri been up to?' they asked, alluding to the fact that cuckolded husbands were often depicted wearing yellow. 'It continued like that for a long time,' he added, acknowledging that he soon grew tired of the teasing he got from his rivals and fans at the roadside.

As a consequence of the fact that none of these original jerseys have survived into the modern era, there is something of a conundrum surrounding them – what shade of yellow were they? The canary reference indicates that they were bright, but in the black-and-white photographs taken of Christophe over the following days his jersey is considerably darker than the light-grey La Sportive tops worn by Lambot, Alavoine and others who are pictured with him. It has no luminous quality whatsoever. In his book *Les Grandes Premières du Tour de France*, former Tour doctor turned race historian Jean-Pierre de Mondenard refers to images that appeared in *La Vie au Grand Air* and says, 'the yellow jersey worn by Eugène Christophe, from the 11th to the 13th stages, and by Firmin Lambot, on the last two [sic], seems to suggest a "waxy yellow", rather than the clear, bright and striking shade of today.'

His evidence for this assumption is the only contemporary colour image from the 1919 Tour, an illustration produced for *La Vie au Grand Air's* cover that portrays a rider in a jersey that's dark mustard in shade and with a black hoop on each sleeve. On his heels is a large car with a French flag on its front wing carrying race officials. It's not clear whether this is a depiction of Christophe, of another rider, or, just as likely, a stylised composite by the illustrator. Yet, the dark shade of yellow used in this cover image would undoubtedly have reproduced as a very dark grey in photographs. However, any yellow will represent as dark grey in black-and-white photos because it is a colour and not on the black and white scale – unlike grey, which will be represented accurately, as it is in pictures of La Sportive's riders.

Christophe, unwittingly, contributed to this puzzle by dyeing all of his original *maillots jaunes* grey during the Second World War. During an interview with radio journalist Daniel Pautrat at the Tour's legend's home in the Paris suburb of Malakoff in the early 1960s, he said, 'I've kept one. Yes, only one, because during the war we were in pretty low spirits and, one day, I said to my wife: "We won't do anything with these jerseys any more, you should dye them." That's what she did and I used them like that, and wore them out.' The Frenchman managed to dig out the jersey in question, Pautrat describing it as, 'the first yellow jersey in history, shrunken a little, a bit moth-bitten and faded, more grey than yellow.'

Jean-Paul Rey adds another layer to this story, relating how Christophe employed his original Tour leader's jerseys as base layers when he went out riding in his post-racing days and wore them out. Discovering this, Jacques Goddet, Desgrange's successor as the race director, had

| *In 1968, Eugène Christophe models the yellow jersey he was given around 1960 to replace his worn out originals*

three replicas made for him in the 1930s, which he wore proudly when coaching cyclo-cross to youngsters. Overuse proved the undoing of these too, and he received at least two more in 1960. Embroidered with the words '1919 Tour de France' on the left breast, which certainly didn't appear on the original yellow jersey, he was buried in one of them at the Malakoff cemetery in Paris in 1970, while another that is very distinctly canary yellow was donated with his diaries and photos by his family to the Hautes-Pyrénées Departmental Archives in Tarbes.

Oddly, while Christophe's 'canary' jersey initially attracted some attention following its introduction in Grenoble, it subsequently went almost unmentioned in the press. In *L'Écho des Sports*, which branded itself as the paper that 'sees everything, knows everything, reports everything – all that the other sporting titles don't say', the report on the Geneva stage described how on the climb of the Galibier, 'Christophe, wearing for the first time the yellow jersey, the distinctive indicator of the leader of the general classification, admits at the summit that he's no longer 20 years old.' *L'Auto*, however, didn't make a single reference to it for a week, although its report on the Strasbourg to Metz stage did highlight that it was still very difficult to pick out the race leader, with Desgrange himself describing a moment when, 'we see a jersey appear that seems, from a distance, to be Christophe's. The jersey gets closer, and closer still, we can't make out its colours, but the style of the man in it seems to be more pressing and brutal than that of the old gladiator Christophe. A bend in the road, then the wearer of the jersey is finally recognisable: it's that bulldog Barthélémy, who is making a tremendous effort.' If the Tour director couldn't recognise his leader of his race, spectators can't have found it any easier either.

Other accounts of the action on that stage also reveal that there was no early blossoming of the principle that has become one of the peloton's unwritten rules in the current era: the yellow jersey shouldn't be attacked if he has stopped for a mechanical or, particularly, for a natural break. When Christophe paused to relieve himself, his rivals all deemed it a reasonable moment to accelerate. Forced to spend the next half an hour chasing after his rivals, the veteran did get back

into the group that was eventually led in for the second time in succession by the only remaining Italian rider in the race, Luigi Lucotti, who was described by the race leader as being 'as fresh as Italian ice cream'.

With two stages remaining and the most significant climbs now well behind the riders, the press were unanimous in proclaiming Christophe the victor when he finished five minutes clear of second-placed Firmin Lambot in Metz to push his overall advantage out to twenty-eight minutes. All, though, included the caveat that the stage between Metz and Dunkirk was probably the toughest on the whole route. Extending to 468 kilometres, the first half ran through the heart of the Great War battlefields, on roads devastated by bombing and heavy military traffic. The second half ran almost entirely on cobbled roads that have remained the region's primary source of renown in the cycling world. Such was the shaking that these roads would deliver that the riders joked it would be a bad idea to drink milk because it would soon turn it to butter and set in their stomachs.

In its preview, *L'Auto* disclosed that the racers had dubbed it 'the stage of hunger' due to the abysmal roads. Rather than the usual two feed stations, the organisers set up four to ensure that the eleven remaining participants could obtain the sustenance they needed in towns flattened almost to non-existence. Despite this, Lambot packed almost twice as much food as he usually carried, his supplies amounting to fifteen ham or cheese sandwiches, fifteen rice cakes and little tarts, ten bananas, a handful of figs and some bars of chocolate.

'They all fear it like the plague!' *L'Auto* revealed. 'To the point where the question has often been asked: "Which stage do you think is the hardest of the Tour de France, the one that you least like?" This elicits the following response: "Make us do the Pyrenees twice, the Alps one and a half times, or any other stage three times, but you will be doing us a service if you suppress the stage of hunger."'

Reminding readers that the late Lucien Petit-Breton had seen his Tour hopes snatched almost at the last when he crashed near Valenciennes in the 1913 race, the paper recalled the intensity of the battle around Mont Kemmel and Armentières, and declared, 'We really hope that our eleven survivors will use all this to their advantage and that nothing will happen that will mean that any one of them doesn't reach the final goal and is even deprived of the applause and huge ovation that awaits the heroes of the 1919 Tour de France at the Parc des Princes!'

Buoyed by a visit from some of his former comrades from the 4th Cycling Group on the eve of the stage, Christophe had one remaining rival: Lambot. A saddler whose whose relative lack of success, suggested one paper, was down to his love of chips and beer, the Belgian had also had to put his racing career on hold during the German occupation of Belgium, when, reported *L'Auto*, 'he had to work for the Boche for 50 pfennigs a day' in his saddlery in Antwerp. Christophe tracked the Belgian closely through the opening half of the Dunkirk stage. Then, just as he had on the road to Metz, Lambot attacked when the Frenchman paused briefly soon after the leaders had reached the cobbled roads. 'The old man's been dropped,'

he shouted, his acceleration quickly lining out the other riders behind him, before each of them dropped away from his wheel as he maintained his rapid tempo over the pavé.

Christophe soon made his way back up to the small group leading the pursuit of the lone leader across the ravaged landscape, where the only people at the roadside were German prisoners of war glumly awaiting repatriation. They were four minutes behind Lambot at the control in Valenciennes. After signing their names, refuelling and replenishing their supplies, they were soon in pursuit again when, negotiating a level crossing in the town's outskirts at Raismes, the race leader heard a crack. 'With a horrified glance [I noticed] that beneath the tape that covered and protected them, the forks were suddenly allowing the wheel to move around dangerously and to sit an abnormal distance away from the bike's headtube,' he would later describe. 'I believe I lost all reason for a time, such was the impact to my morale. My yellow jersey and first place were slipping away from me.'

Desgrange had been following the leader's group in an official car. Rey describes him shouting 'Noooonnn!' and slamming his fist on the dashboard, causing his driver to jump with alarm. A glance from the rider revealed that the repair required for his forks was more complicated than the one undertaken in 1913, when only the steerer needed to be reworked. This time both sides of the fork had broken. His angry yells attracted the attention of a small boy, who led him off the main route to a workshop that sold and repaired bikes, where the repair could be carried out. Totally meticulous in his preparation, which had included exhaustive preparation prior to the Tour for every manner of mechanical breakdown, Christophe set to work and completed the repair in an hour and ten minutes. Both the speed and correctness of his repair astonished the workshop's owner, Léonard Persiaux, who offered him a position as foreman when the Tour was over because 'being a cyclist is not a proper profession'.

It was this incident – featuring a French sporting hero halted by a repeat of a catastrophic mechanical failure when on the verge of victory and with the Tour founder and director looking on – rather than the low-key presentation in Grenoble that marked the beginning of the myth of the yellow jersey. It is, however and a little surprisingly given its eventual consequence, still overshadowed by the very similar incident on the Tourmalet in 1913.

By now, Christophe was the last rider on the road, but knew that he might have a chance to recoup some of his lost ground if he could catch up with someone ahead. Eventually, he chanced on Belgian Jacques Coomans, the pair pacing each other on the road north of Lille where the German army had launched its final offensive before opening the sluices on the network of dykes and

A depiction of Christophe's most celebrated repair at the forge in Sainte Marie de Campan in 1913

flooding the countryside, making it more forsaken than ever. As the pair raced across the ruined landscape, now being lashed by driving rain, Lambot rode into Dunkirk where an estimated 20,000 spectators saluted his victory. It had taken him twenty-one hours and four minutes to complete the stage, the longest in Tour history in terms of the winner's time.

Despite the downpour, several thousand stayed on to acclaim Christophe when he arrived with Coomans two-and-a-half hours later. The pair had taken just twenty-six minutes short of a full day to reach Dunkirk. The yellow jersey had been lost, but its first legend had been written.

ANTONIN MAGNE
TOUR DE FRANCE
1934

2 REMAKING YELLOW
Le Maillot Jaune

Lucien Aimar 1966

**'I DEDICATE THIS YELLOW JERSEY TO COLONEL CRESPIN',
SAYS LUCIEN AIMAR, PAYING TRIBUTE TO THE EX-SOLDIER WHO
HELPED TO RESTRUCTURE FRENCH SPORT IN THE 1960S**

Le Rire

LE NUMÉRO
2 Fr. 50

Numéro spécial sur le TOUR DE FRANCE

— T'as beau avoir le maillot jaune, faut pas te f'gurer que tu es le premier.

Dessin de R. GUÉRIN.

| You may have got the yellow jersey, but don't go thinking you're the first

Cycling's Holy Grail

In Eugène Christophe's still immaculate, paisley-coloured hardback racing diary, just beneath a log of the gearing he used on the 1919 Tour's penultimate stage (a 44 chainring with a 17 sprocket on one side of his rear wheel that could be flipped on hills so that he could use the 18 on the other side), his entry on the day is brief: 'Broken fork in Valenciennes.' Naturally, the press was not so succinct, least of all hyperbolist-in-chief Henri Desgrange, who anointed him 'the glorious loser'.

The Tour relishes a drama, the chance to indulge in pathos, and this is the first instance involving the yellow jersey. Desgrange's report first sets the scene for the drama that engulfed Christophe. 'The sky is sad and watery. Large grey, dirty clouds speed towards the horizon. Nature seems to be in mourning,' he begins. 'On the outskirts of Valenciennes, Christophe is standing on the pavement surrounded by five or six kids muted by the emotion that is going to embrace us all. He is pushing in front of him,

its saddle turned towards the ground, his machine with its broken fork. It is as I see it nothing less than a great lyre with broken strings evoking the final misery.'

Inevitably, Desgrange can't resist the obvious post-conflict comparison as he turns to Christophe, who is 'like a great warrior, defeated by fate, but continuing and looking straight into the eyes of Destiny that has just knocked him down and snatched everything from him after a month of effort when he was on the point of obtaining the goal, the small fortune and the pride that would have been his on being inscribed on the glorious list of Tour de France winners.'

Desgrange highlights Christophe's meticulous work in the forge, but adds that the time required there 'will put him in third place in the general classification, and the morning after tomorrow, at the moment he leaves Dunkirk for Paris, where there will be a triumphal entry onto the track, he will have to cede to another rider the yellow jersey, which has already become legendary, which marks him out as the first to receive the crowd's applause…'

removes his headgear and slowly pulls the muddy, bloodied, coal-darkened jersey over his head. There's barely a hint of yellow to be seen. He holds it out to Lambot, turns on his heel and walks out, not hearing the Belgian call after him. 'Thank you "Cri-Cri". I'll never forget…'

The setting for Robert Coquelle's version of the handover in *Les Échos des Sports* is similar, but takes place on the morning of the final stage into Paris. The article under the headline 'La Remise du Maillot', begins with an exchange between Baugé and Lambot, the former saying: 'My dear Lambot, you need to go and get Christophe's yellow jersey.'

'there hasn't been in the history of our sport a misfortune as great as that which befell Christophe today'

The mention of the yellow jersey is significant as it is the first reference to it made by the Tour boss. Surprisingly, though, there is no follow-up story on its initial handover. Rey describes Christophe going straight up to Lambot's room in Dunkirk's Hotel des Arcades, knocking on the door and finding the Belgian stretched out in his nightwear on the bed. Going in, Christophe unwinds the three tyres wrapped around his shoulders,

'I wouldn't know how best to do that,' Lambot replies. 'I haven't got the courage.'

'Ah well, old man, Christophe will bring it to you,' Baugé responds.

A couple of minutes later, the Frenchman appears with the yellow jersey and hands it over, telling Lambot, 'I hope it brings you more luck than it did me.'

Five minutes later both men were at the control

point, ready to start the final stage to Paris. In
his *Le Miroir des Sport* memoir three years later,
Christophe effectively confirmed the Coquelle
story, recalling he presented it to Lambot the next
morning.

All commentators agreed, however, that by
playing the long game in riding defensively with the
overall title his target, Christophe had taken a risk
and paid at almost the final moment. In *La Vie au
Grand Air*, Jacques-Charles Sels described Christophe as 'what one could call the race's prudent
man. Not concerning himself with winning a stage,
he based his effort on the final result that ought
to have brought him glory, honour and wealth.
Sport's ability to disappoint meant that in just a
few seconds his dream was shattered.' The loss,
the Frenchman later confessed, 'amounted to
the worst disappointment of my entire sporting
career.' To rub salt into his wounds, he punctured
early on in the final stage and spent most of the
next 300 kilometres to Paris riding on his own.

While this was undoubtedly a sporting
catastrophe for the Frenchman, the Tour and
particularly his part in it had galvanised the nation
in exactly the way that Desgrange hoped it would
when he decided to reprise it so soon after the war.
There was a huge turnout as the eleven survivors
raced into the capital. Box-office receipts at the
Parc des Princes broke all records. In Les Échos
des Sports, Coquelle estimated – perhaps over-
zealously – that 100,000 people had crammed
into the arena, and proclaimed that he hadn't
seen such a throng even in the days when African
American track sprinter Major Taylor's popularity
had been at its peak almost two decades before.
When Christophe arrived thirty-five minutes after

| *Firmin Lambot, eventual winner of the 1919 Tour de France*

Jean Alavoine had claimed his fifth stage win on the track, the crowd spilled over the barriers and mobbed him with shouts of 'Vive Christophe!' Overwhelmed, the rider sought sanctuary in the time-keeper's perch on the edge of the circuit.

The struggles endured on the roads of the Tour de France by 'Père Christophe', as the veteran racer had been described throughout the race by *L'Auto*, mirrored those of the country around which he had just completed a 5,560-kilometre lap. Most significantly, he had worn the yellow jersey through the provinces of Alsace and Lorraine, lost in the Franco–Prussian War of 1871 and restored to France by the Treaty of Versailles signed the day before the Tour had begun. This mattered enormously in a country that had spent half a century living with the trauma of this loss and the fear that it might be repeated with more territory ceded. Yet, here was confirmation that France was whole again, provided by an ex-serviceman who had relentlessly pursued his goal.

As Lambot received the victory garlands, telling Baugé at one point that he wanted to share his prize money with Christophe, the Frenchman slipped away. He had gambled with his strategy and lost the yellow jersey, but had rallied the nation. When he got to the control at Abbeville on the final stage, the last of the eleven survivors on the road, 'I was received like a god... They had made a collection for me in the town... I was so moved that my eyes filled with tears. When I arrived at the Parc des Princes, the crowd, which seemed to be waiting just for me, surged forward, knocking over the barriers... and I was carried in triumph as if I was the winner.' Inspired by his determined

performance, *Le Phare du Nord* opened a public subscription, which *L'Auto* was quick to imitate. Between them, they raised 13,300 francs (the average weekly wage was about 100 francs), twice Lambot's winnings and six times Christophe's share of the Tour prize money.

Amid the commotion of this astonishing finale, the yellow jersey was completely eclipsed. During an interview at *L'Auto*'s office in central Paris the next day, neither Lambot nor the organising newspaper made the slightest mention of it. What would now be an inconceivable lapse was reasonable given its novelty. But, allied to a comical degree of forgetfulness, it resulted in one of the oddest tales about the *maillot jaune*, a tale that suggests it dates from the pre- rather than the post-war period and that Christophe wasn't the first to wear it.

Philippe Thys, the defending champion in 1919, insisted on several occasions that he had been presented with and worn a yellow jersey during one of his two pre-war Tour victories. Interviewed in 1953 by *L'Équipe*'s Pierre Chany in *La Fabuleuse Histoire du Tour de France*, the Belgian, described by this doyen of cycling writers as still being of very sound mind, was adamant that he was the race's first yellow jersey.

In *Le Tour de France a 50 ans*, published in 1953, Thys gave Marcel Grosjean and Fernard Paisse a full description of the incident: 'One night, Desgrange dreamed of a jersey that was gold in colour and suggested that I wear it. I refused because I already felt like I was the centre of everyone's attention. He insisted, but I stood firm. He was stubborn, though, and more so than me. He came at his target via another tangent. What happened

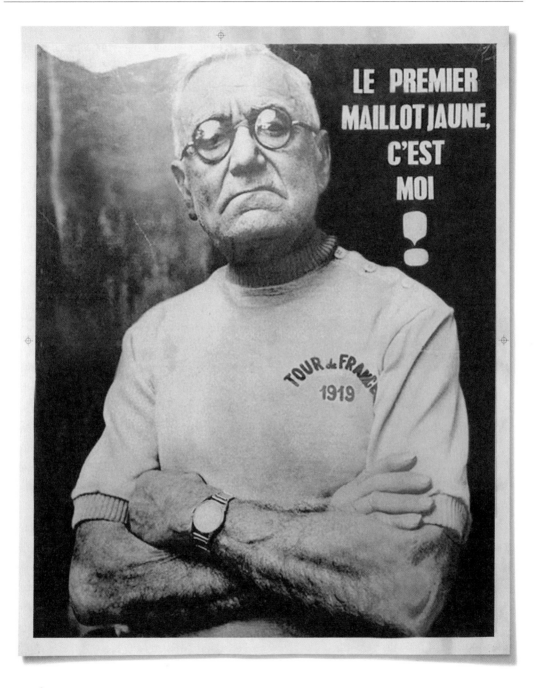

LE PREMIER
MAILLOT JAUNE,
C'EST
MOI
!

Eugène Christophe – I was the first yellow jersey!

was that a few days later, my directeur sportif at the Peugeot team, the unforgettable Alphonse Baugé, advised me to yield. Consequently, a yellow jersey was purchased in the first shop we came across. It was a bit of a tight fit, tight enough indeed to require the cutting of a bigger hole at the neck so that I could get my head through it and that's why I covered several stages with what appeared to be a woman's scoop-necked top. It didn't prevent me from winning the Tour de France.' During that

same period, Christophe added to the doubts over the jersey's origins in an interview in the pre-1951 Tour edition of *Le Miroir des Sports*, describing himself as 'one of the first to wear it' and recalling that he first pulled it on not at Grenoble but Les Sables d'Olonne, where he had first taken the lead in 1919.

It's an intriguing tale, but one typical of the mythical perspective on history often adopted by some of the Tour's most renowned writers. In short, it's hokum. These memories of a pre-war yellow jersey are simply misplaced, as Jean-Pierre de Mondenard neatly highlights. 'If the photos of his stage victory at Nice on 13 July 1920 are to be believed, it can be seen that the Belgian's Golden Fleece has been put over the top of the jersey of his La Sportive team, and that the torn neck is right open as if to accommodate a large lady's cleavage,' he says. Cycling historian Serge Laget also refutes the story, pointing out that Thys repeated it in interviews between 1948 and 1960, more than three decades after the event. Laget backs this up by highlighting how Thys got other facts completely wrong when talking about his Tour wins, confusing years and opponents.

In Thys's defence, there was good reason for him to recall receiving a yellow jersey midway through a Tour that he went on to win, as that was precisely what happened in 1920, when he became the first rider to claim the title on three occasions. *L'Auto* made no mention at all of the leader's jersey when Louis Mottiat won the opening stage, nor when Thys took it from him on the next. The two Belgians remained tied on time at the top of the general classification until the race reached the

Opposite: Phillipe Thys won the Tour in 1913, 1914 and 1920

Right: Phillipe Thys by Gonzague-Privat, '...qu'aurais-je fait... sans mon Peugeot...' ...What would I have done without my Peugeot..., 1920

Pyrenees at the end of the fifth stage, although there was still no clarification at all about which of them was in yellow. Indeed, the jersey didn't merit a single mention during the first half of the race.

It was not until the issue that appeared on the rest day in Nice, two-thirds of the way through the race, that the words *maillot jaune* appeared, specifically in Fernand Mercier's *La Journée des Coureurs* column, in which the final paragraph revealed that it had either been left behind in Paris or completely forgotten. '*L'Auto*'s yellow jersey has been solemnly presented today by Baugé to Philippe Thys, his protégé… the ceremony was infinitely touching,' it read, concluding, 'What it comes down to is that everyone will now more easily recognise Thys passing.' Just like the year before, the race leader hadn't been wearing anything that distinguished him as such until most of the route had been completed. In *Il Etait une fois le Tour de France*, Jean Roussel shed more light on the mix-up, explaining, 'That year, the organiser had forgotten to have the golden jersey made. It was only at the end of the ninth stage, from Aix-en-Provence to Nice, that the Belgian, who was the leader, finally received his yellow jersey. It had been messed around with a bit because the official jersey still hadn't been delivered. That only happened in Metz, two stages before the finish.'

As more than a week passed before *L'Auto* referred to the leader's jersey again, Thys's mistake is easier to understand. On the second page of the 25 July issue under the small headline '*Le maillot jaune*', the uncredited author – Desgrange perhaps? – wrote: 'We remind the hundreds of thousands of sports fans who will be on the route towards the

Parc tomorrow that just one rider has the yellow jersey, and that is the current leader of the Tour de France, Philippe Thys.' That's it, two mentions in a month. Rather than a grail, it was an afterthought.

Following its mid-race birth in 1919 and belated reappearance in 1920, the yellow jersey became properly established in 1921, when Léon 'The Locomotive' Scieur, who hailed from the same Walloon town of Florennes as Lambot, took the lead at the end of the second stage from compatriot Mottiat and held it right through to Paris. In *L'Auto*'s 30 June edition, Desgrange referred to it in his daily review of the action for the first time, stating that 'Scieur is going to defend *L'Auto*'s yellow jersey that he is now wearing with savage energy.'

Two days later, the race director's stage review revealed that spectators were becoming more aware of the significance of the leader's jersey. 'Scieur must have felt pretty good when he went through a level crossing on the Brittany line yesterday. The crossing attendant's young daughter was dressed up, almost certainly on purpose, in a yellow jersey of exactly the same shade as the jersey worn by the leader of the general classification,' he described, adding that Scieur had cut down the collar of the jersey given to him by the race organisation and told Desgrange that he wished he could cut down the passes in the Pyrenees and Alps just as easily.

On the next stage, the Tour director highlighted the growing impact of what had been dubbed '*le toison d'or du muscle*' – the golden fleece of strength. 'The yellow jersey that we oblige the first rider in the general classification to wear is

| *Léon Scieur, winner of the 1921 Tour*

finally looking a success. Not only are the public aware of its significance and as a result give the rider wearing it an especially warm reception, but the mechanic responsible for our Dietrich, Drouet, on seeing several young women in yellow jerseys, shouted out: "Look, there are the Scieurs!"'

The Belgian became not only the Tour leader but also 'the holder of the yellow jersey'. As the duel between the leader and fellow Belgian Hector Heusghem for the title intensified, the mythification of the *maillot jaune* developed. 'The famous yellow jersey, reserved for the rider who heads the general classification on each stage, is now being lovingly worn by Scieur. Yes indeed, he is carrying a slice of glory with him, and his eyes like those of a faithful and courageous hound seem to be lit up with the kind of joy and great sense of well-being that have hitherto been unknown to him,' reported *Le Miroir des Sports*. Recently all but forgotten, it was now famous and glorious, set not only to be coveted by every racing cyclist, but also to change the stigma long associated with yellow.

Soon after I started working as a journalist with *Cycling Weekly* in the early 1990s, the magazine received a collection of Tour de France jerseys for test and review. The King of the Mountains polka-dot version was bagged almost instantly, the green points and the white best young rider jerseys were claimed soon after. But nobody was interested in wearing the yellow. At that time, the Tour leader's jersey was quite orangey in colour and generally associated with being on the shoulders of five-time champion Miguel Indurain. It was, says Richard Virenque, who also wore it during that period, 'très flashy', the colour almost unmissable in its brightness and hue. It would, I thought, be the perfect replacement for the day-glo yellow, non-brand jacket that I used when cycling to and from work.

I had just arrived at the office one morning resplendent in the jersey when a voice bellowed out, 'You can't wear that, Cossins. You haven't won the Tour de France.' Initially, I laughed along with what I assumed was a joke. 'I'm not kidding. Unless you've at least led the Tour, you shouldn't be seen dead in that jersey,' my colleague asserted. Bewildered, I trudged off to the showers and stuffed the jersey in the bottom of my bag. That evening, I washed it and put it in a drawer. Twenty-five years later, it's still there, pristine, almost unused, suffused with the scent of a Laura Ashley summer breeze drawer liner.

Exclusiveness is one of the primary characteristics of the yellow jersey. Among the millions of spectators that line the roadsides at the Tour each year, only a handful will be seen in yellow. At the same time, you usually don't have to travel too far along the Tour route to observe fans and cyclists decked out in polka dots or Peter Sagan green. According to *Libération's* Pierre Carrey, 'It is forbidden to wear the yellow jersey in France, for anyone to ride in it. It belongs to the Tour leader, and him alone. He's like the Louis XIV, the Sun King, reincarnated in a cycling jersey.'

That might be the case in the modern era, but certainly wasn't when Eugène Christophe first modelled the yellow jersey in Grenoble in July 1919. Rather than feeling regal, the Frenchman was embarrassed, a figure of fun, mocked by his fellow racers and spectators. Their barbs highlighted the general antipathy towards the colour yellow that can be traced back more than a thousand years and persisted well into the twentieth century, when it was transformed by its significance within sport and by the Tour in particular.

'The yellow jersey has contributed to a re-evaluation of a colour that did have a bad reputation for a long time,' says Michel Pastoureau, a professor of medieval history at the Sorbonne in Paris, who is an expert in Western symbology and renowned within France for his books on the history of the colours red, blue, black and green – he has his own feelings of reticence about yellow, and has yet to dedicate himself to publication of an extended work on this colour. Interviewed by *Ouest France*, Pastoureau explains there isn't a definitive answer to the question of why yellow attracted such disfavour, but he and other experts suggest that it may stem from the unreliability of yellow dyes and paint in the Middle Ages. Produced using the bright yellow flowers taken from broom as the base, these yellows didn't penetrate fabric, canvas and other materials very well and, as a consequence, tended to fade comparatively quickly. More resistant yellows could be made using saffron, but the spice imported from Asia was expensive and only available to richer members of society, reinforcing the exclusiveness of the colour. Sulphur, in addition, is yellow, and the chem-

| *Judas in yellow: Juan de Juanes, 'The Last Supper'*

ical's association with the devil and all things diabolical is another reason for this distaste.

While other colours maintained a balance of good and bad associations, these negative aspects became inextricably associated with yellow, while the colour's more positive attributes attained a more golden hue. 'Gold acquired all of the good aspects of the colour (heat, light, wealth, power) and left yellow with the bad parts,' Pastoureau explains. 'For a long time in the West, yellow's symbolism was more negative than positive. It was the colour of sickness, of autumn. The colour of lies, of deceit, of treason. The colour of Judas.'

The change came gradually. In Roman times, yellow often featured in clothes worn at weddings and other important ceremonies. In China, it was reserved for the emperor and regarded as a

The colour of Judas

symbol of power, wealth and wisdom. In Europe, however, its status gradually changed as it became increasingly linked with decline and deception.

The journalist and writer Dominique Simonnet, co-author with Pastoureau of *Le Petit Livre de Couleurs*, has detailed this shift in the colour's fortunes. 'This can be seen very clearly in medieval imagery, where debased characters are often adorned in yellow clothes,' he explained to French news weekly *L'Express*. Simonnet highlights the example of Ganelon, the French knight who betrayed Charlemagne's army to the Muslims,

| *Left: Giotto, 'The Kiss of Judas'; Right: Stamp depicting Emperor Taizang of Tang*

who was often depicted in yellow, and also points to the portrayal of Judas in paintings in England and Germany. 'Over time, this figure accumulates ignominious attributes: initially he's depicted with red hair, then, from the 12th century onwards, he is represented in a yellow cloak and, to top it all, he's then made left-handed,' he explains, adding that there is no mention of the colour of Judas's hair or clothes in religious texts. 'It's purely a construction of medieval culture,' Simonnet says. 'Other texts from this period make it very clear: yellow is the colour of traitors.'

By the middle of the medieval period, yellow was associated with liars, cheats and anyone who could not be trusted. 'It also became the colour of ostracism, placed on those who everyone wanted to condemn or exclude, such as the Jews,' says Simonnet, this isolation via colour stemming from

the association with Judas and exemplified in the decree issued by Louis IX, the thirteenth-century king who was the only French monarch to be canonised, forcing Jews to wear a yellow cloth circle on their clothes. In other instances during that period, Jews had to display a yellow star, the symbol reintroduced and imposed by the Nazis in the 1930s. Members of the Cathar movement in southern France were persecuted in a similar way between the eleventh and thirteenth centuries. Condemned as heretics by the Roman Catholic church, Cathars who refused to recant were often burned at the stake, while those who did were required to sew a yellow cross into their clothing.

Yellow's negative connotations spread to other parts of society. In the late fourteenth century, Venetian prostitutes dressed in yellow in order to be more easily noticed by prospective clients, and the practice gradually reached into other regions of what later became Italy. Over subsequent centuries, both red and yellow became associated with prostitutes, yet from the eighteenth century onwards the latter became more prevalent in France, where some town councils required them to wear a yellow ribbon or belt. Dressing in yellow garments also made practical sense on dimly lit city streets, enabling prostitutes to stand out to prospective clients.

By the late eighteenth century, even the term 'yellow' had taken on a pejorative sense. Often associated with Hollywood Westerns as a way of describing a coward, who might also be described as 'a yellow-belly', the description in this sense is believed to have been used first in England, perhaps in Lincoln-shire. According to Francis Grose's *A provincial glossary, with a collection of local proverbs, and popular superstitions*, which was published in 1787, 'Yellow bellies. This is an appellation given to persons born in the Fens, who, it is jocularly said, have yellow bellies, like their eels.' That same year, *Knight's Quarterly Magazine* records an account of life in the Staffordshire coalfields and includes an attempt by a lady to guess the nickname given to the locals, with 'yellow-belly' among the options provided along with 'lie-a-bed', 'cock-eye' and 'pig-tail'.

Although yellow's usage in these instances may stem from its link with illness and be disparaging rather than designed to taint, its association with cowardice soon became prevalent. A report in an 1842 edition of the *Wisconsin Enquirer* describes

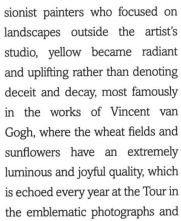

the Texan forces readying to face a rival force from Mexico. 'God send that they may bayonet every "yellow-belly" in the Mexican army,' a Captain Wright exhorts, although it is not known whether the reference refers to skin colour, ill-health or an association with snakes or reptiles. In 1856, American showman and politician P. T. Barnum wrote in *Struggles and Triumphs*, 'We never thought your heart was yellow.' By the Second World War, the words 'yellow' and 'coward' had become inter-changeable among American soldiers.

In France, attitudes gradually began to change from the 1850s. Due in part to impressionist painters who focused on landscapes outside the artist's studio, yellow became radiant and uplifting rather than denoting deceit and decay, most famously in the works of Vincent van Gogh, where the wheat fields and sunflowers have an extremely luminous and joyful quality, which is echoed every year at the Tour in the emblematic photographs and images of the peloton passing between fields of dazzlingly vibrant blooms.

Yet for most of the French population, unaware and untouched by impressionism and abstract art, yellow essentially retained the long-established negative motifs, illustrated by the barbs shouted Christophe's way in Grenoble on that early morning when the first leader's jersey was presented. Comic and satirical publications still depicted their villains in yellow scarves and shawls.

Around the turn of the century, in an increasingly industrialised and unionised France, 'yellow' also described a strike breaker and, by association, a traitor to the cause of the working-class. The first 'yellow union' was established in 1899 by a group of miners at Montceau-les-Mines in the east of the country. Unlike 'red unions', which had links to socialist and communist groups, this new group endeavoured to advance its rights without resorting to strikes or direct action against business owners. More emerged, and in April 1902 the Fédération Nationale des Jaunes de France was founded, headed by Pierre Biétry.

Thanks to financial support from leading industrialists, the yellow movement flourished and attracted up to 100,000 members. In 1908, Biétry set up a political party and a federation uniting the nation's 'yellow unions', both of them firmly in favour of the long-standing divide between the owners and workers and against workers having any kind of ownership of the means of production.

It is interesting to note that when *L'Auto-Vélo*, as it was originally entitled, was established in 1900, its funding came from a large number of very prominent and wealthy industrialists angered by the political stance and partisan editorial support of *Le Vélo*, the market-leading title printed on green paper, and of its editor Pierre Giffard. Although there is no evidence that *L'Auto-Vélo*'s founders deliberately chose yellow paper for their new title, a yellow described by Pastoureau as 'one of those pale, drab yellows that were used to colour cheap paper, destined for short-term usage and mass consumption, a yellow that was neither valued nor rewarding', it is surely an intriguing coincidence, especially because under Desgrange's leadership it adopted a very conservative approach to socio-political matters.

Equally intriguing is the decision to create a leader's jersey that was apparently waxy yellow in hue, rather than in the pale but brighter colour on which *L'Auto* was printed. As noted earlier, more luminous shades had featured in pre-war jerseys and several of these remained unchanged following the Great War. Consequently, there doesn't seem to have been any issue in manufacturing what would now be recognised as yellow. Could Desgrange have ordered a golden jersey on purpose? Did he want to boost the status of his race's leader by clothing him in a colour that suggested nobility and authority, rather than in one that might be ridiculed because of more inappropriate and associations?

There is, unfortunately, no evidence one way or the other. Desgrange may have put in his request without having the slightest idea what shade it might be when it was delivered. However, given the absolute control he exercised over his event, it seems extremely unlikely that the Tour director wouldn't have had a say on the precise nature of the colour used, and it's absolutely certain that he would have had it changed quite quickly if he hadn't approved of it.

What can be confirmed is that by the time Louis Mottiat, for a day, and Léon Scieur, for the rest of the race, donned the yellow jersey during the 1921 Tour, it had taken on a more familiar shade and *L'Auto*'s association with it had developed to the point where the paper was widely known as 'Le Jaune'. When Ottavio Bottecchia wrapped up the first of two consecutive victories in 1924, the jersey featured the name of his Auto-

| *Ottavio Bottecchia displaying the Automoto-Hutchinson branding*

moto-Hutchinson team, although branding of this type was dropped when the event returned to a national team format in 1930. Inevitably, there has been further tinkering.

In 1948, the Tour's second director, Jacques Goddet, paid tribute to his predecessor by adding Desgrange's initials to the jersey. 'Embroidered in black, next to the heart, the initials H.D. in the style of the father of the Tour's handwriting. This was the homage I wanted to make to the designer of the cathedral,' Goddet explained in his autobiography. The practice, he complained was subsequently abandoned 'by others and not by me, to leave the entire jersey free for branding that's judged obligatory. It's a decision that upsets me, but one that has to be understood, because it is by increasing its financial gains that the Tour can become an even more perfect event in terms of sporting status... Nevertheless, I deplore the fact that the decision was taken not to retain this symbolic logo in a fitting place on an official document.'

Dropped in 1984, Desgrange's distinctive initials reappeared on both the front and back in the one hundredth Tour in 2013 when Le Coq Sportif remodelled the jersey, brightening it and adding a transparent Corsican Moor's head emblem to

EN 1903
HENRI DESGRANGE CRÉAIT
LE PLUS GRAND ÉVÉNEMENT CYCLISTE
DE TOUS LES TEMPS

celebrate the race's first visit to the island. Reflective spots were included in the design, making it stand out even more in the lights during the first night-time finish on the Champs-Élysées. As a final tribute to the Tour's founder, these were complemented by a reflective dedication: 'En 1903 Henri Desgrange créait le plus grand événement cycliste de tous les temps' – In 1903, Henri Desgrange created the greatest cycling race of all time.

On occasions faded as if, like much of the French countryside, bleached of its vitality by July's fierce sun, and on others quite psychedelic in tone when touched by the orange end of the yellow palette, the Tour leader's jersey has steadily contributed to a re-evaluation. Introduced, says Pastoureau in *Dictionnaire des couleurs de notre temps*, 'to better highlight the link between the organising newspaper and a cycling race that was already very popular', it was initially 'neither valued nor rewarding'. Yet, as Pastoureau points out, the magic of the Tour de France would soon come into play:

'As soon as it was put on, the jersey became an object of desire, almost mythological (although it still didn't have any history). It gave birth to a syntagma – Yellow Jersey – the use of which spread not only within cycling but also beyond the sporting domain. There were and there still are yellow jerseys in finance, the economy, universities, etc.' Being the Yellow Jersey now signifies "being in the lead" in any area, whatever kind of competition or means of classification is involved... The Tour de France has consequently contributed to the re-evaluation of the

In the late 1920s and, particularly the 1930s, Tour fever raged, its importance reflected not only in huge newspaper sales, particularly for *L'Auto*, but also within popular culture. Each year in the decade up to the Second World War, a song was released to coincide with the race, *Le Maillot Jaune* gracing the 1936 edition. Italian-born Swiss accordion player Frédo Gardoni composed and played on several of these songs, including *P'tit gars du Tour* in 1932, *Et vas-y Théophile!* in 1934 and *La Fleur au guidon* in 1937.

Gardoni had established his reputation in the 1920s, playing with legendary French singers such as Maurice Chevalier and Mistinguett as well as releasing a number of recordings in the musette style was that popularised by accordionists introducing faster rhythms into traditional dances such as the waltz and polka. Musette music and dancing gained mass appeal in France during the first half of the twentieth century. Yvette Horner, the accordionist who for many years performed within the Tour's publicity caravan and on occasion presented the yellow jersey, was among other noted musette performers.

Le Succès du "Tour de France"

LE MAILLOT JAUNE

Chanson sportive
créée par

Enregistrée dans
toutes les grandes
marques de disques

Piano & Chant: 6 fr.

Chant seul: 1f 50

FREDO GARDONI
(DISQUES PATHÉ)

PAROLES DE
CHARLYS

MUSIQUE DE
F. GARDONI & CH. JARDIN
Arr. pour orchestre par RICK

EDITIONS RENÉ RAILLET
12, PASSAGE DE L'INDUSTRIE, PARIS. X°
Tous droits réservés

| *Above and overleaf: Sheet music for the 1936 song 'Le Maillot Jaune'*

Le Maillot Jaune

Chanson du " TOUR DE FRANCE "

Paroles de
CHARLYS

Musique de
Fredo GARDON
& Ch. JARDIN

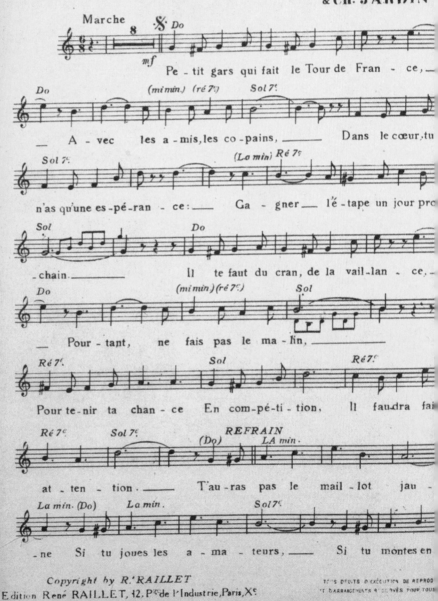

Marche

Pe - tit gars qui fait le Tour de Fran - ce,

A - vec les a - mis, les co - pains, _____ Dans le cœur, tu

n'as qu'une es - pé - ran - ce : _____ Ga - gner _____ l'é - tape un jour pro

chain _____ Il te faut du cran, de la vail - lan - ce,

_____ Pour - tant, ne fais pas le ma - lin, _____

Pour te - nir ta chan - ce En com - pé - ti - tion, Il fau - dra fai

at - ten - tion. _____ T'au - ras pas le mail - lot jau -

ne Si tu joues les a - ma - teurs, _____ Si tu montes en

Edition René RAILLET, 12, P⁼ᵉ de l'Industrie, Paris, Xᵉ

Sol 7e ... **Do**

a - ma - zó - ne, En dan - seuse ___ En sau - teur, ___ Pour ne

La min. ... **La 7e**

pas qu'on te dé - trô - ne, Fais voir que t'es un cou -

Ré min. ... **Si 7e** ... **La min. (Do)**

reur. ___ A - lors ___ t'au - ras le mail - lot jau - ne,

Do) Sol 7e ... **Do**

___ C'est le mail - lot du vain - queur. ___

2

a veux gagner l'étape à Lille,

Alors ménage ton effort,

rras que ce n'est pas facile.

-bas sur les pavés du Nord.

veux te risquer en Bretagne

rs prends garde à tes boyaux,

Car dans la campagne

Les vieux matelots

Ont des clous à leurs sabots. *(Au Ref.)*

3

Si tu prends le chemin de Marseille,

Prends garde au soleil du Midi,

C'est par là que les yeux de Mireille

Ont mis à plat plus d'un ami.

Si tu ne peux rien faire en Province,

Tu peux même encore espérer

Que le Parc des Princes

Te verra premier.

Au grand poteau d'arrivée.

DERNIER REFRAIN

Tu l'auras le maillot jaune,

Parmi les bravos, les fleurs,

Si tu peux, comme un cyclone,

Dépasser les coureurs.

Il te faudra sur la "zône"

Faire encore un tour d'honneur,

Alors t'auras le maillot jaune,

C'est le maillot du vainqueur.

Abonnez-vous à l'ARTISTE AMATEUR ! Ce journal vous tiendra au courant des nouveautés et vous aidera à devenir ARTISTES. Vous y trouverez chansons, monologues, sketchs, revues et pièces, avec les détails d'une interprétation pour vous produire partout avec succès, et vous serez invités à une collaboration pouvant révéler vos capacités. Numéro spécimen contre 2 fr. 50 timbres ou mandat.

_ Les accords indiqués entre parenthèses n'étant que de passage sont facultatifs : si on a une
ulté à les exécuter, on peut les sauter et pour la facilité garder l'accord précédent.

(CHARLYS)

'La meute après le Maillot Jaune',
The pack chase the yellow jersey, illustration by André Galland

colour yellow and of it becoming the colour of victory, and even of excellence. It's no longer the yellow that used to be used for *L'Auto*'s paper, but a luminous, striking yellow, a new gold.'

Tour de France director Christian Prudhomme agrees with Pastoureau's evaluation. 'It has taken on wider significance so that people will talk about someone being the yellow jersey in politics. It's become part of common parlance. It's like the green jacket at Augusta, it's something immense in the world of sport.' Asked if the Tour leader's jersey would ever change colour, he laughs freely. 'That's my reply to that question,' he says. 'It would never happen. It's completely unimaginable. It would be sacrilege.'

Once a taint, yellow has become the colour of success, thanks in no small part to the *maillot jaune*, Brazil's yellow-and-green shirt, and other iconic sporting strips, their glow augmented by the development of colour film and television pictures. Vibrant and often very fashionable, it has retaken many of the positive attributes that it had lost to gold, which has become gaudy, sickening, associated with excess and greed, exemplified by the likes of New York's Trump Tower, a palace of lurid kitsch and bad taste. Yellow, on the other hand, is the colour of summer, of holidays, of happiness, of the Tour de France.

However, while Brazil's football shirt is democratic, suggesting liberation, fun and flamboyance, the yellow jersey evokes a quite different rule and hierarchy. As I was brusquely made aware by my colleague, it is exclusive, the preserve of an honoured few, the modern-day emperors and kings who are the rulers of the professional peloton and stand apart from the pack because they have won the Tour de France. As Prudhomme suggests, it is cycling's equivalent of the green jacket presented each year to winner of the US Masters at Augusta.

'It's interesting that amateur riders rarely wear the yellow jersey. In order to do so you have to have earned that right,' says Prudhomme. 'I, for example, don't like to sign the yellow jersey and generally refuse to do so because the people who should be signing yellow jersey are those who have worn it at the Tour. I'll sign pretty much anything else but I don't like to sign the yellow jersey because it is something sacred, reserved for those riders who fought for it and have earned it. It requires sweat, blood, sometimes tears and joy as well. An incredible effort is required to take the yellow jersey, even if it's only for a single occasion. There's no doubt that the rider who's in it has fully deserved it.'

The same can be said about many sporting shirts or jerseys, including Brazil's iconic yellow-and-green kit. However, the difference in attitude or affection can partly be explained by football being a team game where some players will stand out but everyone contributes to success and shares it equally. The fans sitting in their yellow-and-green replica shirts in the stadium and watching on television are also part of that success. The team is everything. Everybody is rooting for it.

The yellow jersey, on the other hand, is a prize, the mythical golden fleece, emblematic of a personal accomplishment. While every professional might want to wear or to win it, and their fans would love to see them achieve that, the jersey doesn't attract any devotion itself. A rider may depend on his team to give him the opportunity to pull it on, but the honour is essentially his alone. His teammates receive reflected glory and perhaps a share of his prize money. Equally, his and his team's fans may be thrilled to see him in the jersey, but their commitment is to the rider or his trade team, and that's what they will buy to show their support.

There is, says *Libération*'s Pierre Carrey, a very political aspect to it. 'Although the yellow jersey does say summer, sun, holidays to the French people, there are mixed emotions involved, some sadness perhaps. It also has an authoritarian aspect, a degree of ambivalence. Yellow is seen as more conservative, the tunic of a king, whereas the polka dot is more like the jester's jersey, representing anarchy and freedom. It is more democratic because less talented riders have a chance of challenging for it, and that makes it more popular with fans and spectators.

'The contest for the polka-dot jersey is always moving, it's more fluid, it ebbs and flows, and it's always colourful,' Carrey continues. 'Whereas the yellow jersey is all about a quest, a holy grail to begin with, which becomes a drawn-out fight, and not usually a swashbuckling one either. The battle for it is quite conservative, even dull sometimes, the peloton's heavy artillery pounding each other until one big gun finds eventually flattens the rest. If you take Roger Walkowiak and one or two other champions out of the equation, it has always been won by very big names.'

LUCIEN AIMAR
TOUR DE FRANCE
1966

3

THE BUILDING OF A LEGEND
Le Maillot Jaune

Eddy Merckx 1970

**THE SECOND OF TWO YEARS
WHEN IT WAS SPONSORED BY BUTTER
MANUFACTURER VIRLUX**

LES LAURÉATS DU TOUR DE FRANCE

1. Jean Alavoine, 2ᵉ du Tour de
France, vainqueur de 5 étapes.

2. Lambot, le vainqueur du classement général, qui gagna la 14ᵉ étape.
(Bicyclette et pneus *LA SPORTIVE*.)

4. L'Italien Lucotti, autre révélation,
7ᵉ du class., 1ᵉʳ des 12ᵉ et 13ᵉ étapes.

6. Henri Pélissier, qui abandonna,
se classa premier dans la 5ᵉ étape.

3. Barthélemy, 5ᵉ du classement, vainqueur des 9ᵉ, 10ᵉ et 11ᵉ étapes. —
5. Christophe, ne gagna aucune étape,
mais resta leader de l'épreuve jusqu'à
l'avant-dernier trajet, finit 3ᵉ en 233 h.
33 m. 45 s. 4/5. — 7. Francis Pélissier,
qui abandonna, triompha dans la 3ᵉ étape.
— 8. Rossius, qui abandonna, vainqueur
de la 1ʳᵉ étape.

The riders garlanded during the 1919 Tour

Nothing Worth Having Comes Easy

On the July morning that Eugène Christophe became the first rider to wear the yellow jersey at the Tour de France, race director Henri Desgrange wrote in *L'Auto* that when he retired he planned to publish 'a little brochure that I will entitle: How to Win the Tour de France'.

He wouldn't, he said, detail the training requirements to be a Tour contender, but stated that there would be a motif running through it: 'qui veut la fin veut les moyens' – if you have the will, you will find the way.

'If the Tour de France represents for a rider glory and a small fortune, he should prepare for it with the fervour the young and future first communicant devotes to his religious retreat.

He has to drive out of himself, at the very least until the last lap of the velodrome, all of the petty vanities, every bit of boastfulness, all puerile pride, every useless shred of nervousness. You have to live in absolute retreat, allowing yourself no licence, no joy, but living in perpetual ecstasy ahead of the glory and money that awaits at the finish if you scoop the big prize!' explained Desgrange, whose monastic approach would have been laughed off by subsequent Tour greats such as Jacques Anquetil and Freddy Maertens, who had developed a taste for mid-race champagne

Having laid out the methodology required to contend for cycling's greatest prize, he illustrated it by highlighting some of the mistakes that contenders in that 1919 race had made. He warned prospective candidates for overall victory that they should avoid the error committed by Jean Alavoine, who had spent a very unsettled night before the first stage thanks to loud music being played near his hotel that led to him bedding down in a ditch for an hour on the road to Le Havre and in doing so lose all hope of taking the title. He cautioned that anyone wanting to imitate Luigi Lucotti should bear in mind that the stage towns, 'including Nice', should be places of rest and not of excitement. He added that the riders should take to the start with their bodies in pristine condition, with no saddle sores, in-growing toenails 'or with their posterior ruined by road gravel'. It should be noted, given the dismay and hyperbole that greeted Eugène Christophe's undoing on the penultimate stage, that Desgrange concluded by saying he was convinced that Alavoine would have won the Tour without his 'dodo' on the first day.

While the Tour's founder never did get around to writing his treatise on how to win the Tour, his analysis of what it took to claim the greatest title in the sport continued from that moment on. Just four days later, he questioned Firmin Lambot's suitability as a potential Tour winner. 'Our Lambot doesn't really stand out in terms of his perceptiveness or decision-making,' he suggested. 'He's very much the poet of our race. He can always be seen wandering about, leaving the peloton without good reason, descending erratically, risking everything, as if it's towards the end of the stage and he's worried about not featuring at the finish... Has he been considering this? Is he, instead, composing sonnets? I don't know!' Perhaps Lambot took note, because on the next stage he raced in a more consistently aggressive way on the 'stage of hunger' between Metz and Dunkirk, claiming his only stage win and, thanks to Christophe's mechanical disaster, the yellow jersey.

The following year, when Philippe Thys led almost from start to finish, but was criticised in some quarters for his lack of flair, Desgrange tackled a question that has remained a perennial issue. 'Panache. Does Philippe Thys have panache? He is one of those people who worries a lot and worries too much about this question, which is, I believe, of mediocre interest... having or not having panache is of no importance,' the Tour boss surmised.

Over the remainder of the inter-war period, the Tour winner generally emerged from the strongest team. After La Sportive's dominance ended when the consortium was dissolved at the close of the 1921 season, Automoto, then Alcyon and subsequently France won four consecutive Tours with three different riders. Having a strong group meant not only being able to support the designated leader, but also having alternative options if that leader came unstuck on courses that were almost twice as long as nowadays and were tackled with bikes on which the use of derailleurs was banned and required the same rear wheel-flipping pauses

| Automoto were the Team Sky of the 1920s, winning the Tour with three different riders

at the top and bottom of climbs that Christophe, Lambot and their peers had carried out.

Change came in 1936 when Jacques Goddet succeeded Desgrange as race director and immediately removed the ban on the use of derailleurs, and continued in the aftermath of the Second World War with the increasing internationalisation of racing and the emergence of Fausto Coppi as the sport's dominant rider. The Italian revolutionised the sport, introducing a new approach to diet, training, preparation and tactics. But even he wasn't fully prepared for what the Tour had to ask of him when he challenged for the yellow jersey in 1949. The first issue that needed to be dealt with was reaching an accommodation with compatriot Gino Bartali, a two-time winner and defending champion. This required all of the considerable diplomatic skills of Italy's team manager, Alfredo Binda. Coppi's second dilemma was just as thorny. According to William Fotheringham in his biography of '*il campionissimo*', *Fallen Angel*, 'Coppi had trouble adapting to the Tour. This was not the schematised, controlled racing of Italy, where the gregari looked after things until the campioni took over.'

Unlike the twenty-first century Tour, the post-war versions could be unpredictably madcap. 'In the Giro there was a kind of arrangement between the riders that you wouldn't really race until the feeding station, whereas in France we would attack as soon as the start flag was dropped. Controlling the race was much harder, because everyone went from the gun, everyone was a danger, breaks could get a huge amount of time; it was more chaotic,' said Raphaël Geminiani.

Coppi's morale, says the Frenchman who later became his teammate, 'fell to bits' when he realised this.

Described by Fotheringham as 'existentially challenged', the Italian was constantly beset by doubt and in need of reassurance. Away from Bianchi where he was the unquestioned leader, in a national team where he was sharing leadership with his arch-rival Bartali, Coppi was unable to control important aspects of racing that he didn't normally have to be concerned with. He didn't know the roads, the climbs, which gears to use, how to pace himself. He could hardly have been any less prepared for the Tour compared to modern-day successors who recce almost every critical point of the route. Almost inevitably, during the opening week of the race, his challenge for the title all but disintegrated.

From the first few days, Jacques Marinelli held centre stage. Dubbed 'the budgerigar' by L'Équipe because of his tiny build, volatile aspect and the green jersey of his Ile de France team, the Frenchman took the yellow jersey on stage four. Rechristened 'the canary', Marinelli pushed his lead out to fifteen minutes the next day by joining a break that also featured Coppi until the two riders collided as they reached for musettes held out to them in the feed zone, the subsequent crash rendering the Italian's bike unusable. The yellow jersey, who admitted later that he'd been at fault, remounted and said he 'stole away like a thief' to extend his lead to fifteen minutes, while Coppi, angered by a long delay waiting for Binda's team car to provide him with a spare and convinced favouritism towards Bartali was at the root of his

En exclusivité :
**LE DRAME
LAPÉBIE**

Téléphoto transmise de Pau
par nos envoyés spéciaux

16 PAGES

LUNDI 11 JUILLET 1949
N° 189

MARINELLI PLEURE SON MAILLOT

20 frs

Afrique du Nord - Avion : 22 frs

Jacques Marinelli wore the yellow jersey for six days in the 1949 Tour before finishing third

YEAR	WINNER		TEAM
1919	**Firmin Lambot**	◖◗	**La Sportive**
1920	Philippe Thys	◖◗	La Sportive
1921	**Léon Scieur**	◖◗	**La Sportive**
1922	Firmin Lambot	◖◗	Peugeot–Wolber
1923	**Henri Pélissier**	◖◗	**Automoto–Hutchinson**
1924	Ottavio Bottecchia	◖◗	Automoto–Hutchinson
1925	**Ottavio Bottecchia**	◖◗	**Automoto–Hutchinson**
1926	Lucien Buysse	◖◗	Automoto–Hutchinson
1927	**Nicolas Frantz**	⬒	**Alcyon–Dunlop**
1928	Nicolas Frantz	⬒	Alcyon–Dunlop
1929	**Maurice De Waele**	◖◗	**Alcyon–Dunlop**
1930	André Leducq	◖◗	Alcyon–Dunlop
1931	**Antonin Magne**	◖◗	**France**
1932	André Leducq	◖◗	France
1933	**Georges Speicher**	◖◗	**France**
1934	Antonin Magne	◖◗	France
1935	**Romain Maes**	◖◗	**Belgium**
1936	Sylvère Maes	◖◗	Belgium
1937	**Roger Lapébie**	◖◗	**France**
1938	Gino Bartali	◖◗	Italy
1939	**Sylvère Maes**	◖◗	**Belgium**
1947	Jean Robic	◖◗	France
1948	**Gino Bartali**	◖◗	**Italy**
1949	Fausto Coppi	◖◗	Italy
1950	**Ferdinand Kübler**	⊕	**Switzerland**
1951	Hugo Koblet	⊕	Switzerland
1952	**Fausto Coppi**	◖◗	**Italy**
1953	Louison Bobet	◖◗	France
1954	**Louison Bobet**	◖◗	**France**
1955	Louison Bobet	◖◗	France
1956	**Roger Walkowiak**	◖◗	**France**
1957	Jacques Anquetil	◖◗	France
1958	**Charly Gaul**	⬒	**Luxembourg**
1959	Federico Bahamontes	⬒	Spain
1960	**Gastone Nencini**	◖◗	**Italy**
1961	Jacques Anquetil	◖◗	France
1962	**Jacques Anquetil**	◖◗	**Saint-Raphaël–Helyett–Hutchinson**
1963	Jacques Anquetil	◖◗	Saint-Raphaël–Gitane–R. Geminiani
1964	**Jacques Anquetil**	◖◗	**Saint-Raphaël–Gitane–Dunlop**
1965	Felice Gimondi	◖◗	Salvarani
1966	**Lucien Aimar**	◖◗	**Ford France–Hutchinson**
1967	Roger Pingeon	◖◗	Peugeot–BP–Michelin
1968	**Jan Janssen**	⬒	**Pelforth–Sauvage–Lejeune**
1969	Eddy Merckx	◖◗	Faema
1970	**Eddy Merckx**	◖◗	**Faemino–Faema**
1971	Eddy Merckx	◖◗	Molteni
1972	**Eddy Merckx**	◖◗	**Molteni**
1973	Luis Ocaña	⬒	Bic
1974	**Eddy Merckx**	◖◗	**Molteni**
1975	Bernard Thévenet	◖◗	Peugeot–BP–Michelin
1976	**Lucien Van Impe**	◖◗	**Gitane–Campagnolo**
1977	Bernard Thévenet	◖◗	Peugeot–Esso–Michelin
1978	**Bernard Hinault**	◖◗	**Renault–Gitane–Campagnolo**
1979	Bernard Hinault	◖◗	Renault–Gitane

TIME	MARGIN	STAGE WINS
231h 07' 15"	**+ 1h 42' 54"**	**1**
228h 36' 13"	+ 57' 21"	4
221h 50' 26"	**+ 18' 36"**	**2**
222h 08' 06"	+ 41' 15"	0
222h 15' 30"	**+ 30 '41"**	**3**
226h 18' 21"	+ 35' 36"	4
219h 10' 18"	**+ 54' 20"**	**4**
238h 44' 25"	+ 1h 22' 25"	2
198h 16' 42"	**+ 1h 48' 41"**	**3**
192h 48' 58"	+ 50' 07"	5
186h 39' 15"	**+ 44' 23"**	**1**
172h 12' 16"	+ 14' 13"	2
177h 10' 03"	**+ 12' 56"**	**1**
154h 11' 49"	+ 24' 03"	6
147h 51' 37"	**+ 4' 01"**	**3**
147h 13' 58"	+ 27' 31"	3
141h 23' 00"	**+ 17' 52"**	**3**
142h 47' 32"	+ 26' 55"	4
138h 58' 31"	**+ 7' 17"**	**3**
148h 29' 12"	+ 18' 27"	2
132h 03' 17"	**+ 30' 38"**	**2**
148h 11' 25"	+ 3' 58"	3
147h 10' 36"	**+ 26' 16"**	**7**
149h 40' 49"	+ 10' 55"	3
145h 36' 56"	**+ 9' 30"**	**3**
142h 20' 14"	+ 22' 00"	5
151h 57' 20"	**+ 28' 17"**	**5**
129h 23' 25"	+ 14' 18"	2
140h 06' 05"	**+ 15' 49"**	**3**
130h 29' 26"	+ 4' 53"	2
124h 01' 16"	**+ 1' 25"**	**0**
135h 44' 42"	+ 14' 56"	4
116h 59' 05"	**+ 3' 10"**	**4**
123h 46' 45"	+ 4' 01"	1
112h 08' 42"	**+ 5' 02"**	**0**
122h 01' 33"	+ 12' 14"	2
114h 31' 54"	**+ 4' 59"**	**2**
113h 30' 05"	+ 3' 35"	4
127h 09' 44"	**+ 55"**	**4**
116h 42' 06"	+ 2' 40"	3
117h 34' 21"	**+ 1' 07"**	**0**
136h 53' 50"	+ 3' 40"	1
133h 49' 42"	**+ 38"**	**2**
116h 16' 02"	+ 17' 54"	6
119h 31' 49"	**+ 12' 41"**	**8**
96h 45' 14"	+ 9' 51"	4
108h 17' 18"	**+ 10' 41"**	**6**
122h 25' 34"	+ 15' 51"	6
116h 16' 58"	**+ 8' 04"**	**8**
114h 35' 31"	+ 2' 47"	2
116h 22' 23"	**+ 4' 14"**	**1**
115h 38' 30"	+ 48"	1
108h 18' 00"	**+ 3' 56"**	**3**
103h 06' 50"	+ 13' 07"	7

LA DOMENICA DEL CORRIERE

Supplemento settimanale illustrato del nuovo CORRIERE DELLA SERA · Abbonamenti: Italia, anno L. 1400, sem. L. 750 · Estero, anno L. 2000, sem. L. 1050

Anno 54 — N. 29   20 Luglio 1952   L. 30.—

Il re del Tour. Fausto Coppi, capitano della squadra italiana al Giro di Francia, ha ancora una volta sbalordito il mondo sportivo per la facilità con cui ha sbaragliato tutti gli avversari nella durissima tappa delle Alpi che comprendeva le aspre scalate della Croce di Ferro, del Galibier, del Monginevro, e del Sestrière. Dopo l'eccezionale impresa, i competenti lo hanno riconfermato il più forte atleta che il ciclismo abbia mai avuto. *(Disegno di Walter Molino)*

'The king of the Tour. Fausto Coppi, captain of the Italy's Tour de France team, has once again stunned the sporting world by the ease with which he has overcome all obstacles on the highly challenging stage in the Alps, which includes the harsh ascents of the Croix de Fer, the Galibier, the Montgenèvre and to Sestriere. After his exceptional performance, experts once again named him the strongest athlete that cycling has ever seen.'

| *Coppi crushes the field in the La Rochelle time trial in 1949*

struggles, felt his morale dive. He finished the stage thirty-six minutes off first place and had to be persuaded to continue.

Convinced by Binda that he could still win and buoyed by an eight-minute gain in a ninety-two-kilometre individual time trial, Coppi served up a performance that was the embodiment of panache. He slashed his deficit in the Pyrenees then confirmed his comeback over two legendary Alpine stages, the first to Briançon where he finished with Bartali, who took both the win and the yellow jersey, and the second to Aosta, where Coppi finished alone, the yellow jersey his thanks to a five-minute advantage over his compatriot. His victory, which sealed the first Giro–Tour double in racing history, was completely with such style and popular acclaim that, according to Tour historian Jacques Augendre, it contributed substantially to post-war reconciliation between France and Italy.

Coppi's second success, in 1952, was far more emphatic. That edition featured the race's first summit finishes, at Alpe d'Huez, Sestriere and the Puy de Dôme. The Italian won each of them as he opened up a gap on second-placed Stan Ockers of almost half an hour, driven on incessantly by his fear of weakness or falling victim to some catastrophe even as the race approached Paris. But even this margin wasn't enough to convince Coppi of the likelihood he would win. His room-mate Ettore Milano recalled his team leader

| Jacques Anquetil and race director Jacques Goddet endured a tense relationship

looking at the yellow jersey lying on the bed prior to the penultimate stage and saying, 'Will I wear it to Paris?' Still afraid that a Eugène Christophe-like misfortune could occur, 'He would not believe he had won until he crossed the line,' said Milano.

Almost two decades would pass before another rider emerged who rode with Coppi's verve and crushing domination. Haunted by the same nagging doubt that had fuelled the Italian, Eddy Merckx cowed his rivals in a similar manner. Yet, when considering what it takes to win the Tour de France, it isn't helpful to focus on who were, arguably, the best riders cycling has ever seen and certainly the two most befitting of the label phenomenal. It is more useful to analyse the rider who became the race's first five-time winner,

Jacques Anquetil, the model for the majority of the race's champions since the 1960s.

Blessed with a conveyor belt of talent in an era when the international challenge was limited to the countries lying on its borders, the French press and fans could afford to be blasé about success in their national tour. Between Louison Bobet's first win in 1953 and Roger Pingeon's only victory fifteen seasons later, France totalled eleven general classification victories, five of them served up by Anquetil. Reminiscent of Coppi in his style on the bike and deadly efficiency in a time trial, the Norman too became embroiled in a rivalry with a compatriot that divided cycling fans within their home country, in his case Raymond Poulidor.

Like the Italian legend, Anquetil also fed off his insecurity. 'I always had doubt in my mind, and that was perhaps what gave me my strength,' he confessed. Machiavellian in his tactics, particularly when it came to undermining 'Poupou', Anquetil was arguably the first of the modern Tour champions, winning with some style but essentially it was down to his application of exactly the right amount of effort in every domain to ensure that he triumphed.

Goddet was often scathing of the Frenchman's approach. Unlike Desgrange, who was more concerned with the purity of victory, his successor lauded panache. Moreover, by the time Anquetil was in his pomp in the late 1950s and early 1960s, coverage of cycling had extended to radio and, more significantly, television. These audiences needed to be entertained, or they would, Goddet feared presciently, switch over to something else that could hold their attention. As a consequence,

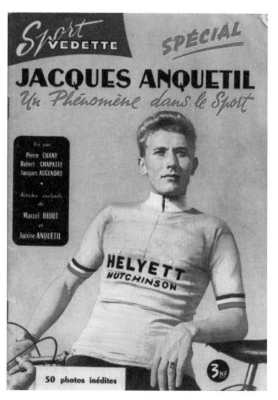

| Sport Vedette 'Special' 1959

the Tour director was caught between his desire to see a Frenchman in yellow and the need to serve up thrilling fare in order to captivate the race's audience.

Ultimately, the Anquetil–Poulidor rivalry guaranteed both objectives could be achieved, but Goddet remained critical of the five-time champion and particularly 'sa tactique d'éteignoir' that 'snuffed out' or suffocated the competition, long before Miguel Indurain and Team Sky were censured for the same approach. Indeed, the race director became so infuriated with Anquetil's conservatism that, in 1963, he revamped the Tour by cutting down the amount of time trialling and moving some finishes closer to mountain summits.

| Merckx, the man with the hammer, quickly became the Tour's 'patron' as a respected rider and unspoken leader

The strategy had mixed results: it delivered a finely balanced contest between the defending champion and 1959 winner Federico Bahamontes, but Anquetil edged it, inevitably, in the final time trial.

It is best remembered for a deceit enacted by the winner and his directeur sportif (DS) Geminiani on the Alpine ascent of the Col de la Forclaz. Switching bikes was prohibited, so in order to enable Anquetil to scale the steep climb with a lighter bike with lower gearing, he faked a mechanical problem, Geminiani jumped out with the spare machine and a hidden pair of cable cutters with which he snipped the rear derailleur of the heavier bike so that the commissaire watching the incident wouldn't think the race rules had been broken. At the top of the pass, Bahamontes had just Anquetil for company and then lost out to him in the sprint, the bonus seconds on the line giving the Frenchman the yellow jersey, which he didn't relinquish.

This small incident, for which he and Geminiani received no censure, encapsulated why Anquetil tended to prevail. He had an instinct for racing and success that his rivals didn't possess, to the extent that he could engineer the action so that his preferred winner did come out on top. In 1959, he schemed with rival Roger Rivière, his co-leader in a top-heavy French team, to assist the chances of Spaniard Federico Bahamontes and thwart those of compatriot Henry Anglade, who the French pair both regarded as being less talented and unworthy of victory. Seven years later, Anquetil was behind another coup, this time with Poulidor as the victim. The beneficiary was the five-time champion's Ford roommate Lucien Aimar, then just twenty-five, who was given free rein to ride his own race once

Anquetil felt that he could no longer contend. By acting as the decoy who distracted both Poulidor and long-term yellow jersey Jan Janssen, he enabled Aimar to establish a race-winning advantage. 'In my whole career, I never let twenty riders escape on a col. There's no doubt that I'll never manage understand Poulidor,' lamented his DS, two-time Tour winner Antonin Magne.

Talking about his second Tour win in 1961, when he achieved the personal goal he had set himself of leading from the first day to the last and extinguished the threat presented by Charly Gaul, Anquetil conceded, 'Yes, I calculated how best to race. I knew that I had to gain six minutes on Gaul away from the mountains. But you can't reproach the yellow jersey for using his head.' It is this quality as much as his beautifully languid technique combined with so much pure power that gave him an edge, most notably over Poulidor, who was, following Rivière's drug-induced and career-ending plunge into a ravine in the 1960 Tour, the only rival of his stature in the cycling's biggest event.

Poulidor, 'the eternal second', may have won the popularity contest with Anquetil and still validly points to the fact that he would never have gained as much notoriety or, significantly for a rider who came from an extremely humble agricultural background, financial reward, but he is the most outstanding example of a rider from the home nation being affected by *l'attraction-répulsion* of the Tour de France's yellow jersey. He wanted it, but was, at the same time, afraid of it. Cyrille Guimard, the managerial mastermind behind six of the seven Tour victories claimed by Bernard Hinault and Laurent Fignon, began his racing

Déro, 'Il survole la course!'
He's flying over the race!
1972: Nicknamed the
'Cannibal' thanks to his insa-
tiable appetite for victories,
Eddy Merckx is considered
the greatest cyclist of all time

career in the late 1960s on the same Mercier team as Poulidor and has said of his former teammate that there is a huge gap between the 'second-hand image' that the public have of him and the reality as Guimard experienced it during the six seasons the pair spent racing together.

'Poupou was fabulous on a bike. But he never asked anything of anybody and especially not his teammates,' Guimard states in his autobiography. 'He was never the one who took the first step, but always his directeur sportif or a faithful teammate. Ultimately, he didn't face up to his responsibilities... Even in criteriums, others took decisions for him. And when we decided to carry out some kind of "coup", we didn't need to warn him. He wouldn't have liked to have been told: "Raymond, in such-and-such a place you've got to attack." He wasn't psychologically disposed to listening to orders of that kind. As a result, he often got caught out, even when it was his own team that was launching major offensives...'

Poulidor was, Guimard suggests, out his depth when up against Anquetil. 'On the bike, he gave the impression of being a poet. A poet who possessed the science of racing, his own science,' says Guimard of the five-time champion. The quote is equally applicable to other multiple Tour winners, including Bernard Hinault, Alberto Contador, Chris Froome and, of course, Eddy Merckx.

Guimard's deconstruction of Poulidor's plucky loser image is supported by his performances in races in between the end of Anquetil's period of hegemony in 1964 and the start of Merckx's five years later. In 1965, he lost out to twenty-two-year-old Tour debutant Felice Gimondi and the next season his understandable fixation on Anquetil led to him being played by the Ford team after Lucien Aimar had slipped into the break on the first day in the mountains to Pau. The escapees gained seven minutes on the group containing the favourites, enough of a buffer for Anquetil's young teammate to fend off Poulidor, who was arguably the strongest rider in the field but ended up third, two minutes off the unlikely winner. Experience, the science of racing, tactical nous, whatever it was, Poulidor was fundamentally flawed by not drawing on it in those moments when it was most required.

With his nemesis Anquetil absent from 1967's return to the national team format, Poulidor began as France's leader but faltered once again, yielding command to another unheralded compatriot, Roger Pingeon. Twelve months later, a yellow jersey hoodoo that was also salted with a good portion of bad luck continued, thanks to the intervention of a race motorbike that knocked him to the ground. With it his hopes of winning the title disappeared for good. Even as Jan Janssen went on to become the second rider after Jean Robic in 1947 to pull on the yellow jersey for the first time after the final stage in Paris, a new era was coming. 'I was happy that Eddy hadn't participated in the 1968 Tour because it was the last chance for a rider like me to win it,' the Dutchman acknowledged.

Merckx had won the Giro earlier that season. Ejected from the same race when on the verge of defending his title twelve months later after a positive drug test that remains the subject of controversy, the Belgian arrived at the Tour determined to restore his reputation and quell his own demons. Like a human tornado sweeping through the peloton, the Belgian left a trail of bewildered rivals stumbling in his wake, his victory as unquestionably dominating as Coppi's in 1952. Nobody has approached the race in the same way since.

There have been Merckx-like cameos, but nothing as brutally sustained as the absolute rule imposed by the Belgian.

Faema's victory in the team time trial on the second afternoon in the Sint-Pieters-Woluwe suburb of Brussels where Merckx had been born and brought up put him in the yellow jersey, which was celebrating its fiftieth birthday. He ceded it to teammate Julien Stevens the next day, who yielded it to Frenchman Désiré Letort when the mountains began with a run through the Vosges to Mulhouse. Then the Merckx Show began. He won alone on the Ballon d'Alsace, taking back the jersey and opening a two-minute lead on GC. He won the short time trial at Divonne-les-Bains a couple of days later, was edged out up a two-up sprint by Pingeon at Chamonix, finished second again at Briançon, beat Gimondi twenty-four hours later in Digne, then finished third in a four-man group in Aubagne. With half the race gone, he led Pingeon and Gimondi by seven minutes, with the rest more than eleven minutes back. It was an annihilation, no matter what the terrain – time trials, flat stages, sprints, medium mountains, high mountains. He was a freak, a coalescence of yellow, green and polka-dot contenders.

There was another time-trial success in Revel. Then, with six days remaining, he served up what was indisputably the most astounding display of individual strength in Tour history. The stage through the Pyrenees to Mourenx began with crushing suppression of what Merckx depicted as an internal rebellion. The evening before, he had discovered that key lieutenant Martin Van den Bossche was leaving Faema. When his teammate moved to the front approaching the summit of the Tourmalet in an attempt to lead the race over the prestigious pass, Merckx, riled by his domestique's betrayal, reacted with an acceleration that took him to the front. 'I just wanted to remind him who was the boss. That's how I ended up alone,' he explained.

Van den Bossche's account of those moments differs significantly, though. He insists no one knew that he had agreed a deal to move and didn't break the news until well after the Tour, when Faema failed to come up with an offer that was anywhere close to the fourfold salary increase he was in line for at Molteni. That evening, Van den Bossche reveals in Daniel Friebe's *Eddy Merckx: The Cannibal,* he searched out his team leader looking for an explanation of events on the Tourmalet. 'I said, "Eddy, today a small rider expected a big gesture from you." He didn't respond and I never brought it up again.' In the same manner as Coppi, Rik Van Looy and other absolutist team leaders, Merckx was only rarely concerned with allowing his domestiques their own moments of glory. They were there to help him, not themselves.

With 140 kilometres still to cover, Merckx descended rapidly, but not at this point with the thought of continuing on alone. Passing through Luz-St-Sauveur having flown down from the Tourmalet, his advantage was less than a minute. He replenished himself and expected the group chasing behind to bridge up to him. But no one appeared. At the foot of the Soulor, he was three-and-a-half minutes clear, had opened his lead to more than five by its summit and almost seven when he reached the adjoining Col d'Aubisque, with seventy-five kilometres still between him and the finish. He sai d later that he began to have doubts about the wisdom of this extraordinary solo exploit coming off the Aubisque and into the valleys and flats below. But the chase behind was flagging. The field had been scattered. A mere seven riders were in pursuit, among them Van den Bossche, who had no reason to contribute. They trailed in eight minutes down in at the finish. 'I lived the stage that I'd dreamed about. The one about which every yellow jersey must undoubtedly dream. But it was so hard!' Merckx confessed.

But still he wasn't done. He was second to Pierre Matignon on the Puy de Dôme, and not at all happy at having missed out on another high-status stage win to the race's *lanterne rouge*, as the rider bringing up the rear in the overall standings is known. True to form, he won the final time trial into Paris, his sixth success of the race in addition to the team time trial to finish almost eighteen minutes ahead of runner-up Pingeon, twenty-two clear of Poulidor and half an hour clear of Gimondi in fourth. It resembled a result from the inter-war years, a rout to compare with Coppi at his peak. However, unlike the Italian, the Belgian's *la course en tête* strategy, of always riding at the front, meant that he dominated everywhere. Although a serious crash later that year on the track at Blois meant that Merckx was never quite the same rider again, he didn't lose the desire to enforce himself whenever the occasion presented itself. He would attack anyone, anywhere. There were moments of weakness, most obviously the humiliating thrashing that Luis Ocaña handed out at Orcières Merlette in the 1971 Tour, but not until Bernard Thévenet stripped him of the yellow jersey for the final time at Pra-Loup in 1975 did anyone ultimately get the better of him.

Many simply opted to avoid goading 'the ogre' (of Tervuren) and picked off the crumbs that Merckx left them. Joop Zoetemelk and Lucien Van Impe, who both won the Tour in years that the Belgian was absent, were frequently accused of doing no more than following, of spineless acquiescence. But, Van Impe told Belgian journalist Éric Clovio, 'When you were up against Merckx, there was nothing you could do... From the start I knew that I was wasting my time trying to battle with Eddy for overall victory. Even if you gave all you had, you still only finished second or third at best. The energy spent in doing so would have stopped me from winning stages and the best climber classification which did so much for my popularity... Personally, I never attacked him on the climbs. It was preferable to have Eddy with you rather than against you, especially on the flat and on descents. I only dared attack him once, on the road to Orcières Merlette. The next day we all regretted it on the famous stage to Marseille...'

Having been humbled by Ocaña, Merckx implemented one of the fundamental tactics from the yellow jersey playbook by striking back immediately. His Molteni teammate Marinus Wagtmans was on the attack even before the starter had waved away the 251-kilometre stage to Marseille. As Merckx and a small group of riders who were by design or pure luck ready for the ambush chased after Wagtmans, Ocaña was being interviewed by a TV reporter at the rear of the field.

The Spanish race leader didn't see the front of the race all day, but ended it comparatively unscathed time-wise, losing just two minutes of an almost ten-minute advantage over Merckx, who jumped from fifth place to second. Yet the Belgian

inflicted a far more significant psychological blow, demonstrating to everyone, and particularly the brittle Ocaña, that they hadn't finished him off, that he was going to harry them at every opportunity. Two days later, trying to respond to the Belgian's kamikaze attack in a deluge that swamped the Col de Menté, Ocaña slid off on a hairpin and, as he staggered back to his feet, was hit by two riders whose brakes had been rendered useless by the rain. His race was over, ended by exactly the kind of calamity that Merckx always feared.

As with Coppi and, to an extent, Anquetil, Merckx's attacks weren't simply acts of panache but attempts, driven by existential angst, to increase his advantage over his rivals when he had the chance to do so and in order to give him as large a buffer as possible. In an interview with Clovio, Merckx explained, 'It's a platitude, but it's compelling: the Tour is only won once the finish line has been crossed. You never know what might happen until that moment. That's why I used to go on the attack as often as possible. It wasn't about brio, but above all to give myself a sufficient buffer. Whether you believe me or not, I wasn't looking to produce great exploits, I just wanted to... put my mind at ease.'

However, those on the receiving end of his compulsion to expel doubt insist Merckx was also fired by another fundamental desire: that of almost incessantly reasserting his dominion over them. Early in the 1974 Tour, Britain's Barry Hoban, a punchy sprinter who claimed eight Tour stage wins over his career, set his sights on the yellow jersey by claiming bonus time in intermediate sprints. In Friebe's book, he recalls racing for one but losing out when Merckx dived under his shoulder at the last moment. 'Eddy, what are you doing? You're going to win the Tour by fifteen minutes. You can give me the yellow jersey for a day or two,' Hoban asked, to which Merckx replied, 'Yes, Barry, but it's *my* yellow jersey...'

As early as 1970, Jacques Goddet was expressing reservations about Merckx, feeling that he pushed himself too hard, too incessantly, that he didn't embody the typical Tour champion, who tended to be more reasoned when it came to their commitment on a daily basis and not so gung-ho. It was even suggested that Merckx was doing a disservice to the race and to the yellow jersey, sublimating them beneath his extraordinary talent rather than raising their legendary status. Following his third consecutive victory in 1971, Goddet returned to his critique, pointing out, 'Bobet and Anquetil are always astonished that Merckx gives so much. A champion must remain parsimonious in his effort. I'm not sure that those well-established dogmas fit with a yellow jersey who doesn't resemble any who has gone before.'

Within a handful of years, another yellow jersey would emerge who would prove to be just as dominant as Merckx and would evoke a similar reproach. Before Bernard Hinault's consecration in 1978, the interregnum between the second and third of the Tour's five-time champions saw Van Impe, heavily prompted by his DS Guimard, finally commit himself to contesting the yellow instead of the polka-dot jersey, although the duel with the equally conservative Zoetemelk was far from a classic. The following year, Thévenet advanced from giant-killer to confirmed champion with a more impressive success over this pair and Hennie Kuiper, and it triggered an unprecedented run of home domination, with France celebrating nine victories in eleven seasons.

Guimard was the guiding force behind six of those home wins, beginning with Hinault's debut success in 1978. Anquetil, who was close to both the Gitane DS and his team leader, said of Hinault that he 'gets his strength from his total certainty'. Guimard agrees, explaining, 'For him, the objective of victory was an exercise in asserting his domination. And he had the means to achieve this!' Often compared with Coppi and, particularly, Merckx for the way that he dominated his rivals and the breadth of his palmarès, psychologically Hinault was the antithesis of this illustrious duo. He didn't need the prop of absolutism within his team and was quite happy to support his teammates in chasing their objectives when they didn't conflict with his own. However, even on these occasions, he couldn't be ignored. 'Hinault either cared or he didn't. When he didn't care about winning he'd bumble round and hurt you just to remind you he was there – you wouldn't know Greg [LeMond] or Miguel [Indurain] were in some races, but with Hinault you always knew,' Robert Millar says of him in William Fotheringham's *The Badger*.

Hinault was, right from the start, the Tour's patron, the rider who imposed discipline on the peloton, and he admitted he took 'a special delight in knowing that you are the boss'. Even before he had worn the yellow jersey in the 1978 Tour, the twenty-three-year-old Breton had been anointed the leader, striding forward in the French champion's jersey, chest and chin thrust out, in the front line of the riders' strike just before they reached the finish line at Valence d'Agen. As the crowd whistled and jeered, Hinault stepped forward to explain

Eddy Merckx, Paris 1969

'Eddy, what are you doing?

You're going to win the Tour by fifteen minutes. You can give me the yellow jersey for a day or two,'

Hoban asked, to which Merckx replied,

'Yes, Barry, but it's my yellow jersey...'

La Gazzetta dello Sport

Una copia L. 150 — Sped. in abb. Post. Gr. 1/70

ANNO 79 - N. 759

MARTEDI' 15 LUGLIO 1975

Seconda tappa alpina - L'ex maglia gialla sferra l'attacco nella discesa del Vars - Thévenet lo insegue, ricupera i 45" di ritardo e con un perfetto colpo d'incontro lo lascia ai piedi dell'Izoard e giunge solo con 2' e 22"

Merckx ancora al tappeto

In classifica Thévenet ha 3'20" di vantaggio

SERRE-CHEVALIER — La smorfia di Merckx dopo la seconda sconfitta consecutiva. (Tel: ANSA)

Comunicato del presidente del Milan

Buticchi rompe «definitivamente» con Rivera

Il colpo a sorpresa non sorprende nessuno - Rivera: «Per me il contratto è stato perfezionato e le ragioni di maggioranza sono mie» - La soluzione ad un Collegio arbitrale?

LOVATI È SICURO

Chinaglia in Italia tra due mesi

E giocherà in una di queste tre società: Inter o Milan o Juventus

Giorgio Chinaglia torna in Italia? Lo dice di sì, ma il direttore sportivo della Lazio, Lovati, che lo conosce bene è sicuro del contrario. E sarà, a suo avviso, il prossimo anno.

INCREDIBILE SPAVALDERIA DELLA MAGLIA GIALLA

Merckx lo lascio andare...

DA UNO DEI NOSTRI INVIATI

SERRE-CHEVALIER, 14 luglio

L'atletica azzurra nella finale di Coppa Europa grazie al «collettivo»

Mennea ha una squadra alle spalle

Sommario

PAGINA 3

Burgnich consiglia all'Inter: Mazzola mezzapunta, Bini libero, Facchetti stopper

PAGINA 8

È Bertoni tra ad arene paura?
(di Gianni Merlo)

PAGINE 6 e 7

Vela - Derivo da «Tortorella» la vittoria degli italiani sulla Francia nella 22.a Giraglia

PAGINE 9

Necessario anche per i piloti un «minimax motodistico»
(di Achille Plucingelli)

Al Mugello hanno vinto le 4 T e del due
(di Nino Zoghi)

ARRIVO

1	Thévenet	3.16'17"
2	Merckx	2'22"
3	Gimondi	
4	Zoetemelk	
5	Van Impe	
6	Romero	
7	Lopez-Carril	
8	Galdos	
9	Janssens	
10	Van Springel	4'08"
11	Poulidor	4'13"
12	FAMBRI	
13	POGGIALI	
17	FONTANELLI	

CLASSIFICA

1	Thévenet	85.6'13"
2	Merckx	3'20"
3	Zoetemelk	6'30"
4	Van Impe	7'36"
5	Gimondi	10'41"
6	Maier	19'08"
7	Lopez-Carril	19'41"
8	Fuchs	27'36"
9	Janssens	29'42"
10	Torres	30'12"

to the town's irate mayor and the race's co-director, Félix Lévitan, the riders' grievance at the number of split stages that meant their day started very early and ended extremely late. 'I'm not going to talk to you!' Lévitan told him. 'Monsieur Lévitan, we're both men and we have to discuss this. If not, we'll go on strike again this afternoon.' Lévitan agreed to listen, and the Tour continued relatively serenely.

Hinault told *L'Équipe*'s Philippe Brunel. 'To be a patron, you have to be capable of winning the race overall, not just the points or the mountains. You hold the key to winning stages and can decide if someone can win. You need the strength to get off the front and catch an attacker, and there may be days you decide to do that even if they haven't wound you up.' Hinault became the embodiment of the patron, 'in order to ensure the riders raced in the way that he wanted to, and – it can be conjectured – to cement the psychological stranglehold he enjoyed over his fellows,' says Fotheringham.

He chased down and chastised those who attacked before he was ready to permit the pace to rise. Unlike Merckx, he didn't have to win every time he raced. He didn't need that affirmation. But in those three or four races each season, including the Tour, that were marked with an X on his race programme, he was determined to impose himself, to ensure that it ran in the way he wanted. 'His pride was his real motor. Often he reacted more like a boxer than a racing cyclist. When he was looking to win, he was at his strongest when he was in a real fight,' says Guimard.

Behaving in this manner could also get him into trouble. On the stage into Angers during

Bernard Hinault, the Badger, enforced his control on the peloton from the outset.

the first week of the 1979 Tour, Guimard recalls Hinault getting irritated by Raleigh's pace-setting at the front, which threatened to split the peloton. In order to get them back into line, he went to the front and upped the pace still further, while behind him Raleigh eased off and let him go clear on his own. He gained almost a minute, not quite enough time for his DS to be allowed past the peloton to reach Hinault and tell him to ease off. In the end, Guimard's only recourse was to get the Renault team to chase down their leader, which mystified the rest of the peloton and didn't go down at all well with Hinault when they reeled him in. When he'd calmed down, Guimard pointed out that he

| *Hinault wins the 75th Tour de France in Paris, France on 22 July 1978*

could well have lost the Tour by riding flat out all day so early in the race. 'In order to prevent his qualities becoming faults, he needed a safeguard. That's what I became,' says Guimard.

Although Hinault leaned much more heavily than Merckx on time trials to construct his five Tour victories, he would commit himself fully on any terrain if he was determined to prove a point or mess with the minds of his fellow racers. He'd get involved and win bunch sprints: in 1979 he fought a stage-long duel with Zoetemelk on the Tour's final stage into the Champs-Élysées where he naturally turned down the Dutchman's plea for a consolation victory, and, in 1981, delivered the racing equivalent of a *bras d'honneur* to the press who had criticised a rather supine performance at Alpe d'Huez with a solo win at the Le Pleynet ski station the next day.

When he brought the curtain down on his career with second place behind teammate LeMond at the 1986 Tour, a race that he stage-managed almost completely just for the sake of his own enjoyment, racing was changing. The salaries of the sport's major stars had grown significantly and were increasingly linked to success in the Tour, the one race that commanded global interest. Rather than racing right through from February to October, they could focus completely on July, using events prior to that as preparation and, if that month went well, ignore much of what came after. Yellow became the only colour that mattered, blinding many to the remainder of the calendar.

EDDIE MERCKX
TOUR DE FRANCE
1970

4

ALL ABOUT YELLOW

Le Maillot Jaune

Bernard Hinault 1978

A CLASSIC DESIGN BY LE COQ SPORTIF WITH
HENRI DESGRANGE'S SIGNATURE
VERY PROMINENT

Le Rire, July 1934

The Only Colour That Matters

Will a climber ever win the Tour de France again, *L'Équipe* asked halfway through the final week of the 2018 Tour?

'Modern cycling has flattened the mountains. In Miguel Indurain's wake, the rouleurs have all but silenced the humm-ingbirds who were once responsible for a substantial part of Tour legend. Take the first four riders on GC this morning. They all share the same profile: rouleurs who, thanks to eating like gazelles and hours of training with their nose glued to their power meters, are now capable of keeping the pure climbers in check,' Gilles Simon said of Sky duo Geraint Thomas and Chris Froome, Slovenia's Primoz Roglic and Dutchman Tom Dumoulin.

This lament about the peloton's high-endurance powerhouses trimming the wings of the mountain specialists is far from new. It was a staple of post-Tour analysis during the Indurain years, when the race's route and action was templated so precisely that those editions between 1991 and 1995 were almost interchangeable. In the run-up to the 1996 race with Indurain aiming for a sixth success to his conveyor belt run of Tour success, he appeared on *Cycle Sport's* cover mocked up as half yellow jersey and half android, the magazine posing the question, 'Is this man a robot?' There was, certainly, a Terminator-like inevitability to Indurain's astonishing time-trial victories, his piston-like legs propelling him at record speeds, his rivals' chances of challenging all but gone even before the mountains had arrived.

That year, his challenge short-circuited, thanks to an unseasonal freeze in the Alps and Bjarne Riis's EPO-fuelled rampage, leaving him on five Tour wins alongside Jacques Anquetil, Eddy Merckx and Bernard Hinault. Each one of this trio was far more flamboyant than 'Big Mig', both on the bike and off it, but raced in essentially the same style. Consequently, *L'Équipe's* intimation that pre-Indurain the Tour was a battleground where darting flyweights ruled, where the likes of Charly Gaul, Federico Bahamontes and Lucien Van Impe consistently dazzled, doesn't stand up, particularly as almost half of the victories that have come since the Spaniard hung up his wheels have been courtesy of specialist climbers, such as Marco Pantani, Alberto Contador, Carlos Sastre and Andy Schleck. Even during the period Sky's riders have hogged the yellow jersey, mountain goats Nairo Quintana, Thibaut Pinot and Romain Bardet have all finished

on the podium, even though they rarely looked like ascending to the top step.

At the same time, 'the French sport daily's suggestion that the Tour, and indeed the whole sport, has changed substantially over the last three decades cannot be denied. When Hinault won his first Tour in 1978, the race began with a peloton that numbered 110 riders in just eleven teams. There were a mere seventy-eight finishers in Paris. Racing, even at the Tour, was freer and more fluid.' Breakaways would go clear and gain ten, fifteen, twenty minutes and more before the peloton took up the chase behind, usually with the goal of keeping the deficit to a reasonable margin. The GC favourites protected their interests by ensuring they had teammates in the break who could win stages and could be used as foils or decoys when the key mountain stages came around. Hinault and LeMond's La Vie Claire team epitomised this approach, DS Paul Köchli judging that it was always better to have riders at the front of the race, in the break, rather than leading the pursuit behind on the front of the bunch. As soon as one break was reeled in, riders would attack off the front of the bunch to instigate the next. As a consequence, there were far fewer bunch sprints – just five in 1985 when Hinault won his final title, and only three a year later when LeMond won his first and the Frenchman bowed out of racing.

It's instructive to note how little Hinault's perspective on racing changed once he stepped away from competition and acted as a pundit. For many years, 'The Badger' filled the role as expert in Tour's annual race guide, analysing the riders and teams. His exhortation to all those who weren't nailed-on podium finishers or among the sprinting elite was invariably a simple one: 'They must attack!' For Hinault and his peers, this was the accepted way to race. Attack often enough and they would create opportunities. By the early nineties, however, tactics had changed considerably for every kind of rider in the peloton.

When Hinault retired, having dominated the 1986 Tour with La Vie Claire teammate LeMond, the American looked likely to become the Tour's new king. However, after he almost lost his life in a hunting accident the following spring, the Tour began with no outstanding favourite and up to a dozen riders eyeing the main prize at a race that was wonderfully chaotic. It was the first to feature nine- instead of ten-man teams, no fewer than twenty-three of them lining up in a 207-strong bunch at the start in West Berlin. Dubbed 'The Waltz of the Yellow Jerseys' by *L'Équipe*, the lead changed hands a record-equalling eight times with no team or rider able to impose control for more than a couple of days. It was exactly the kind of Tour that current race director Christian Prud-homme would love to serve up, unpredictable and brilliant. Stephen Roche was the unlikely winner, having taken the Giro title the month before, drawing on every ounce of his racing nous and sheer bloody-mindedness to edge Pedro Delgado into second place.

In 1988, the Spaniard rose from runner-up to champion, but didn't make a significant impression when defending his title after a disastrous opening few days when he missed his start time in the prologue and got dropped by his Reynolds teammates in the team time trial. As he floundered,

former champions LeMond and Laurent Fignon took centre stage, their see-saw duel as thrilling as any of four spectacular Tours that preceded Delgado's victory and eventually tipping just in the American's favour.

Guimard, who had previously worked with LeMond at Renault but as Fignon's DS was on the wrong end of this verdict, subsequently dismissed all of the American's three titles as flukes. 'In my opinion, he never won the Tour de France. What I mean to say is that on three occasions he should have lost it,' he says in his autobiography, adding, quite viciously, 'At no moment did Greg LeMond win a Tour by going on the attack and dropping

| *Stephen Roche stalks Pedro Delgado on the 1987 Tour*

| *Roche winning the 1987 Tour*

his rivals. His only barometers were his intelligence and his resistance. And he also knew how to remain serene and calm in every kind of situation. Don't they say that you never win the Tour de France by mistake? Well, he won three of them.'

Stemming it would appear from sour grapes at Fignon's loss of the 1989 race by a mere eight seconds on the final time trial into Paris, it's a laughable statement. Guimard backs it up by highlighting LeMond's use of tri-bars in the time trials and Fignon being affected by a suppurating saddle boil in the closing days. Yet he makes no mention of the American's two-year hiatus after being shot, nor of him coping with the glaring deficiencies of his ADR squad and defying the well-established convention that the Tour winner must have a strong team around him. Often isolated from teammates, LeMond had little option but to ride defensively, gaining ground in the time trials and taking other opportunities when they presented themselves, notably on the uphill finish in Briançon, where he gained a useful thirteen seconds on Fignon, and three days later in Aix-les-Bains, where he outsprinted his rival to take victory, his success the only road stage claimed by any Tour champion between 1987 and 1995.

Indurain, of course, dominated most of this period. His summit victory at Luz-Ardiden in 1990, when he rode in support of Delgado but often looked to be the stronger of the pair in the mountains, concealed his strength as a GC contender. An excellent climber, he was also an exceptional time triallist. Equipped from 1991 with Pinarello's state-of-the-art aerodynamic frames, and installed as Banesto's leader with Delgado now his first lieutenant in the mountains, 'Big Mig' emerged. Driven not by doubt or inner demons like Coppi, Anquetil and Merckx, nor by the braggart self-confidence of Hinault, Indurain found a new way to bend his rivals to his will. 'He had a politician's understanding of the Tour and the peloton which was far more subtle than theirs, yet it made his domination of his rivals every bit as complete,' says Ed Pickering in *The Yellow Jersey Club*.

Caricatured as a lumbering farmer's son who depended on brawn rather than brain, Indurain was among the most skilled of diplomats to grace the peloton. Charismatic, polite and, for the most part, unflappable and unruffled, he presided over the most benign of dictatorships, allowing other riders, including some of his most significant rivals, to divide up the minor spoils on the tacit understanding that the major prize would go his way. His first Tour success exemplified this perfectly. Although defending champion LeMond appeared to be in control over the opening half of the race, an initial indication of change came in the seventy-three-kilometre time trial to Alençon, where the Spaniard beat the American by eight seconds. In the Pyrenees, and specifically on the Col du Tourmalet, the middle of five big ascents on a stage to the tiny resort of Val Louron, LeMond's abdication began when he was unable to follow the acceleration made by Indurain and Claudio Chiappucci. At the finish, the Italian climber took

the stage and Indurain his first yellow jersey, his lead a healthy three minutes, which he maintained quite serenely through the Alps and extended a little with a second time-trial triumph on the penultimate day.

Over the next four years, the pattern continued. There were eight further time-trial victories and as many top-three finishes on road stages, but never a victory among the latter. Breakaway riders knew that they had a chance of staying clear if they were no threat to Indurain's lead. GC rivals were equally aware that he wouldn't deny them the fleeting glory of a stage win if they failed to drop him in the mountains. It was an insurance policy that he drew on when problems did occasionally arise, most evidently the stage to Mende in the 1995 Tour when Spanish rivals ONCE attempted a coup. Taking advantage of a fast start that left Indurain with just two teammates for support on a long stage over very lumpy roads through the Massif Central, they smuggled Frenchman Laurent Jalabert into the break with two teammates and three other riders. Their advantage stretched out to more than ten minutes, making Jalabert, whose label as a puncheur well described his aggressive style, the yellow jersey on the road. The moment had come for Indurain to cash in his insurance policy. 'A lot of people helped Indurain that day simply out of kindness, in exchange for nothing,' Jalabert later reflected. He was only half right: Indurain had dispensed favours to so many that there was no hesitation in paying him back. The Frenchman was, ultimately, foiled. He gained six minutes and won the day, but Big Mig remained on his Tour throne.

'Caricatured as a lumbering farmer's son who depended on brawn rather than brain, Indurain was among the most skilled of diplomats to grace the peloton.Charismatic, polite and, for the most part, unflappable and unruffled, he presided over the most benign of dictatorships, allowing other riders, including some of his most significant rivals, to divide up the minor spoils on the tacit understanding that the major prize would go his way.'

Miguel Indurain rides to victory in front of the Arc de Triomphe, 1994

| *Jan Ullrich feels the heat in 2005*

In his calculating style, Indurain was similar to Jacques Anquetil, but, unlike the Frenchman, lacked a rival with the Poulidor factor who could spark him to legendary feats of achievement, with the consequence that he usually left spectators hoping for more but knowing that they were very unlikely to get it. In 2000, he was voted Spain's sportsman of the twentieth century, but at the same time didn't even make the top 100 in L'Équipe's ranking of the world's best, judgements that sum him up neatly: lauded by his compatriots but still unfathomable to the rest of the world. He defended his method that by emphasising that his Banesto team weren't paying him for fireworks. 'My priority was bringing the yellow jersey to Paris. Pleasing the public wasn't our goal. Nothing mattered except Paris. I did everything possible to reach that goal, but nothing more,' he said. 'Of course I was criticised for it. You are who you are and that's that, like it or not. I could never be like Pantani. Had I attacked in the mountains like he used to I wouldn't have lasted very long.'

He was also a product of the Tours during that period. The routes devised by race director Jean-Marie Leblanc were entirely predictable: a prologue time trial, half a dozen stages for the sprinters interspersed by a team time trial, a long time trial, the first mountain stages, two or three transition days before returning to the climbs, a couple of flatter stages to get the race back towards

Paris, a final time trial and, ultimately, a sprinters' jamboree on the Champs-Élysées. Once Indurain had proved his method in 1991, he replicated it again and again.

Changing dynamics within the bunch also worked in his favour. The twenty or more teams participating were better organised and more focused on specific objectives, some of them built almost completely around a new breed of sprinters, protected from the wind and the possibility of a breakaway going the distance by a string of strapping and self-sacrificing rouleurs who would lead them into the final few hundred metres. The Dutch Superconfex team featuring Jean-Paul van Poppel popularised the trend, the Saeco team featuring the inimitable Mario Cipollini perfected it. By strictly managing the peloton, restricting time gaps gained by breakaways and ensuring that the bunch finished en masse during the first week, they enabled Indurain's Banesto teammates to save resources for the mountains.

For those first ten days or so, the specialist climbers could do no more than try to hold a place in the bunch. In a race run at faster averages than ever before, most had either dropped out of contention or had much of the explosive vim sapped from their legs when the Tour reached the mountains. Needing to recoup minutes on rouleurs like Indurain and Tony Rominger to contend for the yellow jersey, and well knowing that this was impossible, they resigned themselves to easier pickings, participants in a completely different race to the GC favourites, who, having been set up like the sprinters by strong outriders, only needed to commit themselves at the very last with a time-trial-like effort. Doping, particularly the increasing use of endurance-enhancing products like EPO, also played a role in levelling out differences in competitive strength in the mountains.

Banesto's yellow jersey-winning method has essentially remained unchanged since. Telekom adapted it for Jan Ullrich, who looked set to establish the next ruling house, but admitted that his success came too young and struggled to cope with the pressure and demands of being a Tour champion. According to his former DS Walter Godefroot, Ullrich had the physical ability to win the Tour again but not the obsessive, almost maladjusted focus required to do so.

'He didn't have the spirit of the great champions, who needed to be killers, and I mean that as a compliment to him,' Godefroot says in *The Yellow Jersey Club*. 'Jan couldn't live for sport twelve months a year. He just wanted to relax at home, eat what he wanted and live how he wanted. The pressure of sport was too much for him, and he didn't have the mentality of a star... All the great champions of cycling have special characters. Jan is not a special man, he's a normal man.'

Ullrich built a palmarès that was the envy of most professionals, but, despite his love of racing, he ended up chasing the goals that his team and fans expected of him. 'I was only twenty-four and everyone was asking me to win the Tour again without understanding that my places of honour had some value. I had to live with that pressure all the time and accept hearing that finishing second was a failure. It's perhaps because of that that I couldn't savour my victory in 1997. Everything arrived too fast and I couldn't do anything to stop

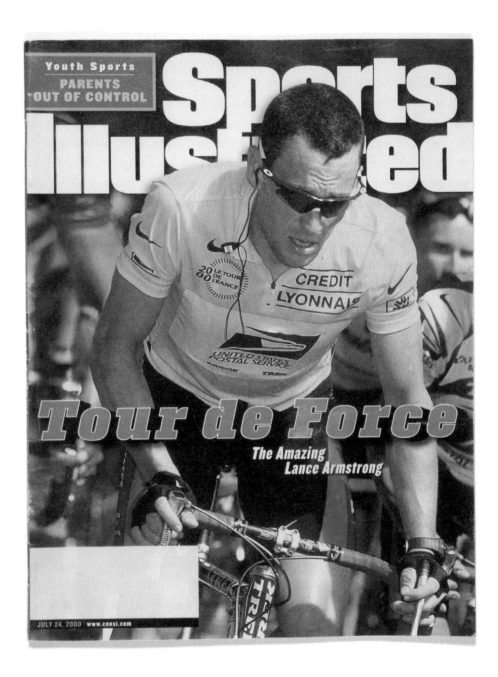

it,' he said in retirement.

Reflecting in his 2018 book *Icons* on what it takes to be a Tour champion, Bradley Wiggins also suggested, like Godefroot, that being 'normal' is not usually an advantageous characteristic. According to the Briton, the yellow jersey winner is 'on occasion, borderline sociopathic' and 'always a very special, very driven human being', adding that he felt 'privileged to be a member of this group of nutters'. The 'icon' he had specifically in mind was, of course, Lance Armstrong, who barged Ullrich aside and became the Tour's most successful champion until compelled, in 2012, to admit his great lie about doping, which led to his name being erased from the race's list of winners.

This made it possible to overlook the Armstrong years when writing about the yellow jersey, as historian Serge Laget essentially does in *100 Ans de Maillot Jaune*. Yet, for many, myself included, who watched and reported on the Armstrong Tours between 1999 and 2005, rubbing out the memories of his performances is not so easy. Just as I can remember exactly where I was and who I was with when I saw Ben Johnson break the world 100-metre record as he won gold at the Seoul Olympics in 1988, a sporting moment the impact of which I will never forget despite the almost immediate taint it gained when the Canadian failed a drug test, I'm also stuck with so many memories of Armstrong's Tour feats – from his first stage win in Verdun in 1993, which was my first day in the Tour pressroom, to him riding off a mountain road and apparently into a void, catching Ullrich in a short time trial, and dishing out a yellow jersey of a bollocking to Filippo Simeoni, who had dared

to diverge from the Texan's warped perspective on the cycling world.

The tale of the Texan's comeback from almost succumbing to cancer to not only racing again but claiming cycling's most iconic prize seven times in succession has already been well told. Extremely sensitive, prickly, quick to take offence and just as fast to deliver it, Armstrong was, psychologically, a hybrid of Merckx and Hinault. Beset by doubt, driven by anger, determined to impose his own certainty on the Tour, he fed off perceived slights, petty grievances, fear of how his rivals might be preparing and the possibility that they might have an edge on him, trawling websites to get any snippet of information on other GC contenders such as Ullrich and Marco Pantani, drawing on comments about their form and expectations to fuel his sociopathic determination.

'The darker side of Lance stressed us out; but as far as the team's performance went it served as fuel,' recalled his former US Postal teammate and close friend Tyler Hamilton in *The Secret Race*, his exposé of the doping, lies and cover-ups that were the foundation for Armstong's and the American team's success. 'He was cold, determined. At US Postal, we only had a professional relationship, and he was one who negotiated everything, who took the decisions, who decided matters,' said another former teammate, Frenchman Cédric Vasseur. 'With his Texan roots, things were always black or white, never grey. He could take you out to dinner one evening, then tell you to fuck off out of the door the next day.'

On the road, Armstrong's tactics were an evolution of those implemented by the four

YEAR	WINNER		TEAM
1980	**Joop Zoetemelk**		**TI–Raleigh–Creda**
1981	Bernard Hinault		Renault–Elf–Gitane
1982	**Bernard Hinault**		**Renault–Elf–Gitane**
1983	Laurent Fignon		Renault–Elf
1984	**Laurent Fignon**		**Renault–Elf**
1985	Bernard Hinault		La Vie Claire
1986	**Greg LeMond**		**La Vie Claire**
1987	Stephen Roche		Carrera Jeans–Vagabond
1988	**Pedro Delgado**		**Reynolds**
1989	Greg LeMond		AD Renting–W-Cup–Bottecchia
1990	**Greg LeMond**		**Z–Tomasso**
1991	Miguel Indurain		Banesto
1992	**Miguel Indurain**		**Banesto**
1993	Miguel Indurain		Banesto
1994	**Miguel Indurain**		**Banesto**
1995	Miguel Indurain		Banesto
1996	**Bjarne Riis**		**Team Telekom**
1997	Jan Ullrich		Team Telekom
1998	**Marco Pantani**		**Mercatone Uno–Bianchi**
1999	~~Lance Armstrong~~		U.S. Postal Service
2000	**~~Lance Armstrong~~**		**U.S. Postal Service**
2001	~~Lance Armstrong~~		U.S. Postal Service
2002	**~~Lance Armstrong~~**		**U.S. Postal Service**
2003	~~Lance Armstrong~~		U.S. Postal Service
2004	**~~Lance Armstrong~~**		**U.S. Postal Service**
2005	~~Lance Armstrong~~		Discovery Channel
2006	**~~Floyd Landis~~**		**Phonak**
	Óscar Pereiro		**Caisse d'Epargne–Illes Balears**
2007	Alberto Contador		Discovery Channel
2008	**Carlos Sastre**		**Team CSC**
2009	Alberto Contador		Astana
2010	**~~Alberto Contador~~**		**Astana**
	Andy Schleck		**Team Saxo Bank**
2011	Cadel Evans		BMC Racing Team

TIME	MARGIN	STAGE WINS
109h 19' 14"	**+ 6' 55"**	**2**
96h 19' 38"	+ 14' 34"	5
92h 08' 46"	**+ 6' 21"**	**4**
105h 07' 52"	+ 4' 04"	1
112h 03' 40"	**+ 10' 32"**	**5**
113h 24' 23"	+ 1' 42"	2
110h 35' 19"	**+ 3' 10"**	**1**
115h 27' 42"	+ 40"	1
84h 27' 53"	**+ 7' 13"**	**1**
87h 38' 35"	+ 8"	3
90h 43' 20"	**+ 2' 16"**	**0**
101h 01' 20"	+ 3' 36"	2
100h 49' 30"	**+ 4' 35"**	**3**
95h 57' 09"	+ 4' 59"	2
103h 38' 38"	**+ 5' 39"**	**1**
92h 44' 59"	+ 4' 35"	2
95h 57' 16"	**+ 1' 41"**	**2**
100h 30' 35"	+ 9' 09"	2
92h 49' 46"	**+ 3' 21"**	**2**
91h 32' 16"	+ 7' 37"	4
92h 33' 08"	**+ 6' 02"**	**1**
86h 17' 28"	+ 6' 44"	4
82h 05' 12"	**+ 7' 17"**	**4**
83h 41' 12"	+ 1' 01"	1
83h 36' 02"	**+ 6' 19"**	**5**
86h 15' 02"	+ 4' 40"	1
89h 40' 27"	**+ 32"**	**0**
91h 00' 26"	+ 23"	1
87h 52' 52"	**+ 58"**	**1**
85h 48' 35"	+ 4' 11"	2
91h 59' 27"	**+ 3' 01"**	**2**
86h 12' 22"	+ 1' 34"	1

members of the five-time Tour winner's club. Time trials, whether of the individual or the team variety, were the ideal place to pick up time on other yellow jersey challengers. With the sprinters' teams controlling the first week ever more tightly on Jean-Marie Leblanc's almost invariably identical routes, Armstrong and US Postal DS Johan Bruyneel would ensure the US Postal leader was well prepped, thanks to expert support with training, reconnaissance trips and precisely timed doping, to deliver a knock-out blow on the first day in the high mountains – in 1999 at Sestriere, in 2000 at Hautacam, in 2001 at Alpe d'Huez, in 2002 at La Mongie, in 2004 at La Mongie again, and in 2005 at Courchevel.

As his run of success extended, Armstrong became more confident, as most Tour winners do, but also more fixated on his rivals, some of whom were former teammates, such as Hamilton and Roberto Heras, who had moved on in order to explore their own GC potential. That obsession to control every aspect of the sport as it impacted on him also extended to cycling's politics, the press, to every little detail that he perceived as being important. He saw conspiracies and threats at every turn, recharging his resources with the indignation and anger he derived from them, as the following curious tale underlines.

In 2004, after refusing for four seasons to speak to *Procycling*, the magazine I worked for as a freelance contributor, following an editorial in the British magazine following the 2000 Tour that had urged Armstrong to cut his links with controversial Italian training guru Michele Ferrari, the American agreed to an interview. A few days

after that had taken place, I followed up with a request via his press officer for some quotes about Heras, who had left US Postal to become leader at Liberty Seguros. I heard nothing for several weeks. Then, in the middle of an Easter Sunday family lunch at my father's house, my mobile rang. It was Armstrong.

'Ah, you're calling about Heras. I'll just find a pen and paper,' I told him.

'You won't need them,' he spat back, 'because I'm not going to give you any fucking quotes, Peter.'

For the next twenty minutes he berated me for a small story that had appeared in the same edition of *Procycling* as his interview. In it, the writer – who was someone else on the staff and not me, although Armstrong refused to believe that because 'that's not what I've been told by my sources' – had taken lyrics from the songs of Armstrong's new girlfriend Sheryl Crow and put a cycling spin on them. It was silly, something that appealed to the British sense of humour, perhaps, but clearly hadn't tickled Armstrong's funny bone. He accused me of organising a conspiracy against him within the pages of the magazine, of poking fun at and upsetting Crow.

'But, Lance, I'm only freelance for the magazine. I don't have any control over the content and I've not seen that story,' I repeatedly told him.

'You've got your version and I've got mine, and I believe what my sources are telling me,' he kept responding. He wouldn't reveal who these sources were, but it was well known that the American had a network of informants both inside the peloton and the pressroom who stoked his boiler of indignation with all kinds of tittle-tattle.

It was a bizarre conversation. On the one hand, there was the truth and, on the other, there was Armstrong's truth. Ultimately, this is what his whole career came down to. When the basis for his truth finally slid away, the reality about the nature of his rule became apparent. He wanted his control over racing, his team and almost everyone connected with the sport to be total. Paranoid, obsessive and yet to recant, Armstrong now floats on the edges of the sport, his seven yellow jerseys hanging in the den of his home, like a big FU to the race and the sport that now refuses to recognise him as anything other than a cheat who carried out one of the most pernicious frauds in sporting history.

Inevitably, he left a huge hole at the summit of the Tour's hierarchy when he retired at the end of the 2005 race, a void so immense in fact that Armstrong ultimately felt he was only one who could fill it, resulting in his decision to return to racing in 2009. In between, the Tour witnessed Oscar Pereiro's ill-starred success after Floyd Landis had been disqualified for doping, Alberto Contador's first victory following Rabobank's decision to withdraw race leader Michael Rasmussen from the 2007 race for evading out-of-competition doping controls, and a Carlos Sastre victory that was beset by an array of doping scandals and was described by Armstrong as 'a bit of a joke', because of what he regarded as the lowly standard of the contenders for the title. An earnest, rather uninspiring, but hugely courteous man who kept his counsel rather than verbally machine-gunning his rivals, Sastre had won the race in fine style, emulating Fausto Coppi's achievement of claiming victory on Alpe d'Huez and then defending the jersey into Paris.

That same year, Christian Prudhomme took over the reins as race director and immediately endeavoured to revitalise the organisation of the route, which Jean-Marie Leblanc had allowed to become staid, bereft of any ingenuity or attempt to test the riders in unexpected ways. While Sastre wasn't the swashbuckling champion Prudhomme had dreamed of, seven different riders wore the yellow jersey. The 'Tinkerman' of Tour directors, Leblanc's successor finds it hard to resist an innovation, which have included the reintroduction of cobbles, summit finishes on the penultimate day, a reduction in the number of time-trial kilometres, and, more recently, gravel roads, with varying degrees of success.

In 2009, the race opened with a time trial rather than a prologue, included two stages where race radios were banned, and a stage finish one day from Paris on top of Mont Ventoux. Prudhomme's remodelling of the Tour, which in the case of the radio ban was opposed and scuppered by the bigger teams, was eclipsed, though, by Armstrong's return and the consequent internecine battle at Astana with Contador. 'The team management had put together a plan designed to ensure that Lance won the Tour rather than me. But, as you well know in cycling, it's always the legs that have the last word,' the Spaniard said of the race, omitting to mention the mental strength he needed to cope with the evident favouritism shown towards the American by Astana's DS Bruyneel, whose orders, designed to keep Armstrong in the contest for the yellow jersey and, ultimately, on the podium, Contador regularly defied.

His success underlined the two principle tenets of Tour success: the strongest rider will generally win, and he will usually be backed by the strongest team. Astana's team directors may have preferred to see Armstrong take the title, but not at the expense of seeing a rival team ride taking advantage. Contador's victory also served as a reminder that pure climbers could still finish on the top step of the podium in Paris, which was underlined by Andy Schleck's success the next year following the Spaniard's disqualification, the result of the latest doping infraction to affect the Tour winner. The hummingbirds were back, flitting colourfully and consistently. Even though the diesel-like Cadel Evans denied them in 2011, Contador and Schleck illuminated a contest that almost produced the greatest upset since Roger Walkowiak and concluded with seven climbers in the top ten. Yet, rather than signalling a renaissance of the unpredictable, it was the final race in another Tour interregnum. A new dynasty was about to emerge.

BERNARD HINAULT
TOUR DE FRANCE
1978

5

TWENTY-FIRST CENTURY TOUR TEAM
Le Maillot Jaune

Geraint Thomas 2018

**BIG ON THE BRANDING BUT THERE'S
STILL ROOM TO HONOUR DESGRANGE**

Blue Sky Thinking

Tour de France dynasties have generally been the result of individual prowess rather than team power and consistency.

No one talks about the La Vie Claire, Astana, Telekom, CSC or Renault era, although perhaps we should in the latter case, given that the French squad won six titles in seven years with two different riders. With Sky, though, the team is greater than any one rider, even a multiple champion like Chris Froome. When Geraint Thomas completed their sixth victory in seven seasons, Sky became the first trade team to win the yellow jersey with three different riders since Automoto in the mid-1920s.

Blessed, compared to many of their rivals, with the wealth of Croesus, Sky have the budget to buy almost any rider they want and employ whatever support staff they deem they need.

However, money doesn't necessarily buy sporting success on its own, particularly in the sustained way in which the British squad has achieved it. In the 1990s, the various configurations of the Mapei team never managed to claim the yellow jersey despite having the deepest pockets in cycling, while in other sports the New York Yankees, Manchester United and Paris Saint-Germain are only the most celebrated of the clubs whose financial resources have failed to deliver comparable success on the field in recent years.

Sky, though, have made their financial clout count and, until the surprise announcement by the broadcasting giant in December 2018 that it would be withdrawing from the pro peloton at the end of the following season, there was no indication that the team was about to relinquish its grip on the yellow jersey. Quite the opposite in fact, as younger riders who had been signed to succeed Froome and Thomas were rising quickly through the British squad's hierarchy, getting to grips with a structure and method that has an invincible sheen.

Guided by Dave Brailsford, who had overseen British Cycling's dominance of track racing, they adopted essentially the same framework that has yielded so much success on the boards, identifying the challenge, establishing quantifiable aims and endeavouring to minimise uncontrollable elements. As part of this process, they questioned almost every accepted tenet within professional bike racing, examining attitudes towards training, equipment, competition and logistics in order to pinpoint potential 'marginal gains'. This became so all-consuming that bewildered team members wondered whether they were in danger of being swamped by inconsequentialities. 'They are trying to do things too differently. I mean, if they could reinvent hot water, they would,' suggested Serge Pauwels during Sky's debut 2010 season.

The Belgian's comment encapsulated the prevailing perspective and attitude towards the new team. Like any organisation with a leftfield approach, they were simply ripe for attack from the establishment. Marc Madiot, whose name alone could signify the traditional side of professional cycle sport, was among those who hit out, dismissing Sky's obsession with psychologists, computers, Twitter and even their love of a press release. 'Every day there is something new with them,' the Française des Jeux team boss complained at one point. 'It's information overload. We too put riders in a wind tunnel to analyse their performance, but we don't make a song and dance about it.' After marquee signing Bradley Wiggins rolled into Paris an also-ran in that 2010 Tour, Sky's oft-stated objective of winning the Tour within five years with a British rider became another rod to beat them with. 'Bye-bye podium' crowed L'Équipe after Sky had set the pace for their leader on the climb up to Avoriaz only to see him drop back from the other favourites, his hopes of contending all but gone.

Appropriately for a sports organisation so focused on innovation and technology, Sky's change in fortunes the following season stemmed principally from its support staff. The reimagining of every detail became more focused, thanks in large part to the increasing influence of performance director Tim Kerrison, whose background was in swimming. During the team's first year, he gleaned all he could about bike racing, watching the tactics and preparation, examining the methods, asking, he admits, a lot of dumb questions in order to further his understanding. In their second season, the Australian coach began to revamp the whole team's approach to racing and training. Among the most obvious innovations, introduced to sniggering from rival teams, was riders warming down on home trainers immediately after racing. There were also changes to diet, hydration, equipment testing and development. Kerrison implemented a programme of reverse periodisation, preparing for major objectives not by racing but with intense training at altitude.

'You assume racing is harder than training because as a cyclist it's engrained in you from when you are a kid,' Wiggins says in his autobiography *My Time*, going on to explain that Kerrison corrected that assumption during the latter part of that 2011 season. 'So the philosophy became: don't go to the race to train, but train first, go to fewer races, and go there to win.' Weeks after finishing third at the Vuelta and playing a key role in the Great Britain team that helped set up Mark Cavendish for victory at the 2011 World Championships

in Copenhagen, Wiggins began to work towards the 2012 season, upping his high-intensity workouts in the controlled setting of training camps often held on Mount Teide in Tenerife, and at the same time radically changing his diet and lifestyle with the aim of boosting his power-to-weight ratio. The goal? To enable him to cope more easily with the darting sorties of the hummingbirds at the Tour, particularly on the upper reaches of the Tour's highest passes, his Achilles heel in 2010.

It was widely suggested that Sky were off beam again when Wiggins, backed by a well-drilled cohort of riders, tore through the opening half part of the new season, winning Paris–Nice and the Tour de Romandie and then defending his Critérium du Dauphiné crown. He had, the critics chorused, peaked too soon. But Sky didn't share

Mark Cavendish riding as world champion in 2012

these concerns. As Wiggins was reiterating in interviews and press conferences, they were sure it was possible to race at a high level all year and that their leader was on track for the goal that he had set himself of victory in the Tour de France. He had won more frequently than in 2011, but had raced considerably less – just thirty days leading up to July instead of the forty-one he'd completed twelve months earlier. The racing was also easier to cope with physically and mentally than the blocks of training Kerrison plotted out for them in camps.

'The idea was to go to those races, perform, treat each one as if it were a Tour de France in miniature, lead the race and get the team around me to do the job as they would in the Tour,' says Wiggins. As well as fostering confidence throughout the team, the strategy enabled the Englishman to become accustomed to the process involved in wearing a race leader's jersey, from defending it on the road through to dealing with post-race media protocols.

In the absence of the peloton's two outstanding climbers, with Contador sidelined by a doping ban and Andy Schleck absent after fracturing his pelvis in a crash at the Dauphiné, the Tour shaped up as a battle of the turbo diesels, pitching defending champion Cadel Evans, leader of an impressive BMC team that was one of the few with funding to compare to Sky's, against Wiggins. It was never likely to be a thriller, especially on a course with 100 kilometres of individual time trialling, considerably more than any other Tour in the Prud-homme era. Sky, of course, wanted to suppress unpredictability wherever they could and, as a

Sky sit on the front and control the race on stage 14 of the 2012 Tour

consequence, smooth their optimal route to a yellow jersey that still had grail-like status for them.

The selection of their nine riders was relatively straightforward. Mark Cavendish and his lead-out man/road captain Bernie Eisel were added to a

line-up forged around Wiggins during the first half of the season. The Manx sprinter had won the green points jersey in the previous year, and Sky didn't play down suggestions that they would help him retain it, in doing so lifting some of the pres-

sure on Wiggins prior to the first summit finish at La Planche des Belles Filles on the race's second weekend.

It quickly became evident, though, that Sky were reluctant to commit much support to Cavendish for the bunch sprints, only changing this strategy midway through the first week when Wiggins sensed he and his teammates were dithering towards the end of stages, unsure whether to set the pace at the front and extract themselves from nervy uncertainty within the peloton, or to hold back, save energy and hope that they didn't get snarled up by a crash. The first option required extra expenditure of physical resources. On the other hand, riding at the front, which Kerrison advocated, lowered stress levels and made it more certain that Sky's protected riders would avoid crashes. It wasn't new for a GC team to race in this way, but it was significant because this was the first indication that Sky were prepared to control the peloton by setting the pace from thirty kilometres out even when they weren't defending the yellow jersey.

The stage to medium-mountain summit of La Planche des Belles Filles in the Vosges proved the turning point. On the eight-kilometre final climb, Sky implemented what would quickly become a very familiar strategy, their domestiques setting the pace with Wiggins the last man in the line. With two kilometres remaining, after first Michael Rogers and then Richie Porte had peeled aside, Froome took over on the front with just a handful of riders including Cadel Evans and Wiggins on his wheel. They finished in that order, Froome neutralising the Australian's late attack with a counter that gave him his first Tour stage win. Wiggins came home on the defending champion's wheel to secure his and his team's first yellow jersey.

After Wiggins had blitzed his rivals in a long time trial at Besançon to push his overall advantage out to almost two minutes, the Sky steamroller crushed most of their opposition once again at La Toussuire's summit finish. That stage featured two instances of a tactic that triggered a huge controversy that still continues. Rather than responding with an instant acceleration to counter-attacks made by GC rivals Evans and Vincenzo Nibali, Sky's riders allowed them to go clear, at the same time maintaining a pace and power output that, Kerrison had calculated, would almost certainly guarantee that they would reel in the attackers. The Australian made his move on the climb of the Glandon, with seventy-odd kilometres still to the finish. For a brief time, it looked as if the 2011 winner might pull off an epic turnaround by getting across to a group containing teammate Tejay van Garderen. The success of the tactic depended on Sky's domestiques panicking, reacting too quickly, burning themselves out and leaving Wiggins isolated and having to chase with just a teammate or two. However, rather than engaging in a frantic chase, they upped their incessant tempo and Evans was inexorably drawn back into the group.

'Our road captain Mick Rogers took it straight up to 450 [watts] and sat at that,' Wiggins explains. 'When you are riding at that kind of rhythm, not far off the limit, if someone is going to attack on a mountain and sustain it to the summit, they have to be extremely good to get away, let alone to open up a decent gap.' Not even the defending champion was strong enough. Having made his Hail Mary halfway through the stage, Evans now had to watch Sky run it back for the cycling equivalent of a touchdown. After repeating the tactic on the final climb to reel in Nibali, Wiggins pushed his lead out even further as Froome moved into second place ahead of the Italian, with Evans relegated to fourth, his title already slipping away.

In essence, Sky were implementing a climbing version of a sprinter's lead-out train, a defensive tactic intended to prevent all bar one eventuality. It was impressive, but far from thrilling to watch, 'the cycling equivalent of putting eleven men behind the ball and sitting on a 1–0 lead, a three-week demonstration of *catenaccio*,' says Ed Pickering. Although Merckx, Hinault and, most obviously, Indurain had implemented the same method, the application of Kerrison's science made it almost infallibly effective, assuming Sky's riders could hit the numbers required of them, and soon led to calls for power meters to be banned from races. 'At Sky, they calculate everything. They lack fantasy,' Nibali has complained, declaring this approach is 'very much the opposite of my concept of cycling'. It is this approach, focusing essentially on being completely professional at the expense of the humanity and spontaneity that attracts most fans to the sport that is right at the root of the team's unpopularity.

Apart from the doubts created by Froome's rabid pace-making at La Toussuire and in the Pyrenees at Peyragudes that saw him briefly ride away from his leader, Sky's command of the second half of the Tour was untroubled. Yet racing in this way did, naturally, take a considerable physical toll on their domestiques. As a consequence, support for Cavendish was pared back and restored only when Wiggins had all but won the title. The Manxman finished with a decent haul of three stage wins, but departed for QuickStep after just a season with Sky,

who have never subsequently selected a sprinter for the Tour. There is no place for one when the overriding objective is to control the action at the race's critical points in order to ensure one of your riders reaches Paris with the yellow jersey on his shoulders.

Like Cavendish, Wiggins also ended up a fall guy when ASO decided to reduce the number of time-trial kilometres and boost the amount of climbing for the 2013 Tour. Froome was now Plan A. Rather than contemplate the awkwardness and potential for a rift that might have ensued from a handover of power on the road, Sky directed their Tour champion towards other goals and filled their roster with eight riders completely devoted to their new figurehead. Froome's path to the Tour was much the same as the one followed by Wiggins the year before. He romped through the initial races on his programme, winning the Tour of Oman, the Critérium International, Romandie and the Dauphiné, and went into July as the favourite for the yellow jersey. Having picked his way carefully through the opening week, he announced himself as the rider to beat with a solo victory at the Pyrenean resort of Ax 3 Domaines, where teammate Porte finished second and moved into the same position on GC. It was, it appeared, 2012 all over again.

'Once you have the yellow jersey, a different race gets under way, the Tour starts for real. Your whole day changes. You're at the race for an hour or an hour-and-a-half longer than most of your rivals, the media pressure and focus is incredibly intense. The attention to detail required in that situation is all-consuming,' says Froome. 'Of course, the other

| *Chris Froome celebrates victory in the 100th edition of the Tour in 2013*

aspect to it is that all of your rivals are looking at you in the yellow jersey and thinking that you're the man to be beat.' He acknowledges being well aware that attacks would come during the mountain stage that followed, but felt that his team were ready to deal with them. The route from Saint-Girons to Bagnères-de-Bigorre meandered through the rugged Couserans region, crossing five categorised climbs before concluding with a fast descent into the finish. It had 'breakaway' written all over it, a day for riders who were unconcerned with the GC battle. But Sky were about to unravel.

Their problems began when Pete Kennaugh, one of their strongest climbers, crashed before the first climb of the Portet d'Aspet and had to wait for a new bike. Minutes later, after the yellow jersey group had swept down the short drop that leads immediately onto the Col de Menté, Richie Porte lost contact with the yellow jersey group, paying the price for his efforts at Ax 3 Domaines. In little more than an hour, Froome found himself with no support at all and four climbs still to negotiate. The result was a scintillating day of racing

That he survived was thanks to him being the strongest rider in the field, to DS Nicolas Portal's strategic nous, and to rivals Movistar, a team renowned for its tactical conservatism, being more concerned with relegating Porte from the contest for podium places than in trying to win the Tour. After mulling how best to limit Froome's poten-

'Has he hung his yellow jerseys on the wall, I ask him?

"No, they aren't framed or anything like that at the moment.
I prefer not to reflect too much on my career at this point.
I'm still very much focused on looking ahead and fighting
for a few more victories before I hang up my wheels."

tial losses, Portal instructed his leader to regard Movistar as his new team and track their leaders Nairo Quintana and Alejandro Valverde at all times, paying particular attention not to lose ground on them in the valleys where he wouldn't be able to regain it without allies to assist him. Prompted and cajoled by his team director, the yellow jersey crossed the line without losing time to any of his GC challengers.

It was exactly the kind of stage that Tour director Christian Prudhomme and most outside Sky would relish seeing far more often, but they've occurred very rarely over subsequent seasons. Principally, this has been the consequence of the British team being very careful to avoid ending up in this situation again and, in addition, being clever about how it has used its support riders, rotating the burden of pacemaking between them depending on their form, the terrain and the resources they've already expended in the quest to win the Tour, keeping them as fresh as possible by giving them 'a day off' when this is practical. The collective ability of these domestiques has increased significantly, too. When Froome ultimately eased his way to the 2013 title, the riders who celebrated with him on the Champs-Élysées were a talented group, but not exceptional, for the most part experienced riders who, between them, provided strength on every kind of terrain.

Since 2015, when Froome wrapped up his second success, the balance has changed. That year, the line-up featured only two riders in Luke Rowe and Ian Stannard who could be regarded as pure rouleurs, who would take on the bulk of the workload on the flat and on the opening climbs in

mountain stages. However, in Porte, Kennaugh, Geraint Thomas, Nicolas Roche, Leopold König and Wout Poels, they had racers who, as was frequently pointed out, either had been or could have been leaders on other teams, and who each had the all-round skillset to contend on every kind of terrain. In short, Sky had changed the ideal when selecting a line-up best equipped to contend and, more significantly, impose control over the course of a three-week race. When Porte moved on to explore his own GC ambitions in 2016, Mikel Landa, third at the Giro the previous year, replaced him. In 2017, Michal Kwiatkowski, the 2014 world champion, a potential winner in almost every kind of race and the epitome of this new class of supra-domestique, was drafted in.

Since succeeding Wiggins as Sky's Tour leader, Froome's status as the pre-eminent stage racer of his era has been cemented, despite some significant setbacks. On the road, his lowest moment was the crash in the opening days of the 2014 race that ended his defence of the yellow jersey before he had been fully tested, which subsequent events suggested he would have been as Vincenzo Nibali cruised to a victory more convincing than any yet taken by Sky. When, in 2018, he lost the Tour title to teammate Geraint Thomas, he acknowledged that the travails he had endured off the road following an adverse analytical finding for salbutamol at the 2017 Vuelta a España had exacted a toll, as had a victory at the Giro d'Italia that made him the only rider other than Eddy Merckx to hold all three Grand Tour titles at the same time.

During his period of Tour supremacy, Froome has shown himself to the master of adaptability, to the point where it has become hard to pinpoint any significant flaw in his racing armoury. Questions about his climbing on steep ascents, his skill as a descender, his tactical awareness and his handling and positioning in the bunch have all been answered. He's rarely flustered, either when racing or in the media's spotlight. Wiggins has described him as not being afraid of anything. He's not, like Fausto Coppi, Eddy Merckx or Jacques Anquetil, driven to excel by the fear of possible failure. 'That's not something I think about a lot,' he says. 'I'm a lot more focused on things going well. I'm trying to focus on the victory side of things as opposed to the fear of not winning.'

He wins, not in order to remind his rivals of his strength and authority, like Hinault, but simply to see how many titles he can accumulate. Has he hung his yellow jerseys on the wall? I ask him. 'No, they aren't framed or anything like that at the moment. I prefer not to reflect too much on my career at this point. I'm still very much focused on looking ahead and fighting for a few more victories before I hang up my wheels. Displaying them somewhere in my home would be a reminder every day of what I'd done, and I think it would take away from what I'm still trying to achieve, so I'm holding off on that front,' he says.

Nothing disturbs his remarkably unflinching focus. Thanks to his training, his recces of the route and the vast experience he's accumulated that have raised his self-confidence, Froome has become the ultimate Grand Tour racer, adapting to the requirements of the route as it changes each year. Even Christian Prudhomme's determination to keep the overall result in the balance until the

Tour's very final days hasn't thwarted him.

Two moments from the 2016 race, the first an attack and the second a calculated decision to hold back, illustrate his talent as a racer. That year, in an attempt to prevent Froome distancing his rivals on the first day in the mountains as he had done in 2013 at Ax 3 Domaines and in 2015 at La Pierre Saint-Martin, the Tour director plotted in a down-hill finale off the Peyresourde into Luchon rather than a summit finish. Nevertheless, Froome won it, attacking on his own just as he reached the top of that climb.

'I caught everyone off-guard with that attack, even Nico Portal,' he says, explaining the thinking behind it. 'I'd won the polka-dot jersey the year before and when we'd gone over the top of a couple of the previous climbs I had pushed on a little bit and taken any mountains points that I could behind the breakaway. I knew my GC rivals had seen me do that. So, in the last couple of kilometres before the summit of Peyresourde, I thought, "We're still all together. They're going to see me push over the top and think that I'm just going to be going for the King of the Mountains points again. If I make a move over the top they might, even if just for a second, lower their guard thinking that I'm just picking up the points. But if I carry on pushing over the other side it will be interesting to see what their response is. So why not? The worst that can happen is that they'll bring me back."' When, as Froome attacked, Nairo Quintana hesitated, a gap opened and Sky's leader accelerated away, victory in Luchon putting him in the yellow jersey.

'It showed he's smart, that he doesn't ride like a robot,' Portal says when he remembers that day,

'I've looked and kept looking for whoever might become the next Chris Froome, the rider who might be our next big leader on the Grand Tours. Egan Bernal was my choice and it was vital that he came to this team. Today he is our future'

Dave Brailsford

before offering the second insight into Froome's racing psyche. 'When he says, "Nico, I feel so good", I immediately think, "Oh my God!" because I know what he's actually saying is, "Nico, I want to attack." At that point, I sometimes have to say, "You can't attack now because it's too early or it's too late." The 2016 stage into Culoz is a good example of that. It was a tough day in the Jura mountains. At the end they went over the Grand Colombier twice – two different ways up and the same route down. The plan was for Froomey to stay with his teammates because there were still two summit finishes and a mountain time trial in the final week just ahead.

'Towards the top of the climb, on the very steepest part, which was 16 per cent or so, Froomey touched his microphone and said: "Nico, I feel really, really good." When Wout Poels, who was one of the two riders we had with him, heard that he thought to himself, "Fucking hell, here we go!" Froomey wanted to split the race open again, but I told him to stay with Mikel [Nieve] and Wout, to let them control the race. He did that, although if you look back he did make a very small attack, just as a test really. When he moved, the other GC guys moved with him, and when he stopped, they stopped. If the likes of [Romain] Bardet and Quintana had been in really good shape, they would have used the fact that Froomey had attacked to counter attack. But they didn't, and why was that? Because they were full on. A couple of years earlier, he would probably have attacked, but the fact that he spoke to me about it showed that he probably knew himself it wasn't the right place to try to gain time.'

For Portal, Froome is essentially a bike rider who wants to race, a modern-day Merckx who would love to attack and drop his rivals, but refrains from doing so because of the damage this could do to his yellow jersey hopes, as was the case that day in Culoz. The Sky leader acknowledges this can be frustrating, but also highlights how the unparalleled level of competition for the yellow jersey and the nature of the Tour route frequently force the contenders to err on the side of caution. It is also, he adds, one of the reasons why he has bucked the long-standing trend among GC specialists to focus entirely on the Tour, and has targeted the other two Grand Tours where there is generally far more opportunity to race aggressively. 'I do enjoy those races because you get more of a chance to race, to actually enjoy competing. That's one of the reasons why the Vuelta is one of my favourite races. Every second day there is a mountain-top finish. In a race like that you get to see a real battle between the GC rivals,' he says. 'They're not afraid to try their hand on any one given day because they know that the next day they can try something different if things don't work out.'

Although many, including Prudhomme, have highlighted race radios, power meters and nine-man teams (prior to the cut to eight-rider teams in 2018) as the principal reasons for the racing between the GC contenders at the Tour often being so sterile, Froome is not convinced. He argues that that the action is tamer than it could be because the favourites know that they are unlikely to be able to recoup any time they lose because the route doesn't allow them to do so, resulting in a safety-first approach in which defence is the best form of attack.

'I believe the Tour has scaled back a lot in terms of in the scale of its mountain stages and big summit finishes. They do still exist, but the Giro and Vuelta have a lot more in comparison, more full-on days in the mountains, which leads to a lot more aggression and a more attacking style of racing compared to the Tour de France,' he says. 'In the last couple of Tours there have only been two or three opportunities to do anything in the mountains. When you're racing, you can sense that the GC riders are holding their cards very close to their chest. You don't really see them going all out on any given day because they're too afraid of the potential downside of losing time, and that's led to very negative racing.'

Froome contends that the Tour organisers can either have an exciting, open race with bigger time gaps between the favourites, or stick to its preferred formula in recent seasons that keeps the gaps tight and the verdict in the balance for longer, but encourages racers to eliminate risk. 'If we did see seven or eight big mountain stages and more mountain-top finishes, I would certainly be more inclined to go on a long-range breakaway to regain time, to launch an all-out attack on a mountain-top finish if I've got an opportunity the next day to try to play my cards differently if it doesn't work out. But I don't think we've had those opportunities in the last couple of Tours,' he insists.

When asked about other ways of pepping up the action at the Tour, Froome and Portal agree with Prudhomme's introduction of shorter stages. 'When you do a really short stage, even if it is flat, it is hard for any team to control it, including Sky,'

says Portal. The sixty-five-kilometre stage to the summit of the Col de Portet in the final week of the 2018 race backed this up. Won by Quintana ahead of another mountain goat, Dan Martin, it created bigger gaps between the favourites than any other road stage. 'On days like that, every rider in the peloton can make an all-out effort from start to finish, and when one of the stronger riders commits in that way the GC leaders can quickly become isolated from their domestiques,' explains Portal, who admits that he dreads stages of this kind because he never knows what to expect, while acknowledging they tend to make for electrifying viewing.

The finish on the 2,215-metre Portet, the one moment in the race when the pure climbers left the power climbers such as Geraint Thomas, Tom Dumoulin and Primoz Roglic in their wake, prompted Prudhomme and his Tour route-finding team to seek out France's loftiest passes in 2019. The race has five summit finishes, three of them at an altitude of more than 2,000 metres. The riders will go above that mark on four other occasions, while there are four more hard days of climbing. As a result, it offers a notable shift from recent editions that demanded a cautious approach, and back towards the kind of format that Froome believes will provide more thrills. It is notable, too, for a proliferation of steeper climbs, following the example of the Giro and Vuelta. Like higher altitude, precipitous ramps are seen as way of weakening the grip of the power climbers, of tipping the scales back towards the angels of mountains, such as Quintana, regarded by many, including Froome, as the favourite for the yellow jersey in 2019.

WINNERS OF THE GENERAL CLASSICFICATION 2012-2018

YEAR	WINNER		TEAM	TIME	MARGIN	STAGE WINS
2012	**Bradley Wiggins**	✠	**Team Sky**	**87h 34' 47"**	**+ 3' 21"**	2
2013	Chris Froome	✠	Team Sky	83h 56' 20"	+ 4' 20"	3
2014	**Vincenzo Nibali**	()	**Astana**	**89h 59' 06"**	**+ 7' 37"**	4
2015	Chris Froome	✠	Team Sky	84h 46' 14"	+ 1' 12"	1
2016	**Chris Froome**	✠	**Team Sky**	**89h 04' 48"**	**+ 4' 05"**	2
2017	Chris Froome	✠	Team Sky	86h 20' 55"	+ 54"	0
2018	**Geraint Thomas**	✠	**Team Sky**	**83h 17' 13"**	**+ 1' 51"**	2

Although Colombia's first Tour victory appears to be imminent, Quintana's position as the man most capable of delivering it is under threat, predictably from Sky. While their rivals have been searching for ways to defeat Thomas and Froome, team boss Brailsford has been hunting for the two Britons' successors. 'My job as manager is to look two or three seasons ahead, and I already have the team that I want in three seasons,' he explains two days from the end of the 2018 race. 'I've looked and kept looking for whoever might become the next Chris Froome, the rider who might be our next big leader on the Grand Tours. Egan Bernal was my choice and it was vital that he came to this team. Today he is our future.'

Just twenty-one when handed his Tour debut, the precocious Colombian is a racing phenomenon. Winner of two big stage races and runner-up at Romandie in 2018, his first season at WorldTour level with Sky, Bernal finished fifteenth on GC, most of his deficit to the riders who finished in the top ten sustained on one stage over the cobbles to Roubaix, where he lost sixteen minutes. In the final week, and notably on the Col de Portet, he was one of the strongest men in the field. 'I was a little afraid of bringing him to the Tour. I wasn't concerned about him physically, but at Sky it can be a very intense experience that comes sometimes become quite negative. For a young South American rider who doesn't have a lot of experience of racing in Europe, it was a risk. I was particularly concerned about the first week. Even a few days ago I wasn't sure I was right, but now I'm happy that I made that decision,' says the Sky boss.

A couple of days prior to that conversation with a beaming Brailsford in Lourdes, L'Équipe had asked the question of whether a climber would ever win the Tour again. Offering his take,

Française des Jeux head coach Fred Grappe said that the sport should consign the idea of the mountain goat to Tour legend. 'What is a climber?' he asked. 'This is all based on how climbers used to be, when they could express their talent in a very different era of cycling. Today racing is stereotyped and they climb passes at very high speed while making as few accelerations as possible. The aim is to save resources. Climbing like they did before, with bursts of acceleration, is very costly. To climb quickly, you have to be linear... Given the Tour's configuration, only rouleurs who have been transformed into climbers can win it.' Thierry Gouvenou, the Tour's route director, was equally pessimistic about the prospect of a pure climber taking the title, suggesting that it would only become possible by changing France's geography and moving some high mountains northwards, thereby avoiding a situation where, 'their legs shot to pieces when they tackle the first passes because the first week is so demanding and oppressively nervy'.

But Bernal may prove to be the rider who proves Grappe, Gouvenou and many other naysayers wrong about the demise of the pure climber at the Tour. Unlike Wiggins, Froome and Thomas, and pretenders such as Dumoulin and Roglic, he isn't a member of the *rouleur-grimpeur* class who climbs passes by reproducing a time-trial effort, sticking to a regular rhythm. He comes more from the Alberto Contador mould, a pure climber with outstanding physiological attributes, always on the lookout for opportunities to attack, and capable of defending himself in a time trial. He has the same confidence and, it appears, mental resilience as Spain's two-time champion. He's certainly in the right team to win the Tour, assuming they can adapt to a new leader for the third time, to one who will require a very different approach when it comes to challenging for the yellow jersey, and that Brailsford can unearth another backer to ensure long-term continuity.

Winning the Tour with a British rider was one thing, but doing so with a specialist climber could mean something quite different, a renaissance that few would have imagined possible that could revitalise the Tour and the legend of the yellow jersey.

GERAINT THOMAS
TOUR DE FRANCE
2018

6

ETIQUETTE AND UNWRITTEN RULES
Le Maillot Jaune

Luis Ocaña 1971

**THE YELLOW JERSEY THAT WAS CUT OFF
AFTER THE SPANIARD ABANDONED THE 1971 TOUR,
FOLLOWING HIS CRASH ON THE COL DE MENTÉ**

Louis Ocaña tumbles out of the 1971 Tour on the Col de Menté

The Self-Policing Peloton

For a sport that has been perennially beset by endemic cheating, cycling has extensive and occasionally bizarre ethical codes.

Although not written down, they are universally understood and, for new professionals, quickly learned. They have evolved in response to the nature of bike racing, which features numerous events across the season, each of them bringing together as many as two hundred racers, who have to compete in very close proximity to each other and, as far as possible, do so without putting each other in danger or causing unnecessary stress or aggravation.

These codes can perhaps be best explained by applying the concept of the 'reasonable person' that exists in British law. Once described as 'the man on the Clapham omnibus', this hypothetical member of society who exercises average care, skill and judgement in conduct is used in court to decide whether a party has acted reasonably, with their character established through interpretation of good practice or policy. In cycling terms, they are the average man or woman in the bunch. Some of the codes are well established and quite strictly adhered to – not attacking when the peloton decides it's time for a pee stop, for instance, or when riding through a feed zone. Others only apply in stage races and, principally, to the race leader or at least to recognised contenders for the title, such as don't attack the yellow jersey when they've crashed or had a mechanical problem and, on Grand Tours at least, refrain from doing so on the final stage even if there's only a small margin between the top two racers.

When it comes to the Clapham omnibus that is the peloton, order is generally maintained by consensus rather than a single conductor. But the *patron*, often the yellow jersey but in some instances a well-respected and very experienced performer like Fabian Cancellara prior to his retirement in 2016, adopts this role and, as a result, may impose their own interpretation of the unwritten codes, provoking debate, argument and, ultimately, acceptance or dismissal. Their evolution is constant and, in recent years, their application follows an increasingly ethical perspective, tying in perhaps with a general acceptance that cheating in its basest form should not be tolerated.

Establishing exactly when and why these codes have been adapted is not straightforward. When Eugène Christophe became the first rider to wear the yellow jersey, the Tour's code was a simple 'every man for himself'. The rules prohibited mutual assistance, including the sharing of food or water. During his brief spell in the *maillot jaune*, his rivals attacked the Frenchman at every opportunity, including when he had a *pause pipi*, punctured, crashed or had a mechanical problem. Staying upright on a properly functioning bike was

'I'll never understand why anyone would attack an injured man'

part of the test. When Christophe saw his Tour hopes evaporate as a consequence of his forks breaking, sympathy for his bad luck was almost universal, but no one begrudged Firmin Lambot his title.

There's little evidence that this anything-goes attitude towards the Tour leader changed during the inter-war years. In 1937, when the Belgian team quit in Bordeaux in protest at the behaviour both of fans on the route and of the race organisation, there was no yellow jersey when the race set off for Royan the next morning. Similarly, following the Italian team's decision to quit in almost identical circumstances in 1950, Ferdi Kübler decided against wearing it until the next stage had been completed. In both instances, the abandon of the riders in the yellow jersey, Sylvère Maes and Fiorenzo Magni respectively, couldn't be confirmed until they hadn't taken to the start line and the stage had got under way without them.

Almost two decades later, the bunch showed no compassion for Raymond Poulidor when he crashed heavily after a race motorbike clipped his rear wheel on the road to Albi in the 1968 race.

| *Raymond Poulidor inspects his injuries after an untimely crash in 1968*

Lying fifth, but best placed of the GC favourites, the Frenchman, his brow, nose and mouth bloodied, managed to limit his losses to a minute and fifteen seconds with the help of his teammates, but railed against rivals who had raised the peloton's speed as soon as they realised that he had been waylaid. 'I'll never understand why anyone would attack an injured man,' he complained at the finish.

Half a century on, the wounds from that day are still raw. Jan Janssen, who went on to win the title, was one of those who benefited from Poulidor's losses and still insists there is no reason to wait for any rider who crashes, even the yellow jersey. 'Tough luck, that's racing! That's cycling! I have respect for everyone, but if the yellow jersey makes a mistake, tough luck for him,' he says in *Secrets de Maillots Jaunes*. Angered by the Frenchman's complaints that made a big stir in the media, Janssen told him the next day, 'Raymond, we're not playing golf or cards. You have to pay attention.' The acrimony from that fallout continues to fester, the Dutchman admitted. 'Since then we've not been all that friendly. We see each other and shake hands. But that's all.'

That 1968 edition also featured a peculiar incident that highlights how the Tour organisers have on occasion employed unwritten rules to ensure the yellow jersey does not end up in a place they felt it shouldn't. On the penultimate day of what had been a race so dull that journalists went on strike in protest, the little-known André Poppe, riding for the Belgium 'A' team who were defending Herman Van Springel's yellow jersey, was among half a dozen riders who joined an early break. To his surprise, they quickly opened up a lead of close to twenty minutes. Thirteen minutes down and well outside the top ten at the start, the Belgian was catapulted into the position of leader on the road.

Seeing the lack of response in the bunch, Tour directors Jacques Goddet and Félix Lévitan contemplated the Tour being won a rider without a pro victory and who had been called into the race late as his team's first reserve, and didn't relish the prospect at all. They began coaxing and then bribing rivals to chase, threatening to confiscate prize money if Poppe prevailed. Among those that responded was Janssen's Dutch team. 'Messieurs Goddet and Lévitan begged us to chase,' said Janssen. 'They would have regarded Poppe winning as a humiliation.' Up ahead, Poppe's breakaway companions, including Belgium B rider Eric Leman, were also ordered to ease off. 'There was no way that a Belgian domestique could win the Tour,' Poppe later remarked. 'I couldn't do anything against the peloton on my own and when they cut the lead back to less than ten minutes my chance of a Tour win was over.'

At the finish, Van Springel remained in yellow, but, according to Poppe, still wasn't happy with the scenario that had almost played out. 'He came to me at the end of the stage and said, "Have you got anything you want to say to me?" But, of course, it was never my intention to do anything but be in the break to defend his interests. We all expected that he would win the Tour the next day because he had never lost in a time trial to Janssen. That was the only one that he did.' This was the only instance in the Tour's history of the peloton, the organisers and even members of his own team uniting against one rider to prevent him winning. Insidious in its organisation and execution, Poppe's ostracisation emphasised the exclusionist attitude towards the yellow jersey club and makes it easier to understand why Roger Walkowiak, widely depicted as an interloper in spite of his heroics on the bike, was treated so harshly after his unheralded triumph in 1956.

Three years later, Eddy Merckx provided what remains the most high-profile application of the ethical code as it relates to the yellow jersey. Humbled by Luis Ocaña at Orcières Merlette, the Belgian spent the following days hounding the Spanish race leader, determined to force him to his physical and psychological limit to secure the title. Famously, despite the torrents hammering the riders as they descended the Col de Menté, on 'a narrow road shaped like vermicelli' according to *L'Équipe*'s Pierre Chany, Merckx's incessant harrying continued, his pace so excessive across the water- and rubble-covered surface that he fell on a hairpin, hitting his knee hard. He remounted and recommenced his descent in the same semi-crazed manner. In attempting to follow, the yellow jersey went down as well, stumbled to his feet, only to be poleaxed first by Joop Zoete-melk and then by a gaggle of hurtling figures comprising Joaquim Agostinho, Bernard Thévenet and Mariano Martinez, whose brakes had been rendered as useless as the Spaniard's. The contest was over, to Merckx's huge disap-pointment.

That evening, thanks to Ocaña's abandon, the Belgian could have pulled on the yellow jersey, but refused the honour out of respect for the Spaniard, who had abandoned. Disillusioned by the loss of his rival, he insisted that he had 'lost the Tour... Ocaña's crash removes any interest from a possible win. I didn't win it by fighting for it.' He considered quitting the race that for him had become a non-contest, uninterested in a victory that would always be qualified with a 'what if...?' Although his Molteni team convinced him that he had to continue, his perspective has remained unchanged.

'Honestly, I'd have preferred to have finished second having battled each day with Luis with equal arms rather than winning by default after his abandon. It's for that reason that I didn't want to wear the yellow jersey the day after he abandoned'

he said in 2017. 'That was a sincere act, decided by no one else but me.' The next day, Merckx once again refused to wear the leader's jersey in tribute to the Spaniard.

Unwittingly involved in Ocaña's downfall, Joop Zoetemelk was the beneficiary on the next two occasions the race leader couldn't continue. In 1978, he inherited the yellow jersey after Michel Pollentier was caught trying to cheat the dope control at Alpe d'Huez. The Belgian's ejection with a two-month ban from competition promoted the Dutchman into first place. Two years later, Zoet-emelk followed Merckx's lead in refusing to wear the *maillot jaune* when Bernard Hinault quit the race in Pau due to tendinitis in his right knee. 'I only look at the general classification. At the top of it is the name Hinault. And Zoetemelk is below that. Sorry, but I don't want the yellow jersey this morning,' he said before the next stage to Luchon.

In between these two editions, the 1979 race concluded with a stage into Paris that high-lighted another unwritten rule. Tradition demands

Ocaña is forced to abandon after a devastating crash in 1971

that the final day is a celebratory parade, the peloton sauntering into the capital with the champion-in-waiting toasting victory with champagne alongside his teammates. Racing only begins when the yellow jersey and his cohort lead the race onto the Champs-Élysées. It's an oddity in a major sporting event, understandable given the distances and hardships endured, but inexplicable because, well, it's a race, not a post-Tour criterium where everyone is well aware there's a script that has to be followed. Like a winning football team keeping the ball by the corner flag to run down time, it denies the spectacle, which could be considerable given the narrow margins often dividing GC contenders in the modern era. There could, instead, be something much more appetising, similar to the drama that Zoetemelk and Hinault served up.

That morning, the Dutchman informed his teammates of his plan to attack the yellow jersey. Prior to the start, he also sought out his rival, telling him that he was going to attack him if he got the chance. Hinault assumed Zoetemelk was joking. Even so, he didn't allow himself to be distracted by premature celebrations. As the race entered the wooded Chevreuse hills south-east of Paris, Joaquim Agostinho and Hennie Kuiper, a minute between them in third and fourth place, respectively, started to joust with each other. Initially Hinault tracked them, then grew irritated with their antics and attacked on the Homme Morte climb, triggering an unprecedented climax.

Crossing the summit, logic suggested the yellow jersey would sit up and wait. But he was having fun. With Zoetemelk the only rider within twenty-four minutes of him on GC, why stick to the script? He persisted and only eased off when he was told that the Dutchman had jumped away from the bunch and was chasing. They joined up, then put on a show of their own, Zoetemelk haring away on every little rise, Hinault chasing him down. The yellow jersey responded strongly on the flat, almost breaking his rival, but Zoetemelk eventually bridged back up. They entered the finishing circuit a minute clear, and the spectacle continued. On the last lap, the Dutchman, with just one stage win to the race leader's six, pleaded for a second. Hinault glared at him, then won by a distance. What was left of the bunch was

more than two minutes in arrears, the rest trailed in several minutes later. 'No one had ever seen a *maillot jaune* do that before,' Hinault said in William Fotheringham's *The Badger*. 'What it showed was that nothing is written in advance in cycling.'

As well as being an astonishing spectacle, it also demonstrated how an exceptional rider can establish their own unwritten code. Like Merckx, Hinault was strong and dominant enough to do what he wanted. But there was a distinct difference in their styles. Merckx depended on his ability and his desire to conquer, which were usually enough to subdue the competition. Hinault had that same competitive instinct, but wasn't so unrelenting in his drive for victory. Instead, he imposed himself through his uncompromisingly forceful personality. He made up his own laws, but was essentially a benevolent despot, determined to protect himself and the rest of the peloton from the rigours of the sport as much as possible by racing only when he deemed it necessary to do so. Whenever this balance came under threat, Hinault would angrily haul miscreants back into line. Yet, if the urge took him, he would annihilate the code completely, simply because he could, because it reasserted his dominance.

When other, more modest racers attempted to diverge from the unwritten code, condemnation for their actions was generally widespread. On the opening day of the 1986 race, Thierry Marie, the prologue specialist at Système U took the yellow jersey, and victory two days later for Cyrille Guimard's team tightened his hold on it. Racing into his home region of Normandy, the Frenchman expected to arrive in triumph, but ultimately ended the stage in tears as teammate Dominique Gaigne sneaked enough bonus seconds in two intermediate sprints to leapfrog him into first place. Questioned by the press about why he hadn't eased off in either case, Gaigne pointed out that Marie wasn't a great sprinter, to which Guimard responded by saying: 'Perhaps, but Gaigne didn't brake either.' In other words, Système U's DS expected his riders to respect Marie's position as the team's leader at that point.

Writing in *L'Équipe*, Jean-Marie Leblanc drew attention to the unwritten rule that a rider doesn't take the yellow jersey from a teammate unless it's relinquished willingly, as was the case in 2013 when Simon Gerrans ceded it to his Orica-GreenEdge roommate Daryl Impey. 'It's a sort of oral tradition that has long been around but hasn't, it would seem, reached Gaigne's ears. On the finish podium, the two "friends" made it look as if nothing had happened, but, whether they wanted to or not, one of them had lost a friend.' According to the new race leader, opinion within the peloton was split, many saying he'd done the right thing but others making it clear that he'd been an idiot. Guimard appears to have been in the second camp, for he opted not to have his team protect the GC prospects of Laurent Fignon and Charly Mottet rather than chase down a break in order to defend the jersey, which passed to Johan van der Velde.

Later in the race, Hinault not only attacked when La Vie Claire teammate Greg LeMond was in yellow and pushing for a first title, but then stated on television that he would continue to do so and defended his apparent disregard for the code by asserting that he was pushing his teammate to his limit in order to embellish LeMond's final success. 'If he doesn't buckle that means he's a champion and deserves to win the race. I did it for his own good,' he insisted. Although the American, his nerves shredded by his teammate's determination to rewrite the code as it suited him, was and remains unconvinced by the argument, Hinault was lauded for having stuck to his pre-race commitment to supporting his teammate's yellow jersey quest and, at the same time, acted as the trigger for what it is often cited as the best Tour of all.

It was no coincidence at all that the first Tour following Hinault's retirement in 1986 was anarchic – brilliant to watch but relentlessly hard for the participants due to the lack of a controlling force. It is entirely fitting that victory went to Stephen Roche, the most Machiavellian of team leaders, cunning and unscrupulous, not only wise to the plan cooked up to destabilise new race leader Jean-François Bernard by racing through the feed on the Villard-de-Lans stage, but happy to contribute to it. Already out of position when the peloton had shown no inclination to slow when he first unshipped and then punctured, Bernard burned through his teammates and then his own resources in a vain bid to regain contact with his rivals, but ultimately his hopes were torched.

Since the start of this century, disputes about perceived breaches of the unwritten rules have become more frequent, suggesting a more principled approach to what's taking place on the road. This was even, and arguably especially, apparent during the long period when, it subsequently became evident, there was little regard for ethics away from the action. Honour among thieves perhaps? It's hard to suppress a smile when thinking back to, for instance, the 2003 Tour and the endlessly debated question of 'Did Jan Ullrich wait?' following the Luz-Ardiden stage. When yellow jersey Lance Armstrong, who had been under pressure from his German rival for days, clipped a fan and crashed to the ground as he attacked on that Pyrenean climb, taking Iban Mayo down with him, Ullrich managed to swerve around the falling bikes and bodies and kept on going. As the stricken pair got up and moving again, a small group bridged up to Ullrich, Tyler Hamilton among them, and he gestured for them to slow. Moments later, Armstrong and Mayo were back with them, and the action kicked off again.

'As he wept, anger mixing with distress, his rivals reminded the media how, at Paris-Nice earlier that season, he had slipped away under the guise of needing a toilet break... and kept on going to take a solo win. Breaking the code had rebounded on him when it mattered most'

The question of whether or not the German waited is now irrelevant. That stage and Tour have no winner as a consequence of the decision to strike Armstrong's results from the records following his admission of doping. Yet it was just one of a number of incidents during that period when riders made an effort to do the right thing, to compete with equal arms, as Merckx put it. Bar the 'chaingate' incident of 2010, when Alberto Contador swept past almost-stationary race leader Andy Schleck after his chain unshipped on the climb of the Port de Balès and stole away to claim the *maillot jaune*, the trend has continued. But its legitimacy has come into question.

The Mont Ventoux stage of the 2016 Tour provided plenty to chew on from this perspective. What was always likely to be a dramatic stage was made more so by extremely high winds on the open part of this exposed peak and forced the organisers to move the finish down from the summit to the Chalet Reynard ski station located seven kilometres below the summit, at the point where the road emerges from the dense woodland on its lower slopes. As a consequence, there was a concertina effect on fans, who all packed into this section. Unfortunately, the barriers used to keep fans out of the road in the final two kilometres of the stage didn't make it down the mountain with the masses. This didn't create too much of a problem for the breakaway group. However, soon after Thomas De Gendt had outsprinted Belgian compatriot Serge Pauwels for victory, it became a very significant issue for the GC favourites, notably race leader Chris Froome.

Scenting weakness in rival Nairo Quintana, the Briton attacked, Richie Porte and Bauke Mollema the only two riders able to follow his wheel. As it

| *In a moment of panic with no spare bike quickly available, Froome begins to run awkwardly up the slopes of Mont Ventoux*

quickly became evident that the trio could benefit by collaborating in the final kilometre or so, Porte came through to set the pace, only to ride into the back of an official race motorbike that stopped suddenly as the crowd surged into the road. The Australian hit the deck and Froome went with him, his rear mech breaking in the impact, rendering his bike useless. He was handed a replacement from the neutral service support vehicle, but couldn't clip into pedals. Rather than wait for his team car, lost in the masses somewhere behind, he took to his feet, jogging awkwardly upwards in his cleated shoes until, eventually, the Sky team car appeared with a new bike. He finished in more conventional fashion, losing a minute and, appar-

ently, the *maillot jaune*, until his team launched an appeal, their case supported by Christian Prud-homme, who told the race jury 'that an exceptional decision could be explained, given the absolutely exceptional circumstances'. They agreed and awarded Froome the same time as Mollema.

The Dutchman, predictably, wasn't happy. 'What's going on? Seems like everybody gets time bonuses. I wonder what would have happened if I would have been the only one to go down,' he wrote on Twitter. Jan Janssen was also nonplussed. 'Froome fell off, and they annulled the race at that moment,' he stated. Amid this commotion, though, a more fundamental rewriting of the code relating to the yellow jersey had passed almost unnoticed.

| Fabian Cancellara, known as Spartacus, asserts his authority

Does the requirement to show respect play in just one direction, towards the yellow jersey?

It appears that in the quest to ensure the rider in the yellow jersey is challenged fairly, with equal arms as Merckx once described it, the dice are being loaded against every other racer in the peloton, who can't play the same 'get out of jail free' card, or at least not with the same consistency.

Equally, while the desire to ensure the contest is a test of athletic ability and not mechanical soundness is understandable and even laudable, the question has to be raised whether it's correct.

This is bike racing after all

| *Aru makes his controversial attack in 2017*

An hour earlier, with thirty-two kilometres to the finish, Simon Gerrans, had been leading the yellow jersey group down a winding descent when his front wheel slipped away on a sweeping left-hand turn. The Australian slid into the barrier and his bike rebounded off it and into the path of Sky's Ian Stannard, Luke Rowe and Wout Poels, who also went down. Almost instantly, Froome moved to the front of the group, waved his hand to signal a cessation of hostilities, before pulling over to the roadside to stop for a natural break, *un pipi* that was tactical rather than out of necessity. He waited for his teammates to get back up to him, then helped pace them back to the group ahead, which had slowed at the subsequent urging of Fabian Cancellara, who had instigated a similar ceasefire when in the yellow jersey early in the 2010 race and his CSC leaders Andy and Fränk Schleck had been among dozens of riders who crashed on a rain-slickened descent in the Ardennes.

The French describe behaviour of this kind as *le fairplay*, but was it in this instance? Or an abuse of the *maillot jaune*'s power? Apart from the riders in the break whose lead quickly extended to a stage-winning margin, the only beneficiaries were Sky. According to American journalist Caley Fretz, 'The rules surrounding such events are situational... The basic tenet is that the yellow jersey should not be left behind due to an incident out of his control – a flat, a crash, a mechanical of some sort – before the race is "on".' In the kilometres before it occurred, the peloton had split in crosswinds, which had resulted in some of the top-ten contenders losing ground. Gerrans was setting a tempo intended to maintain this gap. So the race

was 'on'. More significant, though, was the fact that the yellow jersey hadn't been left behind. He stopped of his own accord, like a footballer feigning injury to prevent the rival team's attack. This left the rest of the group with a dilemma. They could press on, distance Froome and, almost certainly, face criticism for attacking the yellow jersey, or sit up and wait to allow him and his teammates to return. Despite Alejandro Valverde's evident frustration, they opted for the latter.

The debate resurfaced in the Tour's next edition on the climb of Mont Chat during the stage into Chambéry. With Froome once again in yellow, Sky's domestiques had adopted their standard attack-is-the-best-form-of-defence strategy, setting a fierce pace heading on to this key ascent, the final one before the finish, whittling down the group of favourites and closing in on the few survivors from the break. Halfway up the climb, Froome raised his arm to signal a rear wheel puncture and, a fraction of a second later, Fabio Aru all but ducked beneath it as he went on the attack. Nairo Quintana, Richie Porte and Dan Martin were quick to respond, but the latter pair quickly indicated to the Italian that they weren't going to collaborate. The offensive fizzled out and Froome soon rejoined the group.

Aru was broadly condemned for his action, but defended himself by saying he had planned to attack at precisely that point. Few were convinced, least of all Froome, who revealed that Porte had told Aru to show some respect. 'Richie said, "This isn't the moment to attack the yellow jersey when he's changing his bike." I want to say a massive thank you to Richie and the rest of the group for not taking advantage of that situation,' said the race leader at the finish. Rather than saving their retribution for a later date as Jean-François Bernard's rivals did in 1987, Aru's peers stuck with the Armstrong/Ullrich precedent, which established that the race ceases to be 'on' when the yellow jersey is waylaid by misfortune rather than poor form. In short, the Italian erred by appearing to take deliberate advantage of Chris Froome's breakdown.

Like the French language, of which it is often said that there is an exception to every rule, moments like this emphasise that bike racing's unwritten code often seems counter-intuitive, particularly at the Tour de France where the stakes are highest. It is, as Fretz put it, 'reliant on the elastic subjectivity of circumstance', which was underlined within a few minutes of the Aru offensive when the yellow jersey group started down towards Chambéry. Two kilometres into a descent renowned for being technical and treacherous, Porte crashed heavily, taking Dan Martin down with him, the Irishman's bike clipping Rigoberto Urán's as he swerved to avoid the mayhem, the impact disabling the Colombian's rear mech to leave him with just a single gear to complete the stage. On this occasion, no one called for a cease-fire for the benefit of the Australian or the Irishman, who a few minutes earlier had been gesturing for Aru to ease off, and none of the riders in the front group would have waited if Urán had opted to change bikes on the run-in.

All three riders affected by the crash were highly placed on GC, within sixty-one seconds of Froome, so why the discrepancy? Does the requirement to show respect play in just one direction, towards the yellow jersey? It appears that in the quest to ensure the rider in the yellow jersey is challenged fairly, with 'equal arms', the dice are being loaded against every other racer in the peloton, who can't play the same 'get out of jail free' card, or at least not with the same consistency. Equally, while the desire to ensure the contest is a test of athletic ability and not mechanical soundness is understandable and even laudable, the question has to be raised whether it's correct. This is bike racing, after all. Like the riders on them, the machines are fallible, especially when pushed right to their competitive limit. It's not only absurd that the contest for the yellow jersey doesn't reflect this, but it flies in the face of historical precedent, which established that bad as well as good luck can influence the identity of the Tour winner – think Christophe in 1919, Victor Fontan in 1929, Jean-François Bernard in 1987, Andy Schleck in 2010, or Raymond Poulidor on frequent occasions.

'Some of these unwritten rules exist as a method of self-preservation. But not this one. This one can't be written down because seeing it in writing would reveal how truly silly it is. Leaving it unwritten makes it no less absurd,' Fretz concluded. It seems even more bizarre given the ongoing debate about how to lessen the control that one team can exercise over the Tour in this era when sport is as much as about entertainment as it is a demonstration of athletic prowess. The race needs this element of uncertainty, the heroes and villains that would emerge from it. It is essentially an unforgiving test that rewards the strongest and most courageous, but needs to reflect that wholly and not become overly sanitised, especially in the context of the battle for the biggest prize of all.

LUIS OCAÑA
TOUR DE FRANCE
1971

7

THE COLOUR OF MONEY

Le Maillot Jaune

Jacques Anquetil 1964

THE FINAL HELYETT YELLOW JERSEY BEFORE
THE TEAM DISBANDED AFTER 29 YEARS.

BANANIA présente LES GEANTS DU TOUR DE FRANCE 1947-1980

Ferdi KUBLER
1ᵉʳ du tour de France 1950

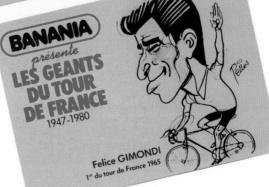

BANANIA présente LES GEANTS DU TOUR DE FRANCE 1947-1980

Felice GIMONDI
1ᵉʳ du tour de France 1965

BANANIA présente LES GEANTS DU TOUR DE FRANCE 1947-1980

Raphaël GEMINIANI
4ᵉ du tour de France 1950 -
2ᵉ en 1951 - 6ᵉ en 1955 -
3ᵉ en 1958

BANANIA présente LES GEANTS DU TOUR DE FRANCE 1947-1980

Jan JANSSEN
1ᵉʳ du tour de France 1968

*Banania – the popular chocolate drink – sponsored
the yellow jersey between 1984 and 1986*

Riding the Brand®

The 2018 Tour de France has pitched up in the Breton port of Brest. One block back from the historic quayside, in the Parc à Chaines that's jammed in between immense warehouses and the imposing ramparts of the old citadel, a steady stream of VIPs, guests and fans is filing through gates of the Village du Tour, the barriered enclave that is home to the race's commercial partners.

Traffic is particularly busy at the LCL (Le Crédit Lyonnais) stand, decked out in unmistakeable yellow and blue, where the bank's director-general Michel Mathieu has arrived for the day. He is ushered by his PR team from one engagement to the next, handing out helmets to local children as part of a campaign to boost cycling within France's towns and cities one moment, greeting race director Christian Prudhomme the next.

But Mathieu isn't the magnet who is drawing most of attention. The pull is being exerted by eighty-two-year-old Raymond Poulidor, who famously never had the *maillot jaune* on his shoulders as a rider but has, since 2001, worn yellow every day at the Tour as LCL's ambassador. Sitting at a table with a stack of postcards in front of him, France's 'eternal second', his hair a shock of white but his face still ruddy with vitality, greets fans with a shake of a huge paw, smiling broadly as he signs his name, never tiring of the questions about his rivalry with Jacques Anquetil and, most regularly, the peculiar twist in fate that has resulted in him becoming emblematic of a jersey he never held. 'I'll only get fed up with autographs on the day that

I'm no longer asked for them,' he says during a very brief pause in his signings, an observation that could be taken as being 'on brand', but captures the essence of Poulidor, who is still as delighted as ever to be part of the Tour.

As the Frenchman retakes his seat and picks up his pen again, Michel Mathieu explains the oddity of having a veteran ex-rider as the face of LCL during the Tour. 'There are good reasons for it. Firstly, even though he never actually wore the yellow jersey, that gentleman is the incarnation of the race for so many people in France. His battle with Jacques Anquetil was one of the great moments in Tour de France history and as a result of that he has still has huge significance for the French people when they think about the yellow jersey,' he says. 'I think one of the interesting things about yellow jersey is that it is emblematic of the Tour and not necessarily of the winner, and Raymond underlines that. It doesn't just highlight the race leader, but has also become the Tour's most important symbol. It's thanks to that, and the fact that the Tour's yellow and blue colours are the same as our own, that LCL has sponsored the *maillot jaune* since 1987. It is an incredibly important for us because of the reach it has. It's a great story, a love affair that continues to thrive.'

This isn't a relationship conducted on the cheap. In 2018, LCL and ASO signed a four-year extension to the sponsorship deal for the yellow jersey, amounting to approximately €10 million (£9 million) a season. In return for that investment, which also covers a number of other races in the Tour organiser's portfolio including Paris–Nice, Paris–Roubaix and the Critérium du Dauphiné,

the bank receives, according to an ASO survey, the equivalent of €140 million (£125 million) in publicity spending based on television and press coverage and is the sponsor most readily associated with the Tour by the French public, with a 31 per cent rate of association. ASO, a private company owned by the Amaury family, also does extremely well out of the association. Its yield from the Tour's sponsors in 2018 was approximately €75 million (£66 million), with a comparable amount estimated to come from the sale of television rights. Factor in merchandising and other sales and the Tour comprises at least 80 per cent of the organising company's turnover, which reached €220 million in 2016, with profits totalling €46 million – to put that into context within ASO's portfolio, the week-long Dauphiné produced a profit of €10,000 in the same year on a turnover of €2.3 million. These figures put the Tour de France on a revenue par with Six Nations Rugby, but some distance behind the Roland Garros Tennis Open in Paris which yielded €230 million (£204 million) in 2017 and light years behind the World Cup, that earned FIFA $3 billion (£2.33 million) in a TV rights deal covering the 2014 and 2018 tournaments.

While the Tour may be among the small fry in sports events in terms of earnings, ASO has made considerable advances in these areas since the Tour agreed its first sponsorship deal with Les Laines Sofil in 1948. Prior to that point, the race had been financed by the organising newspaper *L'Auto* in what was a mutually altruistic arrangement. The more interest the race attracted, the higher the paper's circulation. This model was sustainable and profitable until the Second World

| *V is for Virlux butter: One of the first examples of a sponsor's branding on the race leader's attire in 1969*

War. However, following the conflict and the dissolution of *L'Auto*, its successor *L'Équipe* and *Le Parisien Libéré*, its partner in organising the Tour, needed to find new revenue streams to maintain and modernise the race as earnings from newsstand sales fell as a consequence of competition from rival publications and radio coverage. Under the Sofil deal (*Laines Sofil, Tricot Facile* – easy knit, claimed their ad), the wool manufacturer paid 10,000 old French francs to the Tour leader each year and provided a yellow jersey, which for the first time featured race founder Henri Desgrange's initials.

The deal ended after a season and another half dozen years passed before the yellow liqueur Suze became the second sponsor of the yellow jersey. Over the next decade and a half, Calor gas, Le Soleil insurance, Shell-Berre refining, Le Toro clothing and Champigneulles beer sponsored the *maillot jaune* for a season. But in most years the jersey had no sponsor at all, largely because the Tour's co-directors, Jacques Goddet, editor-in-chief at *L'Équipe*, and Félix Lévitan, sports editor at *Le Parisien*, were both stronger on the editorial than the commercial side and focused primarily on boosting circulation and, on the back of that, advertising revenue. It wasn't until 1969, when Virlux butter became the first partner whose name actually appeared on the leader's jersey, that the yellow jersey began to bring in a regular income, but even so the race ran at a loss until 1974.

Writing about Lévitan in *The Cycling Anthology*, former *Wall Street Journal* correspondent Sam Abt revealed that the race made a profit of US$3 million over the next decade. It was, he said, 'just peanuts, but not to Lévitan. He never bothered about seeking big money for television rights; he was a newspaper man who did not anticipate his audience's shift to television in those distant days when few Frenchmen owned a set. Want to know who was doing what in the race? Read about it in *L'Équipe* or *Le Parisien*. Nor did he try to attract big corporate sponsors. He thought small, satisfied with the income from the publicity caravan that preceded the race with its swarm of hucksters for soap, sausages and sweets.' The Tour was essentially a sporting circus, the riders often performing two or occasionally three shows a day in towns that had put up the money for the right to host a start or finish, the prizes on offer paltry. The teams paid the organisers for their hotels and evening meals, which were often pitiful. Even as late as 1987, riders were often lodged in dormitory rooms, sleeping in beds designed for children.

This shoestring set-up began to change that same year when Goddet stepped down from his position as race director and Lévitan was fired from his and put under investigation for fraud, although the case was settled three years later 'to everybody's satisfaction'. As the old guard departed, in came Jean-François Naquet-Radiguet, a former sales manager for a cognac producer, who set about changing every part of the race's infrastructure and finances. He was surprised to discover that the sale of television rights had only recently appeared on the Tour's income statement. 'They were not important. Lévitan was talented at obtaining money from host cities and sponsors, but the economics of a modern sporting event were fairly out of his understanding,' he told Abt. Within that year of change, the Tour received close to £1 million from West Berlin, which hosted the Grand Départ and Crédit Lyonnais (as it was until its takeover by Crédit Agricole in 2003) and replaced the Banania chocolate drinks company as the principal sponsor of the *maillot jaune*.

Over the subsequent three decades, as the Tour's audience has increased across the globe, its income has grown steadily. However, its sponsors haven't reflected this change. Of its four main partners in 2019, points jersey supporter Skoda is the only one that is recognisably multinational. LCL focuses its banking operations on the French market, new King of the Mountains backer E. Leclerc is a domestic supermarket chain and cooperative society, and Krys, whose name appears on the white jersey of the best young rider, is a cooperative of French opticians. In addition, three-quarters of the race's official partners and suppliers are also domestic companies. Some are corporates with a multinational reach such as Orange and Le Coq Sportif, but most have a very French aspect, such as the Century 21 estate agency chain, St Michel pastries and Cochonou sausage. They reflect what remains, despite the financial and economic strides made since the Goddet–Lévitan era, very much a French race, with home sponsors, many of them very long-standing, able to connect with spectators at the roadside via the publicity caravan and in their homes and work places through the media.

For much the same price as its €10 million per year collaboration with the *maillot jaune*, LCL could achieve these objectives by supporting a very competitive team at WorldTour level, a status that guarantees a place in the Tour line-up. But it stands to reason that buying the rights to association with the yellow jersey is bound to deliver far greater visibility than supporting a team that's trying to get a rider into it, perhaps only for a day or two, and is likely never to achieve this. What's more, while backing a team comes with an element of risk given cycling's frequent flirtations with scandal, partnering with the race is the ideal way to minimise this possibility. Consequently, LCL's is a canny investment and arguably a cheap one considering the reach of the yellow jersey.

'The issues with doping did give us cause to reflect but we never ended the link with the Tour,' says LCL director-general Mathieu. 'Some of the race's partners did withdraw when it was hit by those scandals, but our perspective was that the problems were to do with attitude within the sport rather than particularly to do with the organisers of the Tour de France. We thought that the Tour was greater than that, and we still feel that is the case. I think that loyalty has really paid off for us and for the race.'

'The Yellow Jersey is the Tour de France, the two are interchangeable.

It's the emblem of this crazy celebration that transforms and moves not only the whole of the French nation but also people and regions way beyond it now. For us, it wasn't just a case of getting the Tour to start in Yorkshire, but in having everything went with it including the most important symbol, which is the yellow jersey.'
LCL Director-General Michel Mathieu

He goes on to explain that the Tour also provides the bank with the opportunity to help its customers directly by promoting the use of cycling as a fundamental part of daily life. 'LCL is an urban bank, a bank of the towns and cities, and we want to help develop cycling within them. It is a new and very important focus for us, not only being involved with the Tour de France, but also with cycling in general. If you take Paris, for example, 50 per cent of the journeys undertaken are less than three kilometres in length but only 3 per cent of those journeys are done by bicycle. At the same time, the average Parisian spends 69 hours each year stuck in traffic jams. If we can help shift that balance, people will save time, will be healthier and it will be great for the planet.' His pitch is well practised, but also likely to be well received in a country where environmental issues have popular resonance and the move towards car-free cities has considerable support.

ASO has found other ways to monetise the impact of the yellow jersey without impinging on LCL's status as the sole sponsor, most obviously the Tour's Grand Départ. The fee charged for this varies depending on the location and length of stay in particular city or region. In 2016, La Manche in northern France paid ASO a fee of €2.4 million (£2.1 million) to host the team presentation, the opening two stages and the start of the third. A year later, the German city of Düsseldorf paid more than twice as much, €6 million (£5.2 million) to take the start of the race outside France, while in 2014 Yorkshire paid a fee believed to be in the region of £10 million to host the race for the presentation and two-and-a-half days of racing.

Gary Verity, CEO at Welcome to Yorkshire which was behind the bid, says that the Tour's visit highlighted the county as a destination for international tourists as well as those in the UK. 'We said before the Tour de France came to Yorkshire

Yellow fever peaked in Yorkshire in 2014

that weren't that many people around the world who could point to Yorkshire on a map, but now there are millions who can do exactly that because of the Tour de France, because of the yellow jersey,' he asserts. Fundamental to that, he adds, was the power of the *maillot jaune* as a promotional tool. ASO's establishment in 2015 of the Tour de Yorkshire stage race has built on the wave of euphoria that swept over the county in July 2014, when an estimated 3 million spectators crammed the roadsides to see the passage of the Tour. In 2018, spectator numbers for the spin-off four-day event reached an estimated 2.6 million. Verity's claim that the Tour and the race it helped give birth to have put the region on the map is backed up by tourism statistics. In 2015, the number of domestic visitors to Yorkshire rose by 19 per cent and has continued to climb. The number of international tourists visiting the county has also risen, reaching a record 647,000 in the first quarter of 2017.

For the pro peloton's riders and team, the Tour evidently offers similar rewards with regard to profile, publicity and earnings, although the outlook is not completely positive. As the biggest annual sporting event in the world and by some distance the most important bike race, the Tour is an obvious goal, offering both the greatest prize and audience all season. At the same time, however, it skews the commercial landscape within cycling. According to a 2013 Repucom/Cyclingnews.com report into the sport, TV coverage at the 2012 Tour provided the top-ranked teams with up to 80 per cent of their exposure for the season, depending on their level of success. For the Europcar team that took full advantage of its wild card invitation by winning three stages and the King of the Moun-

tains jersey, this figure rose to almost 96 per cent, underlining the extent by which the Tour is a race apart.

When it comes to the yellow jersey, the sponsors backing the team that holds it are sure to benefit from the considerable glow that it delivers in the form of a significant PR return, an increase in brand awareness and recognition, and a conse-

'No professional sport can sustain itself based on this kind of model. There's no longevity with it, and certainly not the kind that other sports have and with whom we're competing for sponsors'

quent growth in sales. However, for the management companies that own and run most teams, the return is harder to quantify. It may encourage their sponsors to commit to further investment or attract new backers, which ensures continuity. But there is no financial return. ASO owns all rights to the race, including the income from TV deals, while any prize money won is shared between the riders and backroom staff.

The fate of the BMC Racing team illustrates the complications that arise from this model. The Swiss-American team, and specifically the Continuum Sport management company behind it, went into 2018 knowing that its title sponsor would be withdrawing at the end of the season. At the start of the Tour, it confirmed there was still no new deal, but that star names such as Richie Porte,

'There is no other popular spectator sport that is so completely dominated by a private company, and ASO hasn't offered the least indication that this situation is likely to change'

Rohan Dennis and Tejay van Garderen would be departing to other squads. All three featured in the team time-trial victory on the third day that put Greg Van Avermaet into the yellow jersey. Could this make a difference?

A couple of days later, with the Belgian still in yellow but still no news of a new sponsor, team manager Jim Ochowicz acknowledged it was difficult to assess what power the yellow jersey

has in attracting sponsors. 'I think historically it's been proven that the yellow jersey works pretty well as a draw for potential sponsors. We've seen performances by the rider leading the Tour change things on the sponsorship side,' he said, recalling Steve Bauer's stint in yellow during the 1990 race that enabled Ochowicz to tempt Motorola to take over from 7-Eleven. 'The yellow jersey obviously brings a global awareness to us and, in terms of creating energy and ideas, that might encourage a company to think that this is the right place for them to promote their products.'

According to the American team manager, the frustration for him and his peers in the pro peloton who have responsibility for ensuring competitive continuity is that the search for sponsors is never-ending. 'I guess one of the things that having the yellow jersey does highlight is that even though you have it, it doesn't bring you any revenue. That's the model that we have in cycling at the moment, with no revenue-sharing with the teams. There's no revenue that we can generate, we are completely dependent on sponsors,' he explained. When the Tour reached Annecy and its first rest day, Van Avermaet had completed a week in yellow and Ochowicz finally had some news. Polish shoe manufacturer CCC had agreed to become his team's title sponsor. The deal, he said, had come together a few days before the Tour when a contact tipped him off that Dariusz Milek, the billionaire backer of the Polish CCC racing team, wanted to step up into the World-Tour in order to guarantee appearances in the top races on the calendar and specifically the Tour. As holders as one of the eighteen WorldTour licences Continuum Sport could provide this. 'It was the

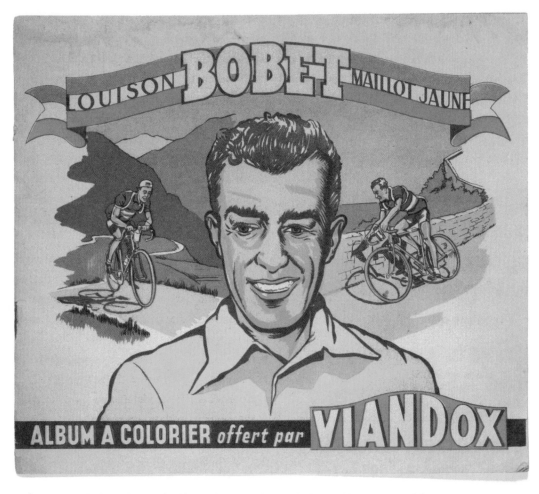

| *A promotional colouring book produced by Viandox, the French Bovril-like drink, and featuring Louison Bobet*

licence that sealed it,' the American confirmed. Van Avermaet's spell in yellow hadn't played a direct role, but did, Ochowicz admitted, reassure his new sponsor that he had made a good decision after backing a team that had spent sixteen long seasons in what is effectively cycling's PR wilderness.

This not only highlights the irresistible pull of the Tour for sponsors, but especially the control that ASO exercises over cycling. There is no other popular spectator sport that is so completely dominated by a private company, and ASO hasn't offered the least indication that this situation is likely to change. Beyond the altruistic argument, there's no reason why it should. From the commercial as much as the sporting perspective, the evocation of the yellow jersey as the 'grail' is entirely appropriate. Every team yearns for it and is pulled inexorably towards it.

There have been mutterings of a boycott. In

2014, Oleg Tinkov, whose bank sponsored the Tinkoff team, told Cyclingnews.com, 'I think we can compare it to a theatre. When you go to the theatre and buy the ticket, you expect the actors are paid for their performance. But when you watch a Grand Tour like the Giro, the Tour or the Vuelta, the actors aren't getting any of the revenue, the teams aren't getting a share of the TV revenue.' When it was put to him that ASO owns the theatre that is the Tour and everyone wants to perform in it or watch them do so, the Russian responded that there is no show without actors. 'If ASO doesn't share their TV revenue, we could boycott the Tour de France,' he declared. The Russian, though, pulled out of the sport before following through on this threat, while pro teams have subsequently given more focus to developing new income streams rather than trying to force ASO's hand.

For the riders who take to centre stage, the Tour is far more benevolent. The race has long

After Sofil became the first company to sponsor the *maillot jaune* in 1948, Louison Bobet refused to
wear their jersey in that year's Tour because it contained synthetic fibres as well as wool.
He believed that racing kit should only contain natural products as these allowed
the rider to breathe and perspire correctly, and therefore were the best way
of remaining healthy. Hearing the news and hearing that the contract with
Sofil might end as a result of Bobet's stubbornness, race director
Jacques Goddet abandoned his dinner and went to see the
race leader, who was "always exquisitely courteous,
but whose head was harder than the granite
plateaux found across his Armorica
homeland". They agreed that special
jerseys would be made for Bobet
that only contained a
symbolic amount
of synthetic
fibres.

been their best opportunity to put themselves in the shop window. In the pre-war years, two-time winner André Leducq was the face of Ovomaltine, the malted drink known as Ovaltine in the UK, while his compatriot and fellow double champion Antonin Magne was associated with Clacquesin, a pine tar liqueur tagged 'the healthiest of aperitifs'. Post-war, as media coverage grew, the leading stars became even more marketable. Louison Bobet promoted Viandox, a meat extract sauce, and Pontiac, 'the yellow jersey of watches', while Lucien Aimar's bounteous locks made him the ideal representative for a brilliantine-like hair gel called Magic Fix.

each held on a closed circuit in front of a paying audience, with professionals often participating in two or three a day, cramming in as many as possible. A Tour appearance would bring a decent fee, a stage win a significant one, while a spell in the yellow jersey meant the jackpot. Since the 1980s, though, salaries have risen considerably throughout the pro peloton and, especially in the twenty-first century, the sale of image rights and other commercial opportunities have ballooned. Although post-Tour crits can still deliver a useful bonus to Tour glory, there are greater gains to be made elsewhere.

'I think the Tour multiplies what you've

| The liqueur, Clacquesin, sponsored Antonin Magne in the 1930s

Until the 1980s, the riders' livelihoods were ruled by a simple equation: the better they rode in July, the higher their fees for appearances in the post-Tour criteriums. There used to be dozens of these,

achieved by three. If you win a stage on the Vuelta or Giro, you're a good rider. If you do so at the Tour, you're a great champion with a rosy future,' 2006 Tour winner Oscar Pereiro says in *Secrets de*

Maillots Jaunes. 'I don't know how to explain it. In the end, the effort you make in racing or training are the same. The suffering on a bike, the sacrifices away from it, the drain on your mental strength are exactly the same... When you win a stage of the Tour, the size of your contract increases, but if you do so on the Vuelta or Giro you don't get anything.'

It is, every rider who has worn it agrees, a transformative experience, beginning with that first rush and exhilaration and bewilderment that Cédric Vasseur described as making him feel like 'Leonardo di Caprio on the prow of the Titanic' and persisting as a permanent label of achievement. 'Once you've been in the yellow jersey, it lasts for eternity,' said Jens Voigt. Reflecting on his eight-day spell in the lead in 2009, Rinaldo Nocentini told *Procycling*, 'People talk about the value of the yellow jersey, and I can confirm that it's colossal. Everything I've done on a bike pales in comparison to those eight days... Maybe they didn't change my life but they certainly changed perceptions of me as a bike rider, my own included. Ultimately this sport is all about visibility and cyclists are judged according to how much of it they deliver. I was still Rinaldo Nocentini but suddenly I was a much higher-profile cyclist. Suddenly I was Rinaldo Nocentini, Tour de France yellow jersey.'

The Italian acknowledged that the longer he maintained his hold on the *maillot jaune*, the more his confidence in himself and his value as a rider grew. Then almost thirty-two, he raced for another six seasons with the French Ag2r team, and even at thirty-eight managed to secure another contract with Sporting Tavira in Portugal, which continued through to 2018, when he set up a coaching business in Tenerife aimed at nurturing young riders hoping to follow his footsteps into the pro ranks. 'I still feel that warmth from the public that the yellow jersey gave me,' said Nocentini, who was the only Italian rider to wear the yellow jersey between Alberto Elli in 2000 and Vincenzo Nibali in 2014.

As was seen in Yorkshire in 2014 where old bikes, pubs and even sheep were painted yellow, the jersey can have a transformative effect beyond the riders who wear it. When Daryl Impey became the first South African rider to lead the Tour in 2013, his compatriots responded with a celebration of their own. 'The next day they had a "yellow Friday" with everyone wearing yellow, and it gave the country a real boost, which was good at that time. I think it gave hope to young kids in South Africa that they could achieve something similar,' says Impey. 'I'm not the kind of guy who can walk down the street in South Africa and people know who I am because the sport's profile is still really small. But in terms of the overall picture, comparing where we were to where we are now, there's been a big change. There's been a South African team in the Tour since 2015, and there are riders on that team who have the potential to contend for the yellow jersey outright. The profile has gone up tremendously. There's even been talk of the Tour starting in South Africa.'

In its home country, too, this sense of the yellow jersey's power to transform remains very evident, particularly in towns and regions within *La France profonde* with which the race has always had a special affinity since the inaugural 1903 edition provided so many of them with their first experience of a major sporting event. During 2018, the small Breton town of Sarzeau hosted a stage finish, largely thanks to the influence of its mayor and UCI president David Lappartient. 'I feel hugely proud of it and all the people in Sarzeau feel proud too,' he said the day before his town's moment in the Tour spotlight. 'We've got a ten-metre-high yellow jersey hanging on the wall of the town hall and just the sight of it enthuses people as they walk past. It is such a huge occasion for our town, like for so many others. We'll never have the World Cup or the Olympic Games, but we can host the Tour de France. That's the strength of this race, that it can visit little towns like ours and offer them notoriety. People all over the world will see the magnificent coastline of the Golfe du Morbihan. We get a piece of the magic that the Tour brings.'

It could sound corny, but Lappartient is almost certainly echoing the sentiment of every other mayor along every Tour route. 'It's funny just how influential it is throughout all parts of French life. I was in a meeting recently and somebody talked about a business being the *maillot jaune* within a particular sector, meaning it being the leader. The reference is not only known in cycling now, it is known absolutely everywhere. That is the power of the yellow jersey.'

JAN JANSSON
TOUR DE FRANCE
1968

8

THE MOTIVATING MAILLOT

Le Maillot Jaune

Thomas Voeckler 2011

A NIKE-MADE YELLOW JERSEY,
SIGNED BY VOECKLER

With a total of twenty, Thomas Voeckler holds as
many yellow jerseys as italian legend Gino Bartali

'**This** Jersey **has special powers**'

In addition to the jersey itself, there is, Thomas Voeckler affirms, only one thing that every rider that has held the *maillot jaune* shares.

'When you first take it, you can't imagine what the yellow jersey will bring to you in terms of attention and recognition,' the Frenchman says. 'It doesn't matter whether you're only likely to have it for a single day or if you're hoping to wear it all the way into Paris, it will have an immense impact on your career. When I had the French champion's jersey in 2004, I thought to myself, "This is cool, being the French champion everyone recognises me." But once you take the yellow jersey that recognition rockets into the stratosphere. It's so completely different it's hard to describe it.

You suddenly become more famous than the president. I was shocked by the intensity of it, by the focus that was on me. It's absolutely mind-blowing and hard to come to terms with.'

Watching Fernando Gaviria's reaction to his opening day success at the 2018 Tour de France in the small Vendée town of Fontenay-le-Comte provides a complete endorsement of Voeckler's assessment. Victory sealed – incidentally the first in a road stage by a Tour debutant since Edward Sels in 1964 – the Colombian has the bullish swagger of any bunch sprinter who has just blitzed his rivals, his elation obvious as he steps out on to the podium to be presented with the leader's jersey. Even after autographing a couple of dozen replicas and conducting a television interview with the host broadcaster, his face remains radiant, his smile broad and beaming, the sunlight frequently glinting on his braces that are testament to recent dental work.

like to win the first stage of the Tour and take the yellow jersey? Is this a dream come true for you? Will you be able to keep it tomorrow? After the adrenalin rush of the sprint that left the rest of the bunch in his wake, and on his very first day in the Tour no less, Gaviria can't escape the media's shackles in the mixed zone.

He reaches the end of the line of broadcasters, websites and bloggerswho have each paid thousands of euros for the right to grill the race's protagonists, his smile broadening for a moment, until ASO's media aide takes his arm. 'Just the written press to speak to now. This way, Fernando.' The fixed smile returns, although he is, at least, well versed in what to say by this point...

The next morning, when the QuickStep bus is directed to its place in the team paddock in Mouilleron-Saint-Germain, Gaviria gets mobbed again.

'Bon courage, Fernando!'

Half an hour later, the Colombian remains resplendent in yellow, but his podium sparkle has waned. Since receiving the cheers and applause of the crowd, he has completed – or endured if his expression is now anything to go by – dozens of interviews, answering a variation of the same two or three questions in all of them. What does it feel

The media are back for more interviews – Will you try to keep the jersey today? Did you sleep in it last night? Do you have a message for everyone back in Colombia? Fans want autographs, selfies, the opportunity to wish 'Bon courage, Fernando!' It's manic, 'like being a movie star, or the king of the peloton,' according to Frenchman Cédric

Vasseur. 'It's really difficult to deal with all the fuss and attention that you get and the thing you most look forward to is the start so that you can have a little bit more peace and quiet by being in the bunch. That's the only place you can really escape it.'

But returning to that sanctuary brings another a new pressure. To every member of the peloton who is not part of his team, the yellow jersey is a bright target that they all have in their sights. Initially, this is surreptitious. The Tour leader can glide through the bunch, his colours opening a passage through the pack. 'You do get a little more space, more respect. You feel like you own the world and that everyone is looking at you,' says Thor Hushovd, who led the race on two occasions. 'But you've got to remember that it's the yellow jersey that they're responding to and that extra bit of room you get will disappear the instant the race is on. At that point, nobody else cares about the fact that you're in the yellow jersey, and you've got to do everything that you can to protect it.'

It is when this moment arrives, as it inevitably does, that the exponential power of the *maillot jaune* becomes apparent. 'It does allow you to transcend yourself, assuming that you're prepared to defend your position tooth and nail,' says Voeckler. 'It's difficult to describe, but you don't feel that you have the right to yield and, as a consequence, you can push your degree of suffering further than normal. It does give you wings.' It is as if, suggests Vasseur, the jersey transfers a particular force to the rider who is in it. 'It's such a powerful motivator, you can do things when you're in it that you would never ever imagine were possible.'

Vasseur points to Greg Van Avermaet as a good example of a rider who has squeezed everything he was able to from his two spells as the Tour leader. In both 2016 and 2018, the Belgian took the unusual step of defending the yellow jersey by attacking, joining the break on both occasions on the opening stage in the high mountains. 'I knew that doing this was only going to give me an extra day in the lead because the GC riders were holding back for the bigger climbs that were just ahead, but it was well worth it. I'm not a rider who is ever going to win the Tour, but I wanted to show off the jersey and hearing the response from the fans at the side of the road gave me even more of a lift and made the experience even more memorable,' says Van Avermaet.

Watching him defying the peloton's big hitters reminded Vasseur of the five days he spent in yellow during the 1997 Tour. While the Cofidis team manager confesses that as a rider he didn't have the same all-round ability as the Belgian Classics specialist, he did feel the yellow jersey instilled him with that same elemental urge to tap every internal resource. 'Perhaps that was partly because I come from a cycling family that's had a long connection with the Tour thanks to my father being a pro and winning a stage in the 1970 Tour. As a child, I used to dream of racing in the Tour de France and just being part of it was quite wonderful,' he explains. 'But being a real protagonist as a result of winning a stage and wearing the yellow jersey was extraordinary because leading the Tour seemed completely inaccessible to me.'

Vasseur's solo win in 1997 at La Châtre provided him with enough of a buffer to fend off the sprinters over the following three days as the race headed down through western France towards the Pyrenees, which began with a Bastille Day stage over four passes to Loudenvielle. 'The twin effect of being in yellow on the Fête Nationale enabled me to go far deeper than I'd ever done before,' says the Frenchman, who got dropped by the GC contenders on the Tourmalet and Aspin, but took huge risks on the descents to rejoin them before the final climb of the Col d'Azet. Once again unable to hold his place in a group containing Jan Ullrich, Richard Virenque, Marco Pantani and Bjarne Riis, Vasseur reached the summit with his lead all but eroded, barrelled down the pass and crossed the line with his lead retained by a mere thirteen seconds. 'The next stage to Arcalis in Andorra is renowned as the day that Jan Ullrich first took the yellow jersey, and with six passes on the menu over 250 kilometres of racing I was never likely to be able to prevent him going into the lead. But I was stung by the fact that the media was writing me off even before we had got under way, and that pushed me into one last show of defiance.'

Dropped by the favourites on the relentless ascent of the vast Envalira pass, Vasseur threw caution to the wind on the long drop into the mountain principality, remained in close contact over the shorter Ordino climb and fought his way back up to the group chasing lone leader Jean-Philippe Dojwa. 'We got onto the first ramps up to Arcalis and I attacked. I managed to get across the gap to Dojwa but in all honesty I had nothing left. When Ullrich went past me just a few minutes later he was going about three times my speed. I'd just been taking it day by day, with each new one in yellow a bonus. Losing it was like passing from the light into darkness,' explains the Frenchman. That light, he acknowledges, doesn't disappear completely, though. 'Being a former yellow jersey opened the door to new opportunities for me, both when I was racing and subsequently,' says Vasseur, who went on to ride for US Postal, Quick-Step and Cofidis, before moving into a new career as a racing analyst on TV and later into team management.

'He's not even won the Tour, he's only worn the jersey, and now he's more popular than guys who have won big races'

Voeckler is on very much the same trajectory, but has been covering that ground far quicker thanks to what were two of the most remarkable spells any rider has had in the yellow jersey in the twenty-first century. Like his compatriot, he talks of a before and after in relation to the yellow jersey, 2004 being the year when everything changed for him, in his case in Chartres where he took it as the best placed member of a five-man group that finished more than a dozen minutes ahead of the peloton. Defending champion and race leader Lance Armstrong and US Postal were delighted at having handed responsibility for defending the jersey to the Frenchman's Brioches La Boulangère team for a few days. Describing himself as the 'little Frenchman' who was fighting against the 'naughty Americans', Voeckler knew full well that the jersey wouldn't remain on his shoulders for long, but delighted the home nation by parrying the inevitable day after day.

'I went through that shock that every first-time yellow jersey is hit by on the podium and in the interviews. We were glad to be right in the spotlight because we were a small team that was looking for a new sponsor, and we had to make the most of that. It meant saying yes to a lot of the media requests, while at the same time trying to do all we could to extend my stay in the lead for another day,' Voeckler explains. 'I remember when I got the jersey that all of the more experienced riders I was racing with said to me, "It will give you wings." I told them, "You're not the one who's on the bike. I know with my legs it's going to be difficult to hold it." But a few days later, at Plateau de Beille, I had to admit to myself, "This jersey has special powers."'

Thanks to a three-minute margin and a run of stages that favoured the sprinters, Voeckler

negotiated tricky days in Brittany and the Massif Central with aplomb. Come the Pyrenees and the summit finish at La Mongie, he pushed his lead out to more than five minutes as his Chartres break-away companions tumbled down the rankings and the GC favourites finally began to emerge, with Armstrong in the vanguard and apparently set to reclaim the jersey at Plateau de Beille, the last of seven categorised climbs on the day's menu. Dropped on the Portet d'Aspet, the Col de la Core, the Latrape, the Agnès and the Port de Lers, Voeckler battled back on each occasion, thinking only of hanging on. On the steep opening ramps of the final ascent, he lost ground again. Rocking all over his bike, grimacing and gurning with tongue protruding, yellow jersey fully unzipped, his features puce with effort, the plucky Frenchman gave it everything. Five minutes after Armstrong had outsprinted Ivan Basso to win, he crossed the line, exhausted and exultant, right fist raised in the air, the yellow jersey retained by twenty-two seconds, enough to let him keep it for another two stages.

'I was often accused of being over-dramatic. But if there's one moment when I certainly wasn't – not even 1 per cent – then it was at Plateau de Beille. Whenever I see that photo of me crossing the line with the jersey wide open... I was young.

That's the charm of cycling, it's the face of the kid who's taken his suffering to its furthest extent. My facial features and body are lined. I wasn't in a good state, but the photo is beautiful,' he says in *Secrets de Maillots Jaunes*.

Reflecting on this career-shaping performance, Voeckler confesses it affected his own perception of himself as well as the attitude of some of his fellow pros towards him. 'There was a short period when I did get big-headed. Certainly not during the second half of the 2004 season, but in the following year, because I'd won a bit of money, because I was recognised in the street. I tried to do my very best from the sporting perspective, but I didn't achieve much success. It didn't last too long, but for a few months, yes, I was full of myself.'

He recognises behaving like this may have coloured the feelings some of his peers had for him, but also believes that the adulation directed his way by fans and the media in his home country, starved of yellow jersey success for so long, was at least equally responsible. 'Because I became very famous through having the jersey, I think a lot of riders were quite jealous of my new status, that there was a feeling among some of them of, "He's not even won the Tour, he's only worn the jersey, and now he's more popular than guys who have won big races." But it wasn't my fault,' he tells me. 'It wasn't if I chose to be in that situation, that I'd decided to be there. It was just fortune looking favourably on me as much as anything. I had the feeling for a couple of years that some people resented me for what I'd achieved, but it didn't change the way I thought about myself at all. I tried not to let it get to me and remain the person

I was, to stick to doing things the way that I'd always done them.'

There is an Hinault-like cussedness to Voeckler. Indeed, it underpinned his success and popularity. The two men also shared a hatred for training and relished racing. They loved beating people and were prepared to hurt themselves quite seriously in order to achieve this. Reflecting on the Frenchman's career as it neared its end, Philippe Bouvet, for many years *L'Équipe*'s chief cycling correspondent, described him as forging his own destiny in spite of obvious deficits in his make-up as a racer. 'He creates opportunities in life and knows exactly how best to seize them. It was said initially that he was a bit limited in terms of his ability, but we've since realised that such an assessment is only half right. He's won some great races because he's so strong mentally. [His team manager] Jean-René Bernaudeau always says that if he had a rider who had the talent of Sylvain Chavanel and the character of Voeckler he would have had a super-champion. Voeckler really is remarkable and quite unique.'

Drawing on this well of bloody-mindedness, Voeckler pulled off feats that seemed close to impossible, defending his corner in what could rightly be described as Badger-like ferocity. 'Attempting those coups has enabled him to achieve greater ones. When he took the yellow jersey for the second time at Saint-Flour in 2011, he didn't set off with that target in mind but looking for the King of the Mountains jersey,' said Bouvet.

Voeckler explains that the only similarity between his second spell in yellow and the first was that he had the jersey for ten days once again.

| Voeckler returns to centre stage as yellow jersey in 2011

'The second time I was ready for it. I knew how to deal with it. I always said to myself after 2004 that if I ever got the yellow jersey again, even though I never expected to, I would try to do things differently. For example, I said to myself, "I won't spend an hour with the press talking about the race after the stage. I'll think about my recovery more, be focused on the race more." It's not that I didn't want to enjoy the moment, I just wanted to make the very most of the opportunity, not only because I wanted to keep the jersey for as long as possible, but also because I knew that this would be the only time that I could finish high up in the general classification in Paris.'

'this motivating factor is particularly significant for racers from the Tour's home nation'

Did this mean improving on his eighteenth place in 2004, a place in the top ten? Finishing in the first five seemed a fantastical notion for a rider whose main asset was his psychological rather than his physical strength. With Cadel Evans a little under two-and-a-half minutes back in third place and the Schleck brothers and Alberto Contador among the other hitters on the Australian's heels, Voeckler had a far smaller cushion when, after another two stages, the race reached the Pyrenees and the favourites readied themselves for the first high-summit finish at Luz-Ardiden, with two significant hurdles to cross before it, the Hourquette d'Ancizan and the Tourmalet.

that any attacks were unlikely to come from so far out on the first significant day in the mountains. Everyone was holding back for Luz-Ardiden, but as they continued to wait Voeckler's confidence increased. When the attacks finally came three kilometres from the finish, he still held his place among the favourites. At the finish, the Frenchman's losses were minimal. Fränk Schleck jumped to second place, but was still close to two minutes down.

'When I had the jersey in 2004, they told me that you become a different rider. You aren't any stronger because of the jersey, but it does change your motivation. What I did today, to suffer like

l'angoisse du maillot

Coming off the first of those passes, Voeckler misjudged a corner and bounced off a car parked on the roadside, but quickly chased back up to his rivals again, unsure and apparently unconcerned about whether he'd done himself any damage. With his Europcar teammates drawing on the energising force of the jersey and doing all they could to keep their leader out of the wind, he tracked the contenders on the Tourmalet, aware

I did on the mountain, I wouldn't do to finish in twentieth position. But when it's to defend the yellow jersey, you have extra resources and that's very important. That's helped me a lot today,' Voeckler stated at the finish.

Sports scientist Ross Tucker has said that in situations such as these, where a rider has pushed himself beyond his normally expected limits, that the brain conducts the physiological equiv-

Voeckler finds himself without any team support on the Col du Galibier in 2011

'I closed my eyes and when I opened them again I was still on the bike'

WINNING THE TOUR DE FRANCE AT THE FIRST ATTEMPT

Eleven cyclists won the general classification the first time they participated in the race.

YEAR	WINNER	COUNTRY	WINNING MARGIN
1903	**Maurice Garin***		**+ 2hr 59' 21"**
1904	Henri Cornet		+ 2hr 16' 14"
1905	**Louis Trousselier**		**+ 3' 00"**
1947	Jean Robic		+ 3' 58"
1949	**Fausto Coppi**		**+ 10' 55"**
1951	Hugo Koblet		+ 22' 00"
1957	**Jacques Anquetil**		**+ 14' 56"**
1965	Felice Gimondi		+ 2' 40"
1969	**Eddy Merckx**		**+ 17' 54"**
1978	Bernard Hinault		+ 3' 56"
1983	**Laurent Fignon**		**+ 4' 04"**

*The first Tour de France, so by definition

alent of a cost-benefit analysis, in which greater motivation enables a higher level of exertion and increased tolerance to physiological strain. 'The classic understanding is that an athlete slows down because they reach the absolute limit of a range of physiological factors – their heart can't supply enough blood to the muscles or they go anaerobic. But even at the very top end of performance, these factors aren't limited by the body's capacity, they are regulated by the brain to ensure there's always a reserve that the body doesn't dip into,' he told *Procycling* in the wake of Voeckler's performance.

'I suspect that the motivation of the yellow jersey is so much higher than it is for a rider finishing in the main group. Voeckler's brain over-rode his normal limits and dipped into the protect-ive reserve through the Pyrenees... A Frenchman wearing yellow in his home race is going to be a powerful driver. It's impossible to know how deep that protective margin is without actually hurting someone but at this elite level it's enough to turn someone good into someone great.'

Voeckler agrees that this motivating factor is particularly significant for racers from the Tour's home nation. 'I think it does lift French riders. It's really quite something to become aware of what it can do for you. You're bound to feel real pride when you wear this jersey, especially when you think a rider like Raymond Poulidor never wore it, even though he won dozens of races,' he says. That day, France's Fête Nationale, the force transmitted to Voeckler by the jersey was especially strong. Foreign riders do receive a similar lift, but it's extremely rare to see a non-French rider raise their performance well beyond expected levels in the

way that Antonin Rolland, Vincent Barteau, Pascal Lino, Georges Groussard and Cyrille Guimard, to name but a handful, were able to when they spent long spells in yellow. Voeckler stands out, though, because he managed it twice.

Two days on from his defence at Luz-Ardiden, he came through an even bigger test on a stage to Plateau de Beille that crossed the same passes on which he had fought his remarkable rearguard action in 2004. 'I benefited that day from the head-wind that was blowing and from knowing the climb,' he says. Initially, the road switches back and forth steeply as it climbs out of the Ariège valley, but the closing kilometres take a more direct line towards the tiny cross-country ski station at the top. With teammate Pierre Rolland not as strong as he had been in the preceding stages, Voeckler found himself under greater pressure. But such was his confidence by this point that he responded to every significant attack. 'It was the only time that I ever felt like the Tour's patron,' he says.

That word that instantly summons up the image of Hinault and is particularly noteworthy at this point because Voeckler's approach to the race began to change. 'I never thought that I would win the race,' he states. 'I always knew that Evans would take the title because of the time trial that came right at the end. I did start to think, though, that a podium finish was possible.' As the race completed the 'transition' stages between the Pyrenees and the Alps, the media were trumpeting this scenario, talking up this '*Tour à la Walko*' where the French underdog could upset the established hierarchy.

When the Tour reached Gap, where Evans sneaked away on the run-in to the finish to gain some useful time on his rivals and move into second place, a minute and forty-five seconds down on Voeckler, the Frenchman had held the yellow jersey for more than a week. But, for the first time, like any other contender for ultimate contender for ultimate glory, he now had something to lose. When Georges Speicher took the lead halfway through the 1933 Tour, he described how doubt started to affect him, making him uneasy, cautious and nervous. 'It's known as *l'angoisse du maillot* [jersey anxiety]. Everyone who has worn the yellow jersey has known all about that. There's no doubt that I had confidence in myself... I felt that I had the strength to keep it, but... you never know... You can't make any mistakes, let your guard down at any moment. I had to watch my rivals at every instant... On the flat, I didn't go looking to make sparks fly. In the sprints, I was afraid of falling, of collisions...'

This anxiety preys on yellow jersey contenders far more than those whose hold on it is certain to be temporary, colouring their thinking and tactics. So lucid in his control of his physical resources and strategy up to that point, Voeckler became more aggressive and it led to mistakes. His first came in the closing kilometres into Gap when he tried and failed to follow a late attack by Contador on the final second-category climb. 'I just wanted to take advantage of the fact that I was on his wheel, but I shouldn't have.' According to Cyrille Guimard, the Frenchman had entered another dimension, one where the yellow jersey inflates the ego and thus diminishes sound thinking. It only cost him twenty-one seconds on Evans in Gap, but it quickly resulted in the loss of his podium hopes.

The very next day, on the tight and twisting descent into the Italian mountain resort of Pinerolo, Voeckler pressed hard on the front of the yellow jersey group, hoping to gain some seconds on his rivals. He almost missed the second bend, but somehow managed to keep the road under his wheels. Two hairpins below, he came into the corner too fast, ran off the road and, very fortunately, bunny-hopped off the bank and into the front yard of the house on the corner. 'I closed my eyes and when I opened them again I was still on the bike,' he said. He escaped unscathed, apart from the loss of another twenty-seven seconds of his advantage.

Twenty-four hours later, the Europcar leader survived his toughest test so far – trial by Schlecks. Andy, the younger and lower-ranked of the Luxembourg siblings, launched a long-range attack over the Izoard pass. Assisted by two teammates, he became the race leader on the road, and went on to claim a courageous solo victory on the summit of the Galibier that was a throwback to another cycling age. When his rivals, and principally Evans, began the pursuit behind him, Fränk Schleck sat on their wheels, got towed most of the way up the final ascent, then jumped away to take second place, ahead of the Australian, with Voeckler another few seconds back, punching the air with elation as he crossed the line, his lead reduced to just fifteen seconds over the stage winner.

Looking back to that stage and the days that preceded, Evans, whose composure crumbled when he led the 2008 Tour, most demonstrably when he threatened a journalist at a stage finish, 'Don't stand on my dog or I'll cut your head off,' has acknowledged that he didn't like having the burden of wearing yellow anywhere but on the Champs-Élysées and was delighted for the Frenchman to have it. 'Voeckler loved wearing it, he loved being the centre of attention for the fans. It was an excellent opportunity for me. I could stay hidden in the shadows until the final stages,' the Australian says in *Secrets de Maillots Jaunes*, but he adds: 'Thomas should have collaborated with me on the climb of the Galibier rather than waiting for the end of the ascent and getting his teammate, Pierre Rolland, to ride. He would have gained more time on Andy Schleck. It was because of his approach on that stage that he lost his podium place.' Voeckler, however, counters that he and his teammate gave everything they had on that stage. It was the next day, he says, he blew his podium chances with the most glaring mistake of his career.

The 109-kilometre stage from Modane to Alpe d'Huez via the Télégraphe and Galibier passes provided the Schlecks with a final opportunity to gain ground on Evans before a long time trial in Grenoble that would follow the day after. But the trigger for a frantic three hours of racing was Contador, whose results were later struck from the records when an appeal against a doping suspension failed. The Spaniard attacked on the Télégraphe, the Schlecks responding and forcing Evans and Voeckler to do the same. As the group caught its breath, Contador went again and again, trying to ride everyone off his wheel. Fränk Schleck was the first to yield. Evans was next to pull aside and drop back. Voeckler hung on, wrongly assuming the Australian, who had suffered a mechanical problem, had cracked. For the first time, he thought

that he could win the Tour. That belief didn't last for long.

He too fell away from the Spaniard's scorching pace, with Andy Schleck the only one able to cope with it. The Frenchman has suggested that Contador's assault was payback after the pair had almost collided and traded insults heading for the finish at Super Besse earlier in the race. 'I found out later that he had cooked something up with Andy Schleck on the Galibier stage with a view to killing me off,' he claimed. Yet, the Frenchman admits he contributed considerably to digging his own grave, that he 'lacked clarity'. Rather than easing off and dropping back to his teammates in the Evans group behind, he continued to chase, a chasse-patate caught in the no-man's-land between the break and the bunch.

'What I saw of him on that Tour was illustrative if what can happen when the yellow jersey – and all that goes with it – lands on your shoulders. For several days Voeckler became his own directeur sportif and, from the moment that he entered the high mountains, he rode tactically in the opposite way to how he should, and as a result his teammates and his management clearly had no idea how to react. Something needed to be said because, very clearly, nobody was capable of giving him racing orders when the stakes were highest,' is Guimard's condemnatory verdict. The Frenchman acknowledges the criticism, describing his foray as an 'idiotic show of panache'.

'Going off the road on the descent into Pinerolo and joining the attack on the Télégraphe were big mistakes. They cost me second place overall, but I'd rather they cost me second place than first place in Paris because there's not so much difference between second and fourth place on the Tour. I think I would struggle to live with it if I thought that those two mistakes had cost me overall victory. That would certainly be very hard. If our team directors hadn't been as intimidated by me and the way I saw the race, they would have ordered me to stop,' he says of Europcar directeurs sportifs Ismaël Mottier and Dominique Arnould, but affirms that he was himself the most culpable during this hour of madness.

Fortunately for Europcar and the French fans who were still clinging tenaciously to the slight prospect of a first Tour victory for twenty-six years, the stage offered the consolation of a Rolland victory at Alpe d'Huez, the first by a home rider at the legendary ski station since Hinault's in 1986. Yet, if it hadn't been for the maddening effect of *l'angoisse du maillot*, Voeckler would have started the final time trial in yellow, perhaps with a minute in hand on Evans. The Australian would surely have taken the title, but what a show Voeckler would have given us in Grenoble, hamming it up for all he was worth, delivering an unambiguous reminder that the yellow should motivate and thrill those watching it as much as those fortunate enough to wear it.

THOMAS VOECKLER
TOUR DE FRANCE
2011

9

THE MADDENING MAILLOT

Le Maillot Jaune

Marco Pantani 1998

**A LONG-SLEEVED VERSION FROM THE
RAIN- AND SCANDAL-HIT 1998 TOUR,
SIGNED BY WINNER PANTANI**

It can be lonely in yellow, as Cadel Evans found out in 2008

Blinded by the Light

In a piece for the *Cycling Anthology* written after Chris Froome had won his first Tour de France title in 2013, Ned Boulting attempted to lift the lid on the enigmatic new champion.

He was, wrote the TV commentator, 'The boy from nowhere, meekly setting about his work, hunched over a bike, head nodding; an unassuming, well-bred beast. He may have the gaze of an accountant, and the manners of a priest, but he is a racer, pure and simple, unquenchable in his thirst, his ambition, curious only to satisfy one particular, driven enquiry. How good can he be? Will Chris Froome be great? Is he already great? Who is he, really? Look straight at him for the answer. Look carefully. It's there, somewhere. But I'm damned if I can find it.'

But Boulting didn't give up. A couple of years later, he took another stab at unveiling the real Chris Froome in a TV documentary. During it, he followed the rider to his winter home in South Africa, where the two of them went to a barbecue hosted by Froome's friends from his school-days. They cooked steak, drank beer, told funny stories about the Tour winner. Throughout it, though, the Sky rider looked like a stranger at his own party, a guest who was desperate to be somewhere else. On his bike, no doubt, preparing for the next yellow jersey defence. Who is he, really?

Froome is relentless, focused, courteous and, most importantly, unflappable. His peers like and respect him, or did at least until his adverse analytical finding for salbutamol at the 2017 Vuelta a España. 'Before the news broke about the control, I was often disappointed in the reaction to Chris because I thought he was making a big effort, speaking French, always smiling, always saying hello. He was a good guy to have alongside you in the peloton, a good ambassador for the sport,' Thomas Voeckler told me four weeks before the World Anti-Doping Agency cleared Froome of wrongdoing resulting from this AAF. 'If he does start the Tour, it will be difficult for him with the public. But I know Chris Froome a little bit and I believe he will be able to deal with this. He's as strong in the head as he is skinny in the legs.'

The Frenchman was right. Froome may have lost his Tour crown, been booed and threatened, but he never wavered until the race's final week, and only then because his efforts in winning the Giro d'Italia title the month before began to tell. He is apparently impervious to pressure, thriving when he scents it. 'I try not to let the impact of the yellow jersey change my thinking,' he says. Somewhere on the meandering path that's led from Kenya, to South Africa, to the UCI development centre in Switzerland and, ultimately, to Team Sky and the Tour de France, he appears to have been inoculated against Georges Speicher's *angoisse du maillot*.

While Froome generally has his inner chimp securely locked away and, as a consequence, rarely looks like getting rattled by yellow jersey fever, it is rare for Tour contenders to be this composed. Many evoke the pressure that comes arm in arm with leadership of sport's greatest races, or even challenging for it. There's another side to it too. As Voeckler showed, wearing the *maillot jaune* undermines rationality. Lucien Aimar has described this particularly well. 'There is a magical side. Everyone is waiting for you. Well, not you in particular, but the yellow jersey. It's like the sun coming up, God himself walking on the Earth... I was in another world, I was twenty-five and leader of the Tour de France. You don't have a rational take on things in moments like that.'

Pushed to their psychological as well as physical extremes, it is hardly surprising that Tour contenders lose control, occasionally very publicly. Following Cadel Evans's progress during the 2008 Tour was to watch a man unravelling. He began it as the favourite, and in an effort to shield him from as many distractions as possible, his Lotto team hired Serge 'The Muscles from Brussels' Borlée, the bodyguard who had previously offered protection to Lance Armstrong and Alexandre Vinokourov. The Belgian minder's presence helped fend off unwanted attention from the press and fans, but couldn't resist the insidious creep of jersey fever. 'Here's your interview,' he said tossing his cracked helmet to journalist Rupert Guinness after crashing heavily on the stage into Bagnères-de-Bigorre. While that was an understandable reaction to an incident that could have resulted in serious injury or ended the Australian's hopes of victory, his behaviour became more erratic after he took the lead at Hautacam the next day.

On the podium, after being helped into the *maillot jaune*, he cuddled the Crédit Lyonnais *lionceau* toy lion like a child hugging a security blanket before walking off without acknowledging the Tour VIPs waiting to shake hands with him. He tossed a water bottle at one motorbike, slapped away the Garde Républicaine piloting another. Encounters with the press became tetchy. He headbutted a camera blocking his path, yelled 'Don't touch my shoulder' at a journalist trying to get his attention, and there was the famous incident with his dog that provoked a threat of decapitation. Amid it all, there was a rest-day press conference in Pau, where he emerged still clutching his yellow lion and with a Midnight Oil song blasting out. 'I don't remember ever having a press conference like this,' he told the bewildered press, who had never seen what felt like a victory parade at the halfway point either.

My final memory of Evans that year is from half an hour after his final drive for glory had come up short in a time trial at Saint-Amand-Montrond. He was behind the barriers surrounding the sports complex where Carlos Sastre was in the middle of his winner's press conference, warming down on his turbo trainer. His wife appeared next to him with his mother, each of them hugging the Australian, who looked happier than he had for days. He wasn't in yellow, but he looked radiant. The heat was off.

Reflecting on that race in which he was one of his compatriot's teammates, Robbie McEwen told Ed Pickering, 'When there's a bit of pressure on him he tends to back himself into a corner. He just gets defensive. You can see the stress building up.' The sprinter describes how Evans would have loved to have ridden with no fans and no media, 'just 200 blokes riding around.' But he stressed the significant point that, 'It's unfair to judge someone during the Tour de France when they are under pressure. You are not yourself – I wasn't either.' It wasn't a coincidence that when Evans did win the title three years later, he took the lead in the time trial on the penultimate day. He had completed what was for him the perfect Tour. Paris was his first day in yellow.

Although a very different character to the Australian, Bradley Wiggins, who succeeded Evans as the champion, shares the same tendency towards prickliness. When he pulled on the yellow jersey for the first time at La Planche des Belles Filles at the end of the first week in 2012, he was overwhelmed, and this despite winning several major stage races over the previous couple of seasons with the precise goal of preparing him for being centre stage at the Tour. 'I'd never had a yellow jersey in my hands; I'd never been in a team that took the jersey. I didn't take it in my stride,' he acknowledged. This wasn't helped by a well-disguised *jours sans* on his first day in yellow to Porrentruy in Switzerland, the result of a cracked frame flexing it was later discovered. After dealing with his rivals on the road, Wiggins' primary concern was getting to Sky's hotel and starting to focus on a long time trial in Besançon the next day that was crucial to his prospects of retaining the lead. 'I didn't want to stick around at the finish doing all the press interviews. But as the yellow jersey of the Tour de France, you have no option,' he says in *My Time*.

That day, the Tour's press tent had been set up adjacent to the finish, offering an ideal opportunity for the written press to ask questions of the

| Bradley Wiggins finds himself the focus of the media pack in 2012

'I didn't want to stick around at the finish doing all the press interviews. But as the yellow jersey of the Tour de France, you have no option'

stage winner and yellow jersey in person within the small, truck-mounted pressroom set up in the technical area adjacent to the final straight. With a little podium at one end for the riders and a translator faced by thirty-odd folding chairs, the closest within touching distance of them, it offers the opportunity to see them up close for ten minutes or so, to check for signs of fatigue, a cough that might hint at weakness to come, to assess their morale, and to ask questions. It was about a third full, most writers choosing to stay in the main press area where questions can be asked via a video link.

When Wiggins came in after stage winner Thibaut Pinot, the initial queries were routine. How was your first day in yellow? What are you hoping for from the time trial? Understandably, at that point he didn't mention how he struggled on the bike and come close to being dropped. There is no reason to ever give your rivals that kind of a leg-up. Over the previous days, Sky's show of power at stage races earlier in the season and at the Tour had been accompanied by sniping on social media. Comparisons had been made to US Postal and Lance Armstrong. Inevitably, this came up.

'There was some chatter in the Twitter-sphere about the comparison between Sky and US Postal,' a journalist asked via the video link. 'I'm wondering your reaction. And, what do you say to the cynics who say you have to be doped up to win the Tour de France?'

Wiggins picked up the microphone and responded: 'Honestly, they're just fucking wankers. I cannot be dealing with people like that. It justifies their own bone-idleness because they can't ever imagine applying themselves to anything in their lives. And it's easy for them to sit under a pseudo-name on Twitter and write that sort of shit rather than get off their arses in their own life and apply themselves, and work hard at something and achieve something. And that's ultimately it.' ASO translator Pascale Schyns, who had been scribbling all this down, was about to deliver this in French, when the Briton added a final message. 'Cunts!' With that, the yellow jersey, stood and stalked out, leaving every eyebrow raised.

It's hard to imagine Froome reacting in a similar way. Abused, spat on, condemned, accused, derided, he's raised his voice, been exasperated, but always answered questions asked of him. It's easy to imagine Wiggins carrying his rage away with him from that Porrentruy presser, perhaps feeding off it the next day as he stomped all over his rivals' hopes in the time trial, but Froome, who it should be noted didn't grow up consumed with racing and the politics of cycle sport, could hardly be any more different. When he walks away from situations of this kind, he's already consigned any angry and negative emotions to a vault in his consciousness from which nothing can escape. Anything that can't enable him to win the Tour is consigned to this Mariana Trench in his mind, including, it would seem, some of that personality that Ned Boulting was trying to identify. Perhaps the politest Tour champion of all time, he is also the most focused on the final objective. Only bad luck or poor form can deflect him.

No other Tour champion or authentic challenger has demonstrated this same equanimity with comparable consistency. Being able to lean on one of the strongest teams the sport has seen does provide a stable foundation for Froome's composure, yet there are numerous instances in the post-war era of leaders succumbing to yellow jersey fever on teams that established the template that Sky have simply adapted.

In 1983, when Renault lost four-time winner Bernard Hinault to injury, their DS Cyrille Guimard believed that in Laurent Fignon he had the ideal stand-in, but was concerned that the twenty-two-year-old Parisian lacked the experience and all-round maturity to cope with the demands of leadership at the Tour. Consequently, he deflected attention from his young tyro by talking up the chances of teammate Marc Madiot, while instructing Fignon to target a stage win, the white jersey of best young rider and a place in the top ten. 'Even as I was saying this, I was thinking, "You are going to remain centre stage and, when I decide the time is right, you will play your card."' That moment arrived when yellow jersey Pascal Simon, who had been racing against doctor's orders with a broken shoulder blade for several days, abandoned on the road to Alpe d'Huez. Fignon inherited the yellow jersey.

There is obvious significance to the first moment that a rider pulls on the yellow jersey, but for those whose objective is to wear it into Paris a successful defence of the lead the next day is at least as important. Just as in football, where a team is never more vulnerable than when it has scored a goal, taking possession of the *maillot jaune* is a wonderful distraction, as the Tour's palmarès underlines. Plenty of big hitters have led the race for just a single day, among them Tom Simpson,

Sean Kelly, Jean-François Bernard, Luc Leblanc and Erik Breukink. But, as Guimard feared in Fignon's case and the rider himself was soon to realise, being able to hang the yellow jersey over the back of the chair in your hotel room for the second night in succession is often a test by fire.

In the bespectacled Frenchman's case, it required him to nullify attacks by his rivals over five big passes as the road weaved 247.5 kilometres northwards from Alpe d'Huez to Morzine. 'I felt a weight on my shoulders that was new to me; a rare honour, a responsibility that seemed to extend deep into the mists of time. It was as if I had finally been given my spurs by generations of ancestors,' Fignon says in *When We Were Young and Carefree*, beautifully capturing the essence and burden of wearing the yellow jersey. On the Colombière, the third of the five climbs, Dutchman Peter Winnen, victor the previous day at Alpe d'Huez, attacked in a group of more than two dozen riders, including Angel Arroyo, Stephen Roche and Robert Millar. Their lead quickly ballooned to four minutes, making the ashen Dutchman leader on the road. Fignon admits he started to panic. Guimard calmed him, his Renault teammates closed the gap, but on the dreaded Joux Plane, the final ascent, Fignon found himself alone. 'It was a nightmare... I was looking into a void; if I didn't pull through I would be sent back where I had come from and there would be no second chance,' he states. 'I don't know whether wearing the jersey helped me in any way or made me freeze. I clung on; it was life or death. With barely an ounce of strength left, I managed to catch Winnen: I'd done what I had to do.'

Laurent Fignon: 'It was as if I had finally been given my spurs by generations of ancestors'

Four years later, Jean-François Bernard, Pedro Delgado and Stephen Roche each felt that same weight that the Frenchman had borne. With Hinault retired, LeMond absent injured and Fignon unable to find consistency in his form after a serious ankle injury, the contest was wide open, a *Tour à la Walko* in the best sense. When Bernard became the sixth rider to don the yellow jersey thanks to a resounding victory in a time trial to the summit of Mont Ventoux, which put him two-and-a-half minutes clear of second-placed Roche going into the final week, he had proved himself the strongest man in the field. That night his rivals watched the young Frenchman tell French TV that he was going to win the title. Hearing this in his hotel room, Ireland's Roche became more determined in his goal of making the leader's first day as leader as hellish as possible. That same evening, a journalist who crossed paths with Fignon asked him if he thought Bernard was his successor. 'Does that mean you've got me dead and buried already?' asked the two-time champion. 'Maybe,' came the reply. 'Well, that's yet another way of getting me to show you that you are wrong,' Fignon responded indignantly.

The next day, a combination of bad luck, poor tactics and bad feeling on the part of his rivals resulted in Bernard suffering a mauling on the stage into Villard-de-Lans. He ended it a spectator on the fringes of a yellow jersey duel between Roche and Delgado. His American soigneur Shelley Verses says in Richard Moore's *Étape* that, 'A part of him didn't recover from what happened at Villard-de-Lans, a part of him dimmed. I've never seen it done to anyone else, that kinda ganging up.

The pressure on him was so intense. The country couldn't handle the gap of losing Hinault… they put so much on this quiet, gifted guy.'

His former La Vie Claire teammate Andy Hampsten has described Bernard acting like a leader off the road, but revealing severe limitations tactically and psychologically when racing. Bernard himself told Moore that he didn't have the maturity as a racer to handle this situation. 'I wanted to become the new Hinault and if he had kept going another year with me then, I don't know, maybe… I had the potential, the motor, but I needed more. There are other things than physical potential. Cycling is like that: there are ten champions with the same physical capacity, who are at the same level, with the same legs, but what makes the difference is the head. I was left on my own a bit too quickly. Like a bird in a nest, if you try to fly too early, you fall.' It's notable too that his DS, Paul Köchli, didn't attempt to coax his fledgling leader through a complicated stage in the Vercors by taking a defensive approach, choosing instead to stick with a strategy where the team always had riders at the front of the race, which backfired when Bernard punctured and then unshipped his chain back in the peloton while three of his teammates were in the break.

Like the Frenchman, Roche also failed to retain the jersey as the Tour continued on to Alpe d'Huez, where Delgado took a twenty-five-second lead. 'I was over the moon on Alpe d'Huez and thought the Tour was mine,' the Spaniard admitted. Given the significant edge he had on the Irishman in the mountains, it should have been. But he too had committed the error of thinking he had the race

'I'll never be a leader. I can't be someone that you can count on 100 per cent, and if you ask that of me I lose half my power'

won when Paris remained a long way off. A third consecutive stage packed with twists and turns followed as the Tour headed for the resort of La Plagne. Roche attacked early, hoping to get onto the climb before the yellow jersey and limit his losses. But Delgado pegged him back at the foot and dropped him almost as soon as it started to climb. The gap between them widened, until, with five kilometres remaining, Roche accelerated almost imperceptibly, wringing every last watt of energy from his body. Three kilometres from the finish, Delgado began to crack. Lost to the TV cameras in the mist, neither knew where the other was until the line, which the Spaniard crossed a mere four seconds ahead of his rival.

The Spaniard pressed hard again on the final Alpine stage over five passes to Morzine, but ended up losing time to Roche on the final descent off the Joux Plane. 'My head had fallen off after La Plagne. I'd given it everything but it hadn't worked. My plan of being ninety seconds ahead of the time trial was down the pan. I hurt him a bit on the Joux Plane but I couldn't shake him. After La Plagne, my heart wasn't in it,' he revealed to jour-nalist Alasdair Fotheringham. Roche, arguably the Tour winner who relied most heavily on psycho-logical strength over physical power, regained the lead in that time trial, which Delgado described as the worst of his career. 'I was feeling so tense and I was sure I'd already lost… Maybe if I'd been a bit more mature I'd have given him a fright… I wasn't totally exhausted, in fact I'd recovered a bit from the mountains during the flat stage the day before, but I went into the time trial so nervous, so demoralised because I couldn't handle the pres-sure. The more nervous I got, the more angry I got with myself and that made it worse.'

The upside of this defeat was that the Spaniard did realise he could win the Tour and achieved that goal a year later. For Bernard, though, there was no second chance. So promising when he broke into the pro ranks, he never threatened at the Tour again and eventually slotted into a more suitable role as a super-domestique for Miguel Indurain. 'I'll never be a leader. I can't be someone that you can count on 100 per cent, and if you ask that of me I lose half my power,' he told *L'Équipe* in the twilight of his career.

'It all went to my head. I began to behave like a guy who looks down on everyone'

It's easy to dismiss a rider like Bernard as lacking some of the right stuff required to win the Tour, of not pushing himself hard enough, perhaps. But, as he pointed, he is the rule rather than the exception. There have always been a lot more Jeff Bernards in the peloton than Chris Froomes. They get talked up on the back of a promising Grand Tour appearance or two, get promoted to team leader, may even win some big races, perhaps even the Giro or Vuelta. At the Tour, though, the level of competition and pressure is unparalleled, and the victor has to be exceptional in his ability, focus, quality of team support, and, in some cases, pure good luck. Even when all these factors align correctly, the champion faces another hurdle to negotiate: dealing with life as the yellow jersey.

This is especially hard for riders who take the title early in their career. Twenty-five when he won, Lucien Aimar admitted that a cocktail of euphoria and sudden star billing turned his head. He returned to his buoyant normality thanks to the influence of Jacques Anquetil and Raphaël Geminiani at his Ford team and a stranger who told him 'Don't act like an idiot, Lucien!' after Aimar had taken umbrage with him unjustifiably. Fignon was similarly affected. 'When reality turns out to be greater than you might have imagined, you run a serious risk: you can believe you are a master of the universe,' he said in *When We Were Young and Carefree*. Just twenty-two, he went through a spell where he described his behaviour as being completely over the top, failing to realise initially that the ecstasy of victory and the recognition that brought had a negative aspect as well as the good one. 'It all went to my head. I began to behave like a guy who looks down on everyone. You know, the sort of bloke who's made it to the top and reminds everyone of it in every word and deed, in case they might have forgotten. I put ridiculous demands on people, said things I shouldn't have said. I thought the world revolved around me, and I have to admit: you come to a point where you genuinely believe that. People kept asking me to do things, and I was ferried here there and everywhere. You are constantly made to feel you are the centre of things, so you begin to think that way.'

Like Aimar, Fignon said the way that people behaved towards him, were so appreciative of him and his achievements, only exacerbated his disconnection from his real self. 'For a long time I couldn't see the difference between the winner of the Tour (the one that all the people wanted to glorify) and the Laurent Fignon who was somewhere inside me – the true me.' He became a caricature, a veritable Sun King who could do and have anything by simply clicking his fingers. 'It was ridiculous, it was vulgar, and it was lousy for my self-respect… In the minds of some of those close to me, I must have become totally impossible for a while.'

Initially unwilling to listen to anyone, not even Guimard, who suspected his young team leader might respond in this haughty, uncontrollable way, Fignon had his feet gradually brought back to ground by the talented young group around him at Renault and his own realisation that the hoopla that arose as a result of his victory was ephemeral. 'I was never the centre of the world, but at most – and only for a few days – the centre of the cycling world.' He felt horrified by his behaviour, but said

YELLOW JERSEY RETIREES

YEAR	STAGE	RIDER	REASON
1927	6	Francis Pélissier	Dropped during a team time trial due to illness
1929	10	Victor Fontan	His bike broken beyond repair, he found an ill-fitting replacement but quit after dropping an hour behind
1937	16	Sylvère Maes	Withdrawal of the Belgian team due to threat from French spectators
1950	11	Fiorenzo Magni	Withdrawal of the two Italian teams due to threat from French spectators
1951	13	Wim van Est	Hospitalised after falling 40 metres when descending the Aubisque
1965	9	Bernard Van De Kerkhove	Sunstroke-induced sickness on the Aubisque
1971	14	Luis Ocaña	Crashed during a flash storm on the Col de Menté
1978	16	Michel Pollentier	Trying to defraud the dope control at Alpe d'Huez having just taken the lead
1980	12	Bernard Hinault	Left the race at Pau due to knee tendinitis
1983	17	Pascal Simon	Quit on the Côte de la Chapelle Blanche after riding for six stages with a fractured shoulder blade
1991	5	Rolf Sørensen	Crashed and broke a collarbone 4km from the line. Finished the stage but quit that evening
1996	7	Stéphane Heulot	Quit on the Cormet de Roselend due to knee tendinitis
1998	2	Chris Boardman	Head and neck injury after a severe crash
2007	16	Michael Rasmussen	Fired by his team due to lying about his whereabouts
2015	4	Fabian Cancellara	Sustained broken vertebrae in a crash
2015	7	Tony Martin	Finished the stage after sustaining a broken collarbone in a crash but quit that evening

| Siro, 1994. 'Never 2 without 3'. Siro suggests a world title for Fignon in 1984 after his French road championship and Tour victories

it could have been worse because it only endured for a few weeks. 'For some guys, it lasts the rest of their lives.'

Among recent Tour victors, Jan Ullrich and Marco Pantani are the most obvious examples of this. Anointed the champion-in-waiting when he finished runner-up behind Telekom teammate Bjarne Riis in 1996, the German duly claimed his country's first *maillot jaune* success a year later. Aged twenty-three, he had laid what was widely suggested as the foundation for the race's next dynasty, but later admitted he had hated every moment of his triumphal ride, which was for him 'a nightmare'. Schooled within the East

German sporting system that co-opted its athletes' successes as a prop for the glory of the nation state, Ullrich emerged from that doping-fuelled set-up where the collective's glory counted more than individual achievement to another that was similarly sinister. Alongside the likes of Michael Schumacher and Steffi Graf, he became a figure-head for German sport, triggering huge enthu-siasm for cycling, while bearing the name of one of the country's most illustrious companies on his jersey, being prodded persistently towards further Tour glory and remaining part of a sophisticated doping programme.

Haunted rather than motivated by the yellow

jersey over the winter following his Tour win, Ullrich put on what some reports suggested was as much as seventeen kilos. This was depicted as an error of youth and inexperience, and laughed off. But unlike Fignon's loss of control, which was fleeting, the German's weight gain hinted at a more fundamental issue. Unlike champions such as the Frenchman or Froome who relished the pressure that the yellow jersey set upon them and approached the challenge of retaining it with tunnel vision, Ullrich was more ambivalent. He loved racing, but was obliged to focus completely on the sport's biggest race to please his team, sponsor and fans more than from a sense of personal achievement. In this context, his overeating could be seen as an attempt to regain a degree of control over his situation, as a reaction to his misery. 'People just kept telling me that I was very strong, and that was enough for me,' he told *L'Équipe* in 2018. Allied to the blood doping that he later admitted, this innate ability might have been enough for Ullrich to win further Tours if he hadn't become the fall guy during Lance Armstrong's incredible and subsequently disqualified comeback from cancer. Yet, a positive test for ecstasy, a drink driving offence, bouts of depression and annual issues with weight gain and loss point indicate an athlete unhappy with a starring role.

In between the German's only win and the first of the American's seven that would later count for nothing in the Tour's official history, Marco Pantani won the 1998 race that stumbled into Paris after three weeks of drug revelations, exclusions and strikes. In the Italian, who in 2013 was identified as one of thirty-three riders found to have used EPO

Marco Pantani in 2000

when their samples were retested following the introduction of new detection methods, it had the ideal champion.

Flamboyant in his style and approach to racing, physically and psychologically fragile, the bald, bandanna-wearing climber who, said *Procycling*, 'looked like Captain Hook but floated like Tinkerbell' was found dead in a dismal Rimini hotel room in 2004 following a drug overdose. Still revered by fans for whom he encapsulated the romance of road racing, Pantani's Tour legend was built around his solo victory in a stormy deluge at Les Deux Alpes that saw him snatch the yellow jersey from Ullrich and offered the perfect manifestation of his swashbuckling approach. Three minutes down on Germany's race leader on GC going into it, Pantani finished it six minutes ahead of the defending champion. Even in the midst of a shambolically illegitimate race, it was widely lauded. The Italian fed off performances such as these, 'harnessing not just physical and mental strength, but also emotional force,' says Ed Pickering. 'But nobody realised that the adulation wasn't a by-product of the primary aim – winning races. Pantani actually needed it.'

In *The Death of Marco Pantani*, Matt Rendell provides not only forensic detail on Pantani's doping, which began in 1993, but also a psychiatric report produced by a specialist in substance abuse, Dr Mario Pissacroia. Along with a diagnosis of depression and bipolar disorder, the doctor describes the Italian as having narcissistic and obsessive behaviours, and concludes that Pantani would have been affected by high levels of stress when competing. In short, the characteristics that enabled the Italian to become an elite athlete, allied to his drug taking, inevitably undermined his well-being. Equally, his exclusion from the Tour and other big races from 2001 due to lack of form or his involvement in doping affairs denied Pantani the acclaim he craved and depended on. While he railed against being scapegoated, he shunned attempts made by those close to him to divert him from his inexorable descent.

Reflecting on the Italian's tragic fate in February of 2004, *Procycling* declared that, 'He was the victim of fudged doping procedures, of insensitive sponsors, of factionalism within governing bodies, of ego, complacency and selfishness,' and urged that 'cycling must change or face extinction'. Over the intervening period those issues have been tackled with varying degrees of success, and while it's impossible to ascertain the level of doping within the professional peloton, the consensus opinion is that cheating of this nature is no longer systematic and is far less widespread. At the same time, however, the inherent pressures that come with life as an elite athlete, the constant flirtation with the loss of status and physical well-being as they pursue excellence, remain. Thanks in large part to the growth of social networks, scrutiny of riders is never-ending. In some cases, criticism has become unremitting and even threatening, and rarely more so than for the man in the *maillot jaune*.

MARCO PANTANI
TOUR DE FRANCE
2008

10

HALF THE ROAD

Le Maillot Jaune

Marianne Martin 1984

FROM THE INAUGURAL TOUR FÉMININ IN 1984

Nous Deux

L'Hebdomadaire
qui porte Bonheur

N° 630 - 60 FRANCS
UNION FRANÇAISE : 60 FRANCS
BELGIQUE : 9 F - SUISSE : 0 F 80
CANADA : 20 CENTS
PUBLICATION HEBDOMADAIRE

"EN ROULANT VERS BAYONNE..."

Égalité? Not yet, but it's coming...

It's the morning of the opening Pyrenean stage of the 2017 Tour de France, and I'm standing with my family on the inside of the first tight hairpin bend on the Col de Menté, the third of five climbs on a long stage weaving into and through the mountains to reach the resort of Peyragudes. Like thousands of others, we've walked for several kilometres to get to this point, carrying bags filled with baguettes, cheese and something fruity to wash them down with – wine for the adults, Orangina for the kids. We've come early, four hours before the race is due to pass, partly because the walk would be even longer given the lack of parking and partly because the children are principally interested in the publicity caravan. When it passes, they rush to collect key rings, hats, bite-sized packets of salami and, handily, giant shopping bags that make it easier to ensure that none of the tat ends up on the roadside. They spend most of the next two hours sorting through it, until the first outriders from the Garde Républicaine herald the arrival of the riders.

First to swish around us on the bend is the breakaway, led by Britain's Steve Cummings, with green jersey Marcel Kittel a surprise presence further back within a group of a dozen or so. A few minutes led, the peloton swings into view, Sky setting the pace, Luke Rowe very comfortable on the front, Chris Froome in yellow looking less so a few places down the line, then a blur of colours, followed by a line of cars so long that I can hear the question before it arrives. 'Dad, why…?'

We start back down, the kids delighted to stumble on the occasional *bidon* that's been tossed to the side of the road, wondering why the riders don't put their 'sweet wrappers' in their pockets. Then, from my eight-year-old daughter:

'Were there any ladies racing with all those men, Daddy?'

'No, it was just men today.'

'Do the ladies race somewhere else on their own? Will we see them as well?'

'No they don't, I'm afraid.'

'But why don't they have a race for ladies? Does that mean I can't race the Tour de France and wear the yellow jersey?'

It's not easy explaining to your child, and almost always to the female one, why they can't do something because of their sex. Perhaps, when I took them into the start village in Saint-Girons the next morning, I should have approached Christian Prudhomme and asked him to give my daughter the answer she was looking for. I'm sure he would have been happy to do so, but I'm not so certain that his answer would have convinced an eight-year-old. Predictably, it's principally a question of money, but with undercurrents that are more sinister. History provides an insight into both aspects.

In the first decade of the twentieth century, Tour founder Henri Desgrange and *L'Auto*, the newspaper that he was at the helm of, opposed women's participation in sport for two reasons.

Firstly, like many in a country still coming to terms with its defeat in the Franco–Prussian War in 1871 and fearful of a repeat as the neighbouring power continued to build up its armed forces, he was concerned by France's stagnating birth rate and how this would inexorably lead to a reduction in the availability of combat troops. Procreation was, he believed, a national duty. He also feared for the physical toll that an event like the Tour would take on any female participants. In 1909, his newspaper, *L'Auto*, dismissed a reader's letter calling for a Tour de France Féminin by suggesting that this would require the bulldozing of all of the mountains across France.

These attitudes endured during Desgrange's reign as Tour director and only began to change in the final years of his successor Jacques Goddet's tenure in the 1980s. When they appeared in the race's narrative, women were wives or mothers waving their husbands or sons away on their great quest for glory or welcoming them back at the end of it. A relic of this still persists in the way that riders are often given a 'pass' to ride on ahead of the peloton to spend a fleeting moment with their family as the race passes through their home town before rejoining the pack again. With the pressroom almost as male dominated as the peloton, the only places that women were obviously apparent were in the publicity caravan and, increasingly, on the finish podium. The claim made by Baron de Coubertin, the founder of the modern Olympics that 'Women have but one task, that of crowning the victor with garlands', was sustained for decade after decade at the Tour de France.

It is not a coincidence that when change finally

came with the running of the first Tour de France Féminin in 1984, it was ushered in by Félix Lévitan, who, as race director, was more interested in the story than the bottom line. His goal was to organise 'something greater than anything that has been done to this point in cycling for athletic women', and the result was an eighteen-stage race running ahead of the men's event and covering about a quarter of the total distance. Six teams of six riders participated, and initially the Dutch dominated, winning ten of the first eleven stages. The Alps, though, brought a new contender to the fore in the USA's Marianne Martin, who was the solo winner at Grenoble and then triumphed even more impressively at La Plagne. That success put the twenty-six-year-old into the yellow jersey, which she held into Paris, with Dutchwoman Heleen Hage second on GC, more than three minutes down, and the American's teammate Deborah Shumway a dozen minutes back in third.

| *A page from 'The Wonder Book of Things to Do', 1957*

Now a Colorado-based photographer, Martin fizzes with enthusiasm as she recalls the race, which took place just before the Los Angeles Olympics, an event that also broke new ground with its first women's road race. 'As soon as I heard there was going to be women's Tour de France, that was all I wanted to do. I had just made it onto the national team and we were on a training camp in Colorado Springs when we heard the news, and it was way more enticing to me than the Olympics. I mean, the Tour de France was a whole month. There's no comparison, it's not even close,' says

'I mean, who gets to race the Tour de France? For me, that was the pinnacle... It's such a shame that they don't have one now'

| *1984 Tour winners Laurent Fignon and Marianne Martin, with Paris mayor and future French president Jacques Chirac (left)*

Martin. 'I hadn't been in the sport that long, but I did know that it was the pinnacle of bike racing.'

As a youngster, the Michigan-born American skied every winter with her father, sometimes in Colorado but often in Europe and had a strong affinity with the mountains. 'I knew that was where I would be at my strongest, but when I started the race I wasn't thinking about winning at all. I just thought that if I finished I'd be a rock star. I took third place on the first stage and I was blown away by that,' she admits. 'Later in the race the top-three riders went to an event with some of the male riders and I was talking to Vincent Barteau, who was in yellow at that point, and he pointed at Laurent Fignon and said, "He's going to win", and somewhere inside me I heard a voice saying, "I'm going to win." I would never say that to anybody because I'm not at all like that, but deep in my subconscious something was going on.'

For Martin, the hardest part of the Tour was dealing with the fatigue that set in after a few days. 'On the rest day I was so tired I couldn't even sit on a bench. I had to lie down because I was totally spent. But the next day you get up because you've got to race. It amazed me what your body can do and how your mind can support it,' she says. The best part? The crowds, not simply the amount of them, but the way that they responded to the riders, which she had never previously experienced. 'I can remember riding up the Joux Plane and seeing people for miles ahead. I loved the fact that in the mountains there were no barriers or anything. I loved the rawness, the realness of it. Going up the Joux Plane, I didn't even know where the road was until the people parted just in front of me. That was so cool – slightly stressful, but so cool. You feed off that excitement. It energises you.'

Although Martin somehow managed to miss a glimpse of the Eiffel Tower when the riders reached Paris, reaching the Champs-Élysées brought a double thrill. 'When we went over the start/finish line on the Champs-Élysées the first time I heard somebody yell, "Go Marianne Martin!" and I could tell it was an American voice. The next time round I looked over and I could see that it was my dad, who'd flown over for the occasion. To see the Champs-Élysées without any cars or anything, well, that was amazingly beautiful. You come around the corner and it takes your breath away.'

Although health issues meant that Martin couldn't defend her title and was subsequently forced into retirement in 1986 when she was only twenty-nine, she looks back on that period with huge fondness. 'I loved racing so much, I loved everything about it – the hard work, the travel, the sense of family within a team, the experiences. It was such a fabulous time in my life and I feel like I was the luckiest person. We had the best races, the Coors Classic, the Tour de France. I mean, who gets to race the Tour de France? For me, that was the pinnacle. Winning it was just over the top. I've got the yellow jersey hanging in my closet next to

the polka-dot jersey and when I see them I still think how fortunate I was. It's such a shame that they don't have one now.'

Interviewed in *L'Équipe* during that first Tour Féminin, Betsy King, one of Martin's teammates who was already renowned for racing and finishing the classic Bordeaux–Paris professional men's race earlier in the 1984 season, felt that the race would create change within and beyond cycling, saying, 'each yellow jersey, each turn of the pedal… has advanced and will advance female cyclists, but also all women.' However, the Tour Féminin barely got the opportunity to become established before ASO reassessed the event. The race stuck to the same format the next season before being trimmed back to fifteen stages in 1986. Two years later, following Lévitan's dismissal, it was cut again to twelve days. In 1990, with ASO focusing on monetising revenue from the men's race, it was detached from the Tour entirely and run in September in conjunction with the Tour of the EEC, as the Tour de l'Avenir was briefly rebranded, for one season. It continued as a twelve-day event for the next three years, Belgium's Heidi Van de Vijver winning the final 1993 edition, the last multi-stage women's race that ASO were involved in.

The year before they pulled the plug, businessman Pierre Boué and the Racing Club Olympique de Toulouse launched the Tour Cycliste Féminin, which was regarded as the spiritual heir to the women's Tour thanks to its length and scope rather than any direct connection between the two. Lasting two weeks, it ran until 1998, when a successful legal challenge by ASO against Boué for infringing their trademark obliged him to rename it the Grande Boucle Féminine Internationale. Beset by organisational and, increasingly, financial difficulties, it ran as a two-week race until 2003, missed a year, then returned in 2005 pruned back to just five days of racing, Britain's Emma Pooley winning the final edition in 2009. Following the demise of the long-running and popular Tour de l'Aude in 2010, that left the Route de France Féminine, established in 2006, as the country's premier stage race until it too disappeared in 2016. Going into the 2019 season, France boasted just one established elite-level multi-day event, the week-long Tour Cycliste Féminin International de l'Ardèche. That was one day more than ASO's entire programme of women's racing for the season, of which just one was set to take place in France, La Course by the Tour de France.

This event came about largely as a result of public pressure in the form of a petition signed by close to 100,000 people calling for a women's race at the Tour de France, which was launched by Le Tour Entier, a campaigning organisation established in 2013 by Dutch Olympic champion Marianne Vos, American pro rider and filmmaker Kathryn Bertine, British Ironman champion Chrissie Wellington, and Emma Pooley. Within a manifesto designed to help harness the full potential of women's road cycling and develop the sport equitably and sustainably, its mission statement declared: 'Our objective is to help create a framework to support the growth of women's cycling and build a sport with greater consumer, media and commercial appeal – starting with a race at the Tour de France.' Or, as Pooley put it more simply, 'Girls should be able to dream of racing the Tour

de France when they grow up.'

As the organisation's name makes clear, their eventual goal is a Tour with full parity in terms of the number of days and prize money. Recognising that this is likely to take time to realise, they called for a shorter pilot version, 'potentially three to ten days long', with the intention of increasing its length annually as the size and strength of the female peloton increased. In February 2014, ASO unveiled La Course by Le Tour de France, a one-day event coinciding with the final day of the men's race and including the same iconic finish on the Champs-Élysées. It was a move in the right direction, but hardly the leap of faith that Le Tour Entier and its supporters had been pressing for. 'We see this as a stepping stone toward a women's Tour. With the 2014 Tour de France less than six months away, we understand time is an issue and we're grateful for the opportunity to make history this year with a one-day event,' said Bertine, the New York-born and Saint Kitts and Nevis-registered racer who has been the organisation's principal campaigning force.

Thanks to its location and timing, the event, fittingly won in its first year by Vos, one of cycling's all-time great racers, presented women's racing to a huge worldwide audience. It was broadcast in more than 150 countries, many showing the final hour live. However, apart from a brief and flawed transformation into a two-day race in 2017, it has not expanded at all and Bertine concedes that initial hopes of progress have diminished. 'They have failed to uphold their promise and they have failed to follow our vision. They've let fans of racing down by sticking to an approach that I like

| The first La Course, 2014: Marianne Vos (Ned) tops the podium, flanked by Kirsten Wild (right) and Leah Kirchmann (left)

to describe as "shape-shifting". The simple fact is that there has been no change apart from the location,' she says, going on to explain what that vision had initially been.

'We said to them that we were happy for it to be a one-day event in the first year but that it needed to grow incrementally: firstly, because that would mean there was a steady rise towards a three-week race, and, secondly, because the women's side of the sport is so strapped financially that springing a three-week race on them made no sense because not many teams would have been able to afford that kind of travel budget.' In meetings with ASO during 2013, Bertine and her colleagues at Le Tour Entier proposed the race expanding to between three and five days in the second year, then to

being a week long, then ten days, two weeks and, ultimately becoming a three-week Grand Tour. 'It made sense to have that ladder of growth so that everybody could benefit. We wanted it to grow and be nurtured, while taking account of the financial element as well,' Bertine explains. 'ASO said to us, "Yes, yes, this is a good idea," and even though we were a little dismayed that they wanted to keep it as a one-day race after the first edition, we gave them the benefit of the doubt because we assumed that they would just do it for one more year and then they would start building it incrementally.'

ASO have been evasive on the question of the possible renaissance of a more extensive Tour de France Féminin, complete with a yellow jersey that La Course, very significantly, does not offer to its victor. On one of the few occasions that Christian Prudhomme publicly entered into to the debate, responding in 2013 to an open letter from Harriet Harman, the then deputy leader of Britain's Labour Party who had been urging progress towards the event taking place, he said, 'We are open to everything. Having women's races is very important for sure. [But] the Tour is huge and you cannot have it bigger and bigger and bigger down the road – it is impossible.'

The Tour is unquestionably far larger than it was back in the mid-1980s, the growth largely occurring outside the peloton thanks to the rising number of backroom team staff and, above all, the huge increase in the media presence. With the addition of extensive hospitality areas and grandstands at stage starts and finishes, the Tour has become a small town, shifting from place to place, its sprawl now too extensive for some once regular haunts to accommodate it. As Prudhomme suggests, adding another race to the mix would be complicated, a fact highlighted by the difficulties the media have encountered when the Tour and La Course have clashed. In 2018, as the women's event was heading towards its finish in Le Grand Bornand, the men were about to get their day under way in Annecy, several Alpine valleys away. Reporting on both was near impossible.

'It has become in vogue to do to call for women's Tour de France, but we had journalists at the Tour in 2018 who had been complaining about the fact that there was no women's race who didn't actually turn up to La Course,' says Sky Sports' Orla Chennaoui, who as presenter of The Cycling Podcast Féminin has followed the debate about the women's Tour very closely. 'They were out there covering the men's race and for logistical reasons couldn't make it to the women's race. Yet they were still filing copy bemoaning the lack of a women's Tour de France, but overlooking the very manifestation of why it is so difficult.'

In addition to logistical issues, there are, contend the race owners, financial concerns too. Jean-Marc Marino, race director of La Course, told *Rouleur* in 2016 that ASO are always on the look-out for new ways to promote both women's cycling, but always struggle to find the backing to help expand their interest in this area. 'For us, women and men are the same. They are professionals, they are cycling, and we want to provide them with the best organisation,' he explained. 'We organise events for women's cycling because we love it, but we also have to show our bosses that we can make money from it, because that is part of the deal too. It would be awesome to have a women's Tour de France. It would be amazing, and I know my big boss would love it. But the problem is to find the sponsor, the partners, the cities, it would cost lots and lots of money. It's difficult to tell the boss we will lose money with an event.'

As a privately owned company that, understandably, does not want to make a loss on any event that it organises, ASO has already closed down a number that have failed to turn a profit, including the Critérium International, Tour of Qatar and Tour of Beijing. Yet, there has been evidence that women's racing is becoming progressively attractive for potential sponsors as companies follow through on policy commitments to equal opportunities. There are signs, too, that the market for women's bikes and equipment is proving increasingly tempting. When American bike manufacturer Trek announced the launch of their women's team in July 2018, CEO John Burke acknowledged that the biggest driver for them was the potential apparent in this fast-developing market. 'There is an altruistic aspect to what we're doing, but our reasons are mainly economic. We've sold an awful lot of bikes to men and we now view the market for women's cycling as having huge potential for growth. We want a part of that,' he told me.

Bertine says that she has also seen evidence of growing interest in women's racing as an investment opportunity, and regards this as vital because this is the area where it has traditionally struggled to get a foothold and, as a result, has held back the development of races. 'It's great to see that more people understand equality is not just the right thing to do but it's also the smart thing to do, and that's why we see this as an epic failure for ASO. We're actually smacking heads and saying, "Can't they see that they would actually thrive if they did this, that everybody would win?"' She has, she says, spoken to companies that are willing to commit to large sponsorship deals and finds it hard to understand why a company with such extensive experience in this field can't lock down similar deals, and goes on to describe a 2017 meeting with ASO in Los Angeles, where they have an office following their purchase of a large stake here in the Tour of California.

'I asked them, "What will it take to put on a race of, say, five days?" A five-day La Course would at least have got some momentum building, and they told me it would cost between $2 million and $4 million to put on a race of that length. I said, "Great, why don't you hire me and I will set about finding the sponsors for you?" And their response was, "Well, we're not hiring at the moment, but if you do find the sponsors just send them our way." Basically, they wanted me to do the work, send sponsors over to them and they would reap the benefit. They have that take where they say, "Nobody is coming to us to invest in women", but I can tell you that is wrong.'

Bertine, who describes herself as 'the world's most annoying person as far as ASO are concerned, I just keep asking, "And? And? And?"', is blunt when asked to assess the Tour organisation's attitude. 'It really boils down to laziness and sexism. They simply don't want to invest the effort into making this race happen,' she asserts. 'When any company finds something that works there are two philosophies. The most successful will say, "Hey, that's great, it works, but what can we do to make it work better?" The other philosophy is, "Great, this works, let's keep it where it is…"' Pooley shares this perspective. 'They have the greatest bike race in the world, and it works well. Why would they change anything?'

Chennaoui also agrees with this assessment of ASO's position and attitude, but argues that it only underlines why efforts to apply pressure on the French race organisation to relaunch the Tour Féminin are misplaced. 'ASO clearly don't have the will to stage a women's Tour de France, so why are we trying to force an organisation that doesn't really want to stage one in order to appease everybody else when inevitably whatever race they put on will be substandard or not of the quality that the women's sport deserves? Unless they are going to do it properly, with the right will, the right backing and for the right reasons, we will end up with substandard product,' she says.

In addition, Chennaoui is not convinced that a Tour Féminin is necessarily the next best step for women's racing. 'If we frame the debate about women's cycling around whether or not we have a women's Tour I think we are doing the sports itself a bit of a disservice because I don't think we need that validation for the sport, which is growing fantastically well,' she adds. 'The danger we have is that every summer we see the mainstream media joining in this handwringing and we assume that the sport is inferior because

to be addressed, such as more equal television coverage, better coverage of the Ardennes Classics, for example, or of the women's Giro, which is a fantastic race, criminally underpublicised, and arguably as an event is much better for the sport than a women's Tour de France.'

Yet the Tour offers a degree of visibility that these races can't. It is the only bike race that is known by people who don't follow cycling, reaching the biggest audience, drawing in new fans, and providing inspiration, which, inevitably, encourages the next generation of riders. Consequently, the argument is often made that the Tour is so exceptional as a showcase that a Tour Féminin is bound to boost women's racing and that it would be detrimental to turn away from it and try

'They have the greatest bike race in the world, and it works well. Why would they change anything?'

of a lack of a women's Tour de France. There are obvious and glaring and urgent inequalities in the sport that need to be addressed, but they're not the result of a lack of a women's Tour, and I think that having one could be detrimental in the sense that it would paper over the cracks and might make people think, "Job done, we must have equality now because we've got both versions of the main race on the calendar." Then, as a result, we don't work so hard on addressing the issues that need

to follow another course, even though the organisation behind it is reluctant to engage in the trend to promote equality within sport. 'If you look at the immense coverage that La Course gets simply because it is part of the Tour machine, it does lend credence to that opinion because the Tour de France is the one race that everyone will have heard of,' Chennaoui acknowledges. However, she is not convinced that is enough of an argument. 'I think we have to be realistic because we're not

'And? And? And?

It really boils down to laziness and sexism'
Kathryn Bertine

In the *#MeToo* era, when the status of women within sport is rising, this De Coubertin-like stance jars. The hostesses do insist that they don't feel degraded by their role, but as the most evident female presence on the Tour, they highlight the race's gender imbalance.

'ASO, FRANKLY, HAVE A PROBLEM WITH WOMEN,'

Emma Pooley stated in *The New York Times* following the decision to retain hostesses.

She compared this with ASO's lack of progress on a women's tour, asking,

'CAN YOU IMAGINE GOING TO THE NEW YORK MARATHON AND THE ONLY WOMEN YOU SEE ARE PRESENTING TROPHIES TO MEN?

AND THE WOMEN'S RACE WAS SOMEWHERE ELSE AND ONLY FIVE KILOMETRES?'

talking about an organisation that is on the cusp of capitalising on women's cycling, but about one that's dragging its heels and doesn't want to come into the twenty-first century to stage a race that's worthy of women's racing. As a result, are we happy to put up with a race that would not be as good as it should be, because that's what we would have to put up with?'

ASO's intransigence in other areas, including its long-running dispute regarding the sharing of TV rights it has with the UCI and the leading bike teams, has demonstrated its determination to stick to its guns. Pertinently, given its stance on a women's Tour, the company has refused to accede to calls to end the use of podium girls, or hostesses as the race prefers to describe them, to hand out jerseys, cuddly toys and trophies to the race's male stars. These demands increased in 2018 after Formula 1 opted to ban 'grid girls'. After intimating it would follow suit, Prudhomme announced that the Tour would be sticking with the tradition. 'They're not wearing swimming costumes on the Tour de France… And they don't just go up onto the podium. In the start village each morning, some of them hand out newspapers, for example, and others welcome guests,' he told French daily *Sud-Ouest*. 'When you speak to these young women, they don't want this to stop. They're often students. They're paid. They aren't forced to come. We get a lot of requests for these positions.'

In the #MeToo era, when the status of women within sport is rising, this De Coubertin-like stance jars. The hostesses do insist that they don't feel degraded by their role, but as the most evident female presence on the Tour, they highlight the race's gender imbalance. 'ASO, frankly, have a problem with women,' Emma Pooley stated in the New York Times following the decision to retain hostesses. She compared this with ASO's lack of progress on a women's Tour, asking, 'Can you imagine going to the New York Marathon and the only women you see are presenting trophies to men? And the women's race was somewhere else and only five kilometres?'

This heel-dragging attitude could also be seen in their dealings, or lack of them, with the Donnons des Elles au Vélo group whose members have, since 2015, ridden the Tour route a day ahead of the men (they're also known as Jour -1) in order to boost women's cycling in France and to push for a Tour Féminin, while at the same underlining that there are no physiological reasons why female athletes can't cope with a twenty-one-day event. Anna Barrero, a doctor in sports science who has been part of the medical team collecting scientific data from participants and has also completed the route twice on the bike, says they haven't had any help or support from ASO, quite the opposite in fact. 'They weren't very happy about the fact that we were using the words Tour de France in our official literature and on our website, and they said we had to remove them. They said there would be problems if we didn't do that,' she explains. 'Every time we've contacted them about a possible women's Tour de France, they don't give any reason for not having one. When we've asked them if it's possible in the future, they always tell us, "For the moment it is not in our plans."'

During the 2018 Tour, the growing roadside

support and the media interest in Jour -1, allied to backing from Tour sponsors Skoda, persuaded Barrero that the 2019 edition of La Course would mark a change of attitude by ASO. 'But then we went to the Tour presentation in Paris and saw that once again nothing had changed. I was confident that they were going to add some extra days to La Course. In actual fact, it seems to have gone backwards rather than forwards. It was extremely disappointing.'

The decision came as a less of a surprise to Chennaoui, although she confesses she's bewildered by ASO's reluctance to engage more fully with women's racing. 'It's difficult to see what the reason is for ASO's lack of interest. Men's cycling is pretty much saturated, it's got its fan base and it's well established. They've completely maxed out the sportive side of things with the Étape du Tour de France. They do a great job with that and create an awful of money with it. I think that the next area to develop would be women's cycling,' she says. 'It's the zeitgeisty thing to do among businesses to support women's sports, so I don't understand why that can't be exploited from the economic point of view because women's sport appears to be growing much faster than the men's side of the sport. I can only put it down to the fact that it is an organisation that is largely run by men who work for men's cycling.'

Once again, though, she insists that rather than focusing on what women's racing doesn't have, principally on the fact that no one is staging a women's Tour de France, its supporters and the media should spend more time drawing attention to its many positives. 'It's easy to forget women's

cycling is in a really exciting phase at the moment and there is so much to celebrate. I feel that the way to help it progress is by highlighting the positives as much as possible as this is more likely to inspire an interest in the sport. You're not going to encourage men to start watching women's sport by saying it's not fair that there is not a women's Tour de France, you're not going to inspire little girls to watch cycling by going on about the fact that there's no women's Tour de France. You're not going to convince anyone to get on a bike by talking about sexism in cycling. It's fine to address the issue but we need more journalists to put women's racing out there. We're getting there, but the sexy topics are still what's not happening and what's wrong with the sport, rather than who won whatever race.'

Chennaoui points out the unpredictable nature of the action in women's races as one of the best reasons for any bike fan to pay more attention to it. 'It's generally thrilling to watch and you cannot often say that about men's cycling,' she says. 'Because women's teams are smaller and there's not the same strength in depth that exists in the men's peloton, it's harder for anyone to control the racing, which encourages more riders to take risks.' As a result of this, a very different sporting spectacle often unfolds, one that is far less formulaic than the standard template in men's racing, which, it should be stressed, ASO would dearly love to change.

'Men's racing could only dream of having the kind of racing the women's side of the sports sees regularly. For me, the priority is showcasing that, showing what we've got and then figuring out

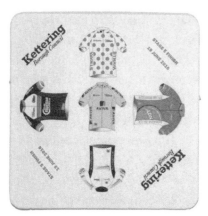

| Promotional beermats from the 2016 Women's Tour

other priorities from there,' Chennaoui explains. 'As a fan if you wanted to showcase cycling to somebody new to it you would show them a women's race rather than men's race, quite frankly. Instead of trying to mirror what the men are doing all the time, I think women have to see that what they have got is good enough, that it can stand alone. I'd love to see the men look at women's racing and think, "What are they doing right? How can they produce much more exciting racing on the same roads?"'

Encouragingly, the sport's ruling body has shown itself to be increasingly even-handed in its focus. When, in 2018, Jour -1's odyssey took them to Sarzeau, where UCI president David Lappartient is the mayor, the Frenchman was, says Barrero, supportive of their ride and cause. Bertine also sees the ruling body as being very much on their side of the argument, her positivity bolstered by the UCI's announcement in November 2018 that a minimum wage will be introduced in 2020 as part of an initiative to strengthen the professionalisation of women's racing, which will also see a rise in minimum standards for prize money and the introduction of codes on ethics and conduct designed to raise awareness of harassment. Speaking in London that same month, Lappartient revealed he had been encouraging ASO to extend La Course. 'I told them, "You are the leading organisation in the world so you have to take your part of the responsibility to support women's cycling,"' he said. 'They are thinking maybe of a one-week stage race. I would support this, but I told them, "Why not the last ten days with the same stages for men and women?"'

On hearing this, Bertine admits her hopes soared, but that optimism is tempered by past experience of the UCI over-promising and under-delivering. 'What I'm fearful of is that somebody who is in a position of power like Lappartient can say all of the right things but then not act on making them happen. We saw that with his predecessor Brian Cookson and with Pat McQuaid before that. Where Lappartient has an edge is that he has come forward and delivered on his promise with the base salary, so I hold him in high regard for having done that,' she says. 'We also know that the UCI and ASO have not been the best of friends, that there's been a power struggle, but it may be that Lappartient is the magic bullet who can resolve this because he happens to be French and maybe that means he has a better relationship behind the scenes.'

If Lappartient does manage to enable the renaissance of the Tour Féminin, whether as a standalone race or as one run concurrently with the Tour de France, its impact on the yellow jersey will be transformative. After so many doping affairs, so much disrepute, it would cast the *maillot jaune* in a new light, as progressive rather than sullied, as a beacon of equality targeted, if not immediately achieved. It would be a feel-good story for the whole sport.

'They say that a rising tide lifts all boats, and I'm sure that not only the women's side would flourish, but the men's side of racing would benefit as well. There'll be new fans, who will attract new sponsors, and that should have an impact filtering down through the rest of the sport,' says Bertine.

MARIANNE MARTIN
WOMEN'S TOUR DE FRANCE
1984

11

TARNISHING THE JERSEY
Le Maillot Jaune

Lance Armstrong 2005

'LIVE STRONG' IS ARMSTRONG'S MESSAGE
FROM HIS 2005 TOUR-WINNING YELLOW JERSEY,
ONE OF SEVEN TITLES HE WAS LATER STRIPPED OF

'THE YELLOW JERSEY IS CLEARED
'Pedro Delgado will once again take to the start in Clermont-Ferrand this morning. He has, indeed, been absolved, as the incriminating substance in his urine (probenecid) is not banned by the UCI although it is by the IOC'

Skeletons in the closet

Radiant, the essence of summer, of holidays and sun, the *maillot jaune* may have helped to transform attitudes towards the colour yellow over the past century.

However, and entirely predictably given the darker side of bike racing, the yellow jersey has more insidious associations with the lust for power. It is the prize in a contest that's fascinating because it has been so often bedevilled by cheating, by dirty tricks. 'It has become in many ways very close to what we see in politics,' suggests *Libération*'s Pierre Carrey. 'To some extent, you could say that the riders trying to win Tour de France, to take the yellow jersey, are like politicians trying to become the prime minister or the president. Watching their antics is disgusting and fascinating at the same time.'

The analogy is well chosen. Just as the popularity ratings of our political leaders tend to plummet once they have progressed from being a prospective candidate with an unblemished image to a leader whose every move is scrutinised and picked apart, riders who are authentic candidates for the title find themselves walking a very narrow line once they pull on the yellow jersey. Hold on to it and the reward is respect and acclaim. Slip off it and the consequences are likely to be severe, and increasingly so in the twenty-first century.

Scepticism and antipathy towards the Tour leader arrived slowly. During the inter-war years, when Henri Desgrange promoted the Tour as a pure sporting contest, ethical concerns were limited to rule-breaking – for instance, riders sharing bottles or pacing each other when they were prohibited from doing so – and didn't extend to any significant concern about doping, which was rife. This was highlighted by investigative journalist Albert Londres in 1924 in his renowned article *Les Forçats de la Route* (The Prisoners of the Road). Published in *Le Petit Parisien*, it detailed his meeting

'From the 1920s through to the 1950s, doping was dealt with in a cursive or humorous fashion, without being totally swept under the carpet'

Jean-Luc Boeuf and Yves Léonard, **La République du Tour de France**

with the Pélissier brothers, Henri and Francis, and Maurice Ville in a café in Coutances after the trio had quit the race because a race official had, without asking permission, lifted Henri's jersey to verify whether he had broken the rule that riders could not discard any clothing when racing.

Pélissier, who had been seen removing a jersey by a rival team manager, approached Desgrange, who refused to discuss the matter until the stage had finished in Brest. Angered by his treatment, the French rider decided to quit and persuaded his brother and Ville to do the same. When Londres found them, they were sitting with a bowl of hot chocolate in front of each of them and, as they sipped, they lifted the lid on the practices they relied on to keep them going through what Henri described as 'a calvary'. He pulled a phial from his bag, saying it contained 'cocaine for our eyes and chloroform for our gums'. Ville tipped out his bag and held out 'horse ointment to warm my knees'. Each of them also had three boxes of pills. 'In short, we run on dynamite,' said Francis. Henri described how they were so juiced that sleep was usually beyond them in the evenings. 'We accept the torment but we don't want the vexations,' said Henri, who had won the title the year before. Although Francis Pélissier later confessed that the trio had kidded Londres a bit with their tales of cocaine and pills, he affirmed that, 'the Tour de France in 1924 was no picnic'.

Another four decades would pass before the Tour and cycling's ruling body, the UCI, implemented the first measures to combat practices such as these. 'From the 1920s through to the 1950s, doping was dealt with in a cursive or humorous fashion, without being totally swept under the carpet,' say Jean-Luc Boeuf and Yves Léonard in their 2003 book *La République du Tour de France*. The race's participants, and above all the victor, continued to be held up as exemplars of individual excellence and success. On the occasions the reputation of the yellow jersey was questioned or criticised, this stemmed from their actions on the road rather than what they might have been getting up to away from it.

When Sylvère Maes abandoned the 1937 edition with the yellow jersey on his shoulders, his Belgian team cited what they perceived as 'French chauvinism' among both fans at the roadside, who had pelted them with rocks and, in one case, thrown pepper in a rider's eyes, and the race officials, who were seen as being lenient in their penalisation of French contender Roger Lapébie, who closed a gap of several minutes on the classic Pyrenean stage to Pau over the Peyresourde, Aspin, Tourmalet and Aubisque passes by hanging on to cars and being pushed by fans.

During the 1950s and the first half of the 1960s, warnings from French national coach Daniel Clément, Tour doctor Pierre Dumas and journalist and ex-pro Jean Bobet about the prevalence and dangers of doping were widely covered but did nothing to change established habits. Nor did the growing number of high-profile cases highlighting the toll these products often exacted on athletes pushing themselves to their physiological limits. These included Jean Malléjac's collapse on Mont Ventoux in 1955 and fellow Frenchman Roger Rivière's crash on the descent of the Col du Perjuret in 1960, which was the result of using Palfium, a medicine that fended off fatigue but also impaired muscular response and reactions. It left Anquetil's rival with a broken back and confined to a wheelchair for the rest of his life.

Performance was everything, both for those participating and for spectators on the sidelines. When, in 1966, the Tour instigated doping controls at the insistence of Dumas, many riders refused to submit to them, this entrenched outlook only changing in the wake of Tom Simpson's death on the Ventoux during the 1967 Tour. Yet, the subsequent 'Tour à la Vittel', the start in the celebrated water-producing town used symbolically to emphasise the pureness of the race, failed to change these attitudes. Ridiculously lenient fines and penalties imposed on miscreants meant that they frequently spent less time out of competition than they would have done as a result of a collarbone break, as was the case in 1978 when Michel Pollentier became the first yellow jersey to be ejected from the race for involvement in a doping affair.

The best friend and perennial leg man of Freddy Maertens, the Belgian had an ungainly style, 'his torso seemingly fixed at one o'clock,' described writer Herbie Sykes. Yet, freed from his near-permanent and fully committed obligation to 'Fast Freddy', Pollentier's ability to turn huge gears on the climbs was often very effective. Winner of the Giro in 1977 and of the Critérium du Dauphiné Libéré prior to the Tour, he took the yellow jersey with an audacious raid on the stage to Alpe d'Huez, attacking just before the summit of the Col de Luitel and continuing with his offensive up the Romanche valley to the foot of the concluding climb, which he started up two minutes ahead of Bernard Hinault and Joop Zoetemelk. By ceding only half of his advantage, he took the stage and the lead.

Following the podium ceremony, Pollentier rode to his team hotel, then made his way back to the finish area for an anti-doping control, where

'Tomorrow... there'll be a storm on the Tour. I have a premonition that something is about to happen...'

Antoine Gutierrez was waiting to be tested. The Frenchman struggled to produce a sample, his odd behaviour attracting the attention of the doctor overseeing the procedure, who lifted the rider's jersey and discovered Gutierrez had been trying to unblock a plastic tube leading down his back and round to his scrotum from a rubber 'container' secured under his armpit. With a squeeze at the top, the device was intended to deliver clean urine into the tester's receptacle at the bottom. Infuriated by the attempted fraud, the doctor lifted Pollentier's jersey to find the same Heath Robinson-like contraption in place.

Later that evening, Pollentier was ejected from the Tour for his attempt to defraud the dope control and banned for two months. In his plea for clemency to Goddet and Félix Lévitan, he pointed out that he hadn't failed a test and hadn't committed a fraudulent act, merely been discovered before he'd had the opportunity to do so. He also insisted that he was far from the only rider who had employed a similar apparatus as word had spread through the peloton that the testers weren't insisting on the riders following the established protocol by dropping their shorts when they urinated. While the decision remained unchanged, Pollentier's defence had authentic substance. Of the 110 starters of that year's race, sixty were involved in some kind of doping affair during their career, making it by some calculations the dirtiest in history.

Although the Belgian's positive test set a precedent by being the first recorded by a Tour leader, he was far from the only contender for the yellow jersey mixed up in doping affairs. Two-time winner Bernard Thévenet admitted at the tail-end of his career that he used cortisone for several seasons, including 1977 when he won the second of his titles. The 1980 champion Joop Zoetemelk failed tests on three occasions, including the 1979 race, although the ten-minute penalty imposed meant he kept his second place behind Bernard Hinault as he was more than twenty minutes clear of third-placed Joaquim Agostinho, who had himself tested positive in the 1977 race.

In their book tracing the similarities between the development of the Tour and that of the French republic, Boeuf and Léonard point to the post-war cult of achievement within Western societies as perpetuating an almost universal acceptance of these practices. They suggest that, as in business and politics, the guiding objective in sport was the end result, which provided a sense of legitimacy. Ethical and health considerations were not important. Consequently, just as industries boomed while polluting the environment, athletes were often prepared to do whatever was required to be successful, the constant demands of their agents, their sponsors and the media pushing them towards this goal, and at the same time encouraging the perpetuation of the established myth that winning was everything. Within this framework, those who were sanctioned, like Pollentier, were scapegoated in order to preserve the façade of authenticity. In short, bike racing was a sport dressed 'in the emperor's new clothes', parading gloriously but undermined by an immense deceit.

This sheen of mythic legitimacy survived well beyond the second instance of the yellow jersey falling foul of anti-doping controls. As Pedro Delgado rode towards victory in 1988, Jacques Goddet, who had stepped down as Tour director the year before, was made aware that the A sample the Spaniard had submitted following the stage to Alpe d'Huez had indicated the presence of probenecid, a medicine employed to extract uric acid from the kidneys when treating gout, but also known as a masking agent hiding the use of steroids. Fearful that the Spaniard would ride into Paris with his success untainted, rather than waiting for confirmation of the positive result to come following testing of the rider's B sample,

Goddet leaked the news to TV reporter Jacques Chancel. Following the stage into Bordeaux, at the end of an interview with the race leader, he theatrically announced to the French TV audience, 'Tomorrow, despite the short stage that will take the race to Limoges, there'll be a storm on the Tour. I have a premonition that something is about to happen...'

Chancel was right about the tumult, but wrong about its timing. Within the hour, his colleague Patrick Chêne revealed that the Tour leader had tested positive. That Delgado survived was down to an administrative error on the part of the UCI, which had failed to bring its list of banned products in line with the International Olympic Committee's. Although the presence of probenecid was confirmed, the Spaniard escaped any penalty because the Paris lab that had undertaken the testing had followed the IOC's guidelines rather than the UCI's, which applied at the Tour.

The yellow jersey, who initially opted for the 'I took a dodgy bottle from someone in the crowd' excuse but later admitted he had taken the product on the advice of his team doctor in order to 'clean the body' and 'get rid of toxins', came under immense pressure to quit the race. Xavier Louy, who had replaced Goddet as Tour director, visited Reynolds team manager José Miguel Echavarri and told him that having a yellow jersey test positive had dishonoured the race and that he wanted Delgado to leave. Echavarri passed this information on to the race leader and told him to make his own decision. The Spaniard decided to brazen it out, and has stuck firmly to this tactic in the decades since. 'At that time, we cyclists weren't

Olympic athletes. We had our own rules. For me, it's very clear. I won the Tour de France according to the rules. The mistake wasn't mine, but the organisation's,' he says in *Secrets de Maillots Jaunes*.

Writing in *L'Équipe*, Jean-Marie Leblanc said, 'The decision that has been taken will please the world of cycling, which has such sensitive skin, and perhaps the wider public, whose memory is short. But look deeper, and it's a dismal verdict. It rewards transgression, it encourages fraud, it lowers sport.' The analysis of the former rider turned journalist who would take over Louy's position at ASO later that year proved, unfortunately, to be entirely correct. When Delgado appeared at the next stage start in Ruelle-sur-Touvre, fans applauded him. 'I couldn't believe my ears! If that had happened in Spain, I could have believed it! But there… in France!' he said. 'It might seem bizarre today, but it was the French public that helped to me to come to the decision not to abandon.' He put this support down to his attacking style on the bike, which might seem far-fetched but appears less so when remembering that the boos that accompanied Alberto Contador during the 2011 Tour while he was contesting a positive test in the previous edition all but disappeared when he lit up the race with his performances in the mountains.

During Leblanc's subsequent two decades at the Tour's helm, the race's mythical status sank, dragged down by scandal after scandal. The Festina Affair of 1998 appeared to be the nadir, but triggered no more than a rearrangement of the chairs on the deck of a floundering ship. For the Tour, though, the consequences were far more far-reaching. As it became clear, during the opening days of that race, that the Festina team that featured the home nation's star rider, Richard Virenque, was involved in systematic doping, Leblanc took the decision to expel them from the event. The day after, it was reported that the French police had found a large quantity of EPO in a vehicle belonging to the Dutch TVM squad. Team buses and hotels were searched, riders detained and arrested, the peloton went on strike, several teams quitting the race in protest. Amid the chaos, there were calls for the race to be stopped. 'The spectacle must not continue. The peloton must stop riding and set about examining its conscience,' an editorial in *Le Monde* asserted. 'If it wants to survive, the Tour de France, a part of the popular heritage which has provided so many legendary stories in sporting history, must admit the truth as soon as possible.'

The race, inevitably, went on, the title disputed by dopers who had been lucky enough to evade the repercussions of the police and judiciary's intervention. The remaining riders took this as a cue to maintain the status quo, but to be more careful about concealing its deceit. While enthusiasm for the race remained, stoked by the incredible story of Lance Armstrong's comeback from near-terminal cancer to win an edition that Leblanc over-optimistically labelled 'the Tour of renewal', its credibility as a legitimate contest continued to diminish. Although the American's regular restatement of the fact that he had never tested positive helped to fend off criticism made during the 2000 Tour of his close relationship with notorious Italian coaching consultant Michele Ferrari, the numerous allegations of doping made

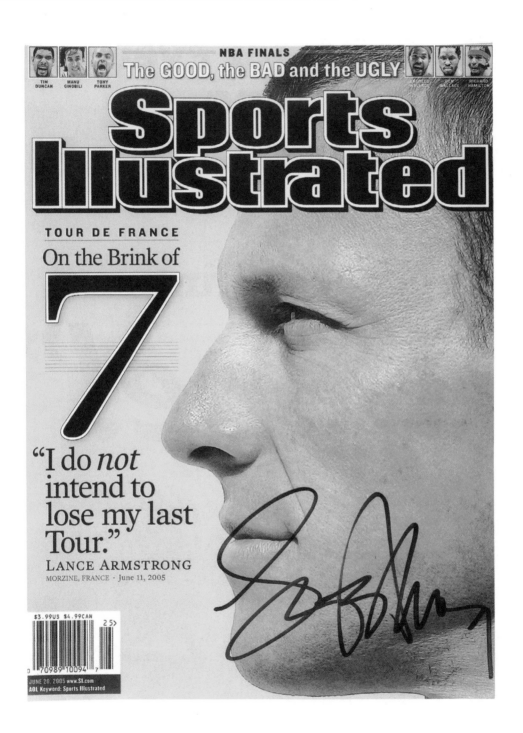

'By 2004, for every fan shouting "Go Lance!" there was another yelling "*Dopé!*"

against him in Pierre Ballester and David Walsh's 2004 book *L.A. Confidentiel: Les Secrets de Lance Armstrong* and *L'Équipe*'s accusation in 2005 that re-testing of samples he had given at the 1999 race had revealed evidence of EPO use, the regular disappearance of his rivals from the playing field as a result of doping infractions indicated either astonishing athletic ability or a Teflon coating on his US Postal kit. Bullying, ruthless and unapologetic, Armstrong turned the attitude towards the yellow jersey toxic. By 2004, for every fan shouting 'Go Lance!' there was another yelling '*Dopé!*'

Since finally admitting that he had taken banned products throughout his seven-year Tour reign, he has said that his only regret was the way that he had treated people who had made what he knew at the time were legitimate accusations against him. Otherwise, he would, he has affirmed, change nothing if put in the same situation once again. 'If I was racing in 2015, no, I wouldn't do it again because I don't think you have to. But if you take me back to 1995, when doping was completely pervasive, I would probably do it again. When I made the decision, when my team made that decision, when the whole peloton made that decision, it was a bad decision and an imperfect time. But it happened. And I know what happened because of that,' he told the BBC.

It is a perspective that some of his most notable rivals share. Asked by *L'Équipe* in 2017 whether he regretted doping for the duration of his career, 1997 champion Jan Ullrich replied, 'That's always the most difficult question, because I didn't think I was doing anything wrong, it didn't occur to me that I was making mistakes… But, I repeat, I didn't

feel like I was acting alone, the context of cycling in that period was such that, unfortunately, you didn't feel guilty. I told myself that I wasn't the only one in the peloton who was behaving in that way and that we would all end up at the same level because we were all cheating to the same extent.'

Michael Rasmussen, who would almost certainly have won the title in 2007 if his Rabobank team hadn't pulled him out of the race in the final few days when it became clear he had lied about his whereabouts prior to the race in order to avoid out-of-competition testing, is of the same mind. 'I don't really regret anything, apart from those moments when I treated people badly and involved people who I should not have involved. I took it because those were the conditions in the playground,' the Dane tells me during the 2018 Tour. Employed for several years as a consultant and columnist for Danish daily *BT* during the race, Rasmussen confessed in 2013 to doping throughout almost the entirety of his professional career, and explains how this reached another level after he turned his back on mountain biking at the end of the 2001 season having taken the world title in that discipline two years earlier.

'In 2002, my first full year as a pro with CSC, I beat Roberto Heras, Francisco Mancebo and Gilberto Simoni on the big stage in the Vuelta a Burgos, which was three weeks after the Tour and I thought that if I could race with those guys at that moment then I was in the place that I needed to be. But, after signing with Rabobank in 2003 I soon realised that I was lagging behind,' he says. 'I was supposed to do the Tour that year but broke my hand during a reconnaissance trip in France and rode the Vuelta instead. I won the stage over the Pyrenees to Cauterets and was basically the best guy for the first ten days of the race. Then, suddenly, I wasn't at the best level any longer. I asked the team doctor to explain what was going on. He told me that somebody had evidently brought some blood bags in and the boost that they had provided to some of my rivals had knocked me down the pecking order. I wasn't aware of blood doping before then, I just did what I'd always been doing, but never any blood doping. I said right away that if that is what it takes then that is what we were going to do, and that's what we did from 2004 right through until it was all over.'

Rasmussen's account confirms that the systematic doping within teams that had become apparent during the Festina Affair continued long afterwards. 'Of course, the team knew everything that was going on. They were complicit right from the start. They were the ones who gave me the phone number of the guy at the blood bank in Vienna, they had a doctor travel to the blood bank to see whether it was OK to send us there. They were the ones who suggested that I could perhaps swap blood with one of my parents because they had done it before within the team. They were the ones transporting EPO around on the bus and handing out certificates for cortisone and whatever else.'

In 2005, the Dane nicknamed 'Chicken' for his scrawny stature, won his first Tour stage and went on to claim the mountains jersey, finishing seventh on GC as Armstrong wrapped up his seventh title. The next year, with the Texan in retirement, the contest for the title was open and, looking back,

Rasmussen believes he could have won it. 'That possibility disappeared when the lab in Vienna threw out six of my blood bags when they cleared everything out after the Winter Olympics. It was all tossed into the river, so my blood values were really low in 2006. I spent most of the race riding in the service of Denis Menchov and on the stage I won, to La Toussuire, my haematocrit level was only thirty-eight.'

In 2007, everything came together for Rasmussen. On the Tour's first mountain stage to Le Grand Bornand he made a show of going for points for the mountains jersey in order to conceal his true intention. 'It was one of those days when I couldn't feel my chain,' he says. 'The next day to Tignes everyone was expecting me to attack again. I remember Fabian Wegmann came up to me and said, "Please don't ride all of us out of the time limit today." I was talking to Levi Leipheimer as we were riding up the valley towards the Cormet de Roselend and we were saying to each other that it was kind of a strange Tour, that it was hard to say who was the strongest. He said, "I think you might be the strongest here right now." I was like, "Whatever, who knows?"'

Towards the top of the climb, the Dane attacked, bridged across to the break and then rode on alone to win and take the overall lead at Tignes. 'I knew when I took the yellow jersey that it was just one step along the way, but I basically felt that I had won the Tour that day, that I was only going to get better from then on and that my rivals would never see me again.' While Rasmussen negotiated the hurdles on the road, away from it the race began to unravel. News that T-Mobile's Patrik Sinkewitz had tested positive in a pre-Tour dope control led to Germany's ARD and ZDF ending their coverage. On the rest day in Pau, it was announced that Alexandre Vinokourov, winner of two stages in the previous few days, had undergone an illegal blood transfusion. As a result, his Astana team withdrew from the race. That same day, Rasmussen's credibility was stretched almost to breaking in a highly charged rest-day press conference in Pau after it emerged that the Danish federation was refusing to select him for the World Championships due to the number of warnings he had received about violations in the whereabouts information he was required to provide to anti-doping agencies.

The next morning, the French and German teams highlighted their concerns about doping by refusing to start at the designated time in Orthez. As the Dane rode through them, fans whistled him loudly. Rasmussen, though, was more focused on his ongoing duel with Alberto Contador. The pair had produced a thrilling contest on the Plateau de Beille, sparring with each other right to the line, where the Spaniard edged the win. 'I'm getting goosebumps just thinking about racing against Contador on that stages even now,' the Dane says, rolling up his sleeve to show the skin pimpling on his forearm. 'For me that's what cycling was all about. Even looking back and knowing the aftermath, I still don't regret it. You don't often see battles like that one I had with Contador, where it repeats day after day. It was well worth spending twenty-five years of my life pursuing a dream even though I didn't succeed.'

As they had at Plateau de Beille, the pair were in the forefront of the action again on the stage to

A tormented Michael Rasmussen

the resort of Gourette, close to the top of the Col d'Aubisque. 'I had one of my best days ever on the bike. I really did Alberto a favour by not winning by two minutes that day because the first time I went all out was with just a kilometre to go. I was afraid of being alone at the front because there was quite a vicious ambience on the mountain. Given everything that had gone on and the fact that ETA had set off some bombs as the peloton rode through Spain, it wasn't the best environment in which to have the yellow jersey. I didn't dare ride close to the roadside, but stayed in between Levi and Alberto,' he explains.

Rasmussen's stage win pushed his lead out to more than three minutes on Contador. For an hour afterwards, he contemplated his success and, barring accidents, the fact that the title was all but won. 'I was sat in the helicopter with Menchov and [DS] Erik Dekker when I got a telephone call from Rabobank team manger Theo de Rooij, who was on the bus. It was a really poor connection, but through all of the noise I heard him asking something about Cassani, and I thought, "Fuck, this is not good news. Surely it can't go wrong now when I've won it?"' While Rasmussen had been racing, ex-pro and Italian TV commentator Davide Cassani had mentioned during the stage that he had seen him training in Italy in June when his whereabouts filing had said the Dane should have been completing his pre-Tour preparations around his in-laws' home in Mexico. His lie had been unwittingly revealed. When the helicopter reached the team hotel, de Rooij informed Rasmussen that he was being withdrawn from the race.

'It was so surreal to have that thought about winning the Tour having worked towards one goal for so long and then, once you've attained it, the people closest to you, who you trust more than anyone else, pull the carpet from underneath your feet,' he says. 'They took me away from the team hotel and I was abandoned in some barn in the middle of nowhere at midnight. That night I walked around and looked for some way to hang myself. Things were really bad for me. If I'd had a gun I would have shot myself, without a doubt. It was almost unbelievable what they did to me considering all that I had done for them.

'At seven the next morning I was picked up and flown to Italy in a private jet paid for by Rabobank. During the flight to Verona I contemplated suicide again. I had a Tour trophy in my backpack that was pretty heavy and I was thinking, "I'm going to go up into the cockpit and knock out the pilot and I'll take down Rabobank's plane." I thought that would make us even. I was that desperate.' Thinking about his eighteen-month-old son kept him alive, he confesses.

'I was the scapegoat for a while. Unfortunately, there is that tendency within cycling,' he says. He's right, but he was a scapegoat with a difference, racing in the yellow jersey at a time when a large part of the peloton had decided that an ethical approach to competition was fundamental and fans were no longer ready to forgive and forget. As Rasmussen flew to Italy, his teammates headed for the next stage start in Pau, where the race would start minus another team after Cofidis's withdrawal following a positive test for Italian Cristian Moreni. Emerging from their bus, Rabobank's riders ran a gauntlet of boos and insults.

Facing the press with Rabobank team manager Theo de Rooij

'I had a Tour trophy in my backpack that was pretty heavy and I was thinking, "I'm going to go up into the cockpit and knock out the pilot and I'll take down Rabobank's plane." I thought that would make us even'

Although, towards the end of the second decade of the twenty-first century, there is almost unanimous agreement that bike racing had become significantly cleaner thanks to more and better testing and a long overdue change of attitude among professional racers, fans have remained cynical. At the Tour, particularly, the catcalls are never far away. They could be heard during another doping-tainted race in 2008, then again when Contador attempted to defend his title in 2011, and with regular frequency during Sky's domination of the yellow jersey. Once tolerated as being an understandable part of sport's most demanding endurance event, doping has become so stigmatised that even the suspicion of it can lead to a rider being heckled and his teammates receiving the same treatment by association. The fall-out from Lance Armstrong's admission in 2012 that he had doped and the subsequent stripping of his titles, combined with the discrediting of many

Oscar Pereiro on being promoted to overall victor after the disqualification of Floyd Landis:

'History will say that I won the 2006 Tour de France, so there is no point in wasting a lot of energy thinking about how things might have been. They were how they were and that's it… I admit winning the Tour did rebound on me because it wasn't a role that sat well with me. It was too much for me. A good lawyer becomes a good lawyer because they spend a lot of time studying. But I think I became a star without having to study. I went from being a normal rider who was fairly well known in Spain to – boom! – being a Tour winner and I wasn't expecting that. It affected me a lot.'

of his rivals, has fostered this mistrust, which has been fuelled further still by far greater scrutiny by the media. The riders have added to this, openly criticising peers caught cheating in dope controls or even when they are perceived as bringing racing into disrepute.

Sky have been the focus of a great deal of this criticism, some of it unjustified, but much of it stemming from its 'zero tolerance' approach to doping and the perception that even if it hasn't broken any anti-doping rules it has pushed the boundaries of legality almost to that point. Even before Bradley Wiggins had claimed Britain's first Tour de France victory in July 2012, the team's stated commitment to clean cycling and the efficacy of its due diligence process was brought into question by the hiring of Geert Leinders as the team's medical consultant. As one of the three-man board that had overseen the Rabobank team during the Rasmussen years, the Belgian doctor had a questionable past within the sport that would be laid bare some months later when the Dane opened up about his transgressions. By that point, Sky had released Leinders from his contract and had carried out internal interviews to root out other staff members with skeletons in the closet.

Yet cynicism about Sky's methods and performances remained, spiking when Chris Froome won on Mont Ventoux to all but seal victory in the 2013 Tour de France, his astonishing kick of acceleration that took him away from Alberto Contador inciting roars of derision in the pressroom at the foot of the mountain and providing more ammunition for those whose faith in anti-doping procedures had evaporated. In his rest-day

press conference the next morning, Froome admitted he could understand why his victory was being questioned. 'I'm also one of those people who have been let down, who's believed in people who've turned out to be cheats and liars, but I can assure you, I'm not.' When, later, he was asked comparisons to Armstrong, he shot back, 'Lance cheated, I'm not cheating. End of story.' Predictably, it wasn't.

Over subsequent seasons, the hostility shown to him and Sky at the Tour continued to grow. In 2015, Froome accused a fan of throwing urine in his face and complained about 'individuals who are ruining the race'. Other team members said they had been hit by spectators. As Froome moved towards his third win a year later, *L'Équipe*'s Philippe Le Gars stated, 'The British have clearly not made many friends. They're criticised for their arrogance and their desire to revolutionise, even dominate the world of cycling.'

This resentment was further stoked by the 'Jiffygate' affair in 2016 and Froome's adverse analytical finding for salbutamol from the 2017 Vuelta that almost led to his exclusion from the 2018 Tour by ASO. The former, a fourteen-month investigation by UK Anti-Doping that failed to show whether a package delivered to Wiggins at the 2011 Critérium du Dauphiné contained a legal decongestant or a banned drug, ultimately tarnished both UKAD, the 2012 Tour champion and Sky manager Dave Brailsford, who first tried to persuade the *Daily Mail* to bury the story and then gave evidence which proved to be wrong on two significant points. The investigation into Froome's use of his asthma inhaler mirrored the

1988 Delgado affair with its leaking of inform-ation that should have remained confidential, but changing times meant the Briton was never likely to receive a warm welcome when he returned to the Tour, in spite of the World Anti-Doping Agency clearing him of any offence. In the wake of these affairs, which dented anti-doping's credibility yet again, the boos resounded louder than ever, the anti-Sky posters and banners were more frequent, the anger far more palpable. The satellite broad-caster's decision to leave the sport at the end of the 2019 season may dissipate this vitriol, but it won't be eradicated it until deep-seated concern about cycling's credibility can be allayed. However, even in this eventuality, the once unimpeachable trust and respect that fans had for the winner and the almost unanimous adulation he would receive winner from the media won't be restored.

Despite these reservations, the Tour's status as one of sport's greatest events will endure, and with it so will respect for its most emblematic symbol, the yellow jersey, because, as Lionel Birnie affirmed in the wake of Armstrong's belated admission of deception and cheating, 'The scandals and disap-pointments are, like the riders themselves, tran-sient. They come and go.' The Tour survives and thrives because it has always been fundamentally resilient. Ultimately, the race chooses who it will favour and it will outlive them all.

LANCE ARMSTRONG
TOUR DE FRANCE
2005

12

BEACON AND TARGET
Le Maillot Jaune

Bernard Thévenet 1975

THE YELLOW JERSEY AWARDED AFTER
THE FRENCHMAN HAD ENDED EDDY MERCKX'S
TOUR-WINNING RUN IN 1975

It's Maurice Garin and he's dressed in black, as he was on the final stage of the 1903 Tour despite usually racing in white. He knew he was under threat from irate fans so changed his kit to fool them

The Dangers of Dominance

When race leader Maurice Garin lined up in Nantes for the start of the final stage of the inaugural Tour de France in 1903, he caused a stir with his outfit. Dubbed 'The White Bulldog' for the colour of his kit and style of racing, this time he was dressed all in black.

It was a canny move on the part of the diminutive Frenchman, whose victory on the preceding stage owed a good deal to him rendering Fernand Augereau's bike useless by stamping repeatedly on its front wheel. As the crowd swelled to several thousand strong, there was huge acclaim when his rival arrived, cries of 'Down with Garin!' mixing with shouts of 'Vive Augereau!' But it was pantomime stuff compared to what the race leader feared might be in store as the peloton numbering just twenty-one survivors raced through the middle of the night towards Paris.

Sure enough, with forty kilometres covered and Garin already alone at the front, a rider appeared at his side from the darkness and asked his name. Wary of revealing his identity, the race leader offered up that of one of his rivals, adding for good measure, 'Garin? We dropped him a long time ago and he must be a long way behind us!' Hearing this, the mystery rider braked and turned, heading back into the night to deliver retribution, unaware that he had just been tricked out of the opportunity to deliver it.

Sixteen years later, the introduction of the yellow jersey made it almost impossible for the race leader to undertake this kind of subterfuge. Indeed, there is no firm evidence that any *maillot jaune* was subjected to verbal or physical threat prior to the Second World War, although it has been claimed that France's Antonin Magne did come under fire from fans as he raced towards his second title in 1934. These stories stem from the assistance extended to him by his twenty-year-old teammate René Vietto, who gave up his wheel to the race leader on consecutive stages in the Pyrenees and in doing so sacrificed his own hopes of glory. On the second occasion, after Vietto turned around on the Portet d'Aspet to aid Magne, a picture was taken of him sitting at the roadside in tears, his bike minus its front wheel propped up against the wall beside him. It quickly became and has remained one of the race's iconic images, legend having it that Magne later requested Vietto ride at his side to appease fans who regarded the young hero as the race's moral victor.

The tale is, however, mostly fabrication. While Vietto was a sensation on his Tour debut, winning four stages and taking fifth place on the general classification, the French climber wasn't in contention for overall victory at any point. When these incidents occurred, he was the best part of an hour behind his team leader on GC and only lost what was then a fairly paltry eight minutes as a result of them. Magne, who led from the second day to the last and took the title by a massive twenty-seven minutes, wasn't the focus of any popular rancour and was, according to *L'Auto*, greeted with an ovation so loud by 50,000 fans at

the Parc des Princes that it sounded like thunder resounding around the arena. The myth appears to have emerged thanks to the emotive photo of the distraught Vietto and, primarily, subsequent claims made by the young rider and his supporters that he had been robbed of overall victory. Radio reporter Georges Briquet, who covered the race and was adamant Vietto hadn't been robbed, asserted that, 'A legend was born and nobody dared meddle with it: it was so moving.'

Until the late 1950s, fans were dependent on print and radio to keep them abreast of the Tour action. While rivalries between the star names did make for good copy, the emphasis tended towards the heroic and, for the yellow jersey at least, idolisation. But as televised broadcasts became more frequent and their audiences grew, fans obtained a different perspective on the race. Rather than using words and radio commentary to summon up the riders' feats in their imagination, they could see and assess performances for themselves, which resulted in more complex, and often critical, judgement of new favourites such as Jacques Anquetil, as stylish off the bike as he was on it, and Roger Rivière.

The two French stars, the former a youthful winner in 1957 and the latter talked up as a future champion, were the first headliners to be subjected to indiscriminate disapproval by fans. Rivals away from the Tour but shoehorned very uncomfortably into the same French team in 1959 that was hyped as the race's strongest ever, the illustrious pair and their teammates were jeered and whistled as they completed their lap of honour in the Parc three-and-a-half weeks later after Federico

Bahamontes had secured Spain's first yellow jersey. Although France's team manager Marcel Bidot had hammered out an understanding between the pair, it quickly became clear that both riders saw themselves as the rightful leader and neither was prepared to help the other or see them win.

As they shadow-boxed, Bahamontes took the lead on the opening day in the Alps and Henry Anglade of the Centre-Midi regional team emerged as his rival. Described by Paul Fournel in his wonderful eulogy *Anquetil, Alone* as a 'mean-spirited, authoritarian little Napoleon riding for a regional team', the Frenchman became the leader on the road when the nervy Bahamontes was dropped on the descent off the Petit-Saint-Bernard. This was the key moment, as Fournel explains: 'The idea that a French nonentity can steal a march on the two great rivals of their time is simply unbearable. Especially as he has chosen as his manager [Roger] Piel, the arch-rival of [Daniel] Dousset, who is their manager...'

When, after the treacherously wet and rocky descent, the Spanish yellow jersey was caught by their group, Anquetil and Rivière, two of the best rouleurs ever to have graced the sport, began to set the pace, determined to support Bahamontes because, says Fournel, 'They see him as a much worthier victor than this young Anglade fellow,' and a gap of five minutes was reduced to less than one at the line, keeping Bahamontes in the lead. Although he proved himself a worthy winner by dropping Anglade on the next stage to Annecy, the home fans weren't fooled. Dismayed by this display of disloyalty towards a compatriot, by Anquetil and Rivière's joint failure to put each other to the test

and by their dishonour of the *maillot jaune*, France's two leading lights were heckled and booed as they circled the track in Paris.

Anquetil made light of the incident, buying a boat to sail on the Seine and christening it *Sifflets 59* – Boos 59. When he returned to the Tour two years later as the undisputed leader of the French team, he determined to put on a show of strength that would erase memories of his mutual surrender with Rivière, whose career had been ended when he broke his back crashing into a ravine in the 1960 edition. He set himself the challenge of leading from the first day to the last. In the break on the opening morning that was led in by teammate André Darrigade and winner of the time trial at Versailles that afternoon, Anquetil took the yellow jersey. Over the course of the next three weeks, the Norman, backed by a twelve-strong team fully committed to his objective, bulldozed the opposition and squeezed any hint of unpredictability from the contest. As the tricolores powered to nine stage wins in addition to Anquetil's yellow jersey and Darrigade's green, the press railed against their control, while fans barracked them for limiting the spectacle. Among the most dominant performances that any team and winner have produced in the post-war era, it actually made Sky appear cavalier in their approach.

Despite the loss of two riders from France's team on the second stage into Roubaix, Anquetil and his band were relentless. Vigorously protective of his lead throughout the first week, they chased down breaks even when they didn't need to, the opposition rallying in vain together to break the stranglehold. As the race left the Vosges on stage seven heading for Chalons-sur-Saône, Tour director Goddet predicted a possible collapse within the French ranks as a consequence of their incessant effort. Instead, Anquetil served up a staggering demonstration of how a rider could impose himself as the patron drawing on nothing more than the power in his legs. When a break gained seventeen minutes, making Jesús Manzaneque the yellow jersey on the road, French DS Bidot suggested to his leader that Jean Stablinski and Georges Groussard ought to drop back from the front group to help set the pace in the peloton. Anquetil refused and rode up to the front of the bunch, where he stayed for the next thirty kilometres, cutting minutes from the gap and saving the yellow jersey on his own. For good measure, Stablinski and Groussard were first and second at the finish.

Later, when Charly Gaul briefly flickered on the first stage in the Alps, Bidot's riders shut down the Luxembourg climber's assaults as well. Anquetil, Goddet complained, 'ruined all the climbs by setting the pace up front and no one wanted to challenge him.' Declaring Anquetil the winner as the race prepared to depart the Pyrenees, he branded the French winner's rivals 'dwarfs of the road, powerless like Gaul has become, or resigned, satisfied with their mediocrity'. The yellow jersey's control was so complete that on the final day he set up teammate Robert Cazala for the stage win in the Parc des Princes. It

'I am there to pedal, not to play the clown!'

was sport as a pure athletic contest, hugely impressive but almost without thrills. It didn't make for captivating viewing, and the crowd registered their disapproval with whistles. The winner, though, was unrepentant, declaring, 'I am there to pedal, not to play the clown!'

The switch back to trade teams from 1962 all but eliminated the possibility of awkward accommodations like the one between Anquetil and Rivière three years earlier. It also, thanks largely to the former's rivalry with Raymond Poulidor, saw the French public adopt a more nuanced attitude towards the yellow jersey, based less on wonderment and adulation, and more on respect and, eventually, suspicion. At the same time, a strong attachment developed for the noble loser, the rider fighting against insurmountable odds, often thrilling in the high mountains but inevitably crushed by the suffocating efficiency of the victor.

The two Frenchmen were typecast into these roles, with Anquetil pitched as the modern champion, defiant, coldly superior and hard to warm to, resolutely focused on success, with Poulidor the simple, downtrodden, ill-starred ordinary man from the sticks who was the incarnation of the underdog. Predictably, the stereotypes don't fit either man neatly. Although Poulidor is most obviously associated with the land, both men were born and raised in the kind of agricultural communities that were for a long time the principal

ETES-VOUS POULIDORISTE ?

Un article de Maurice VIDAL

MIROIR SPRINT

40 PAGES

N° 940
8 JUIN 1964
1,50 F

...OU ANQUETILISTE ?

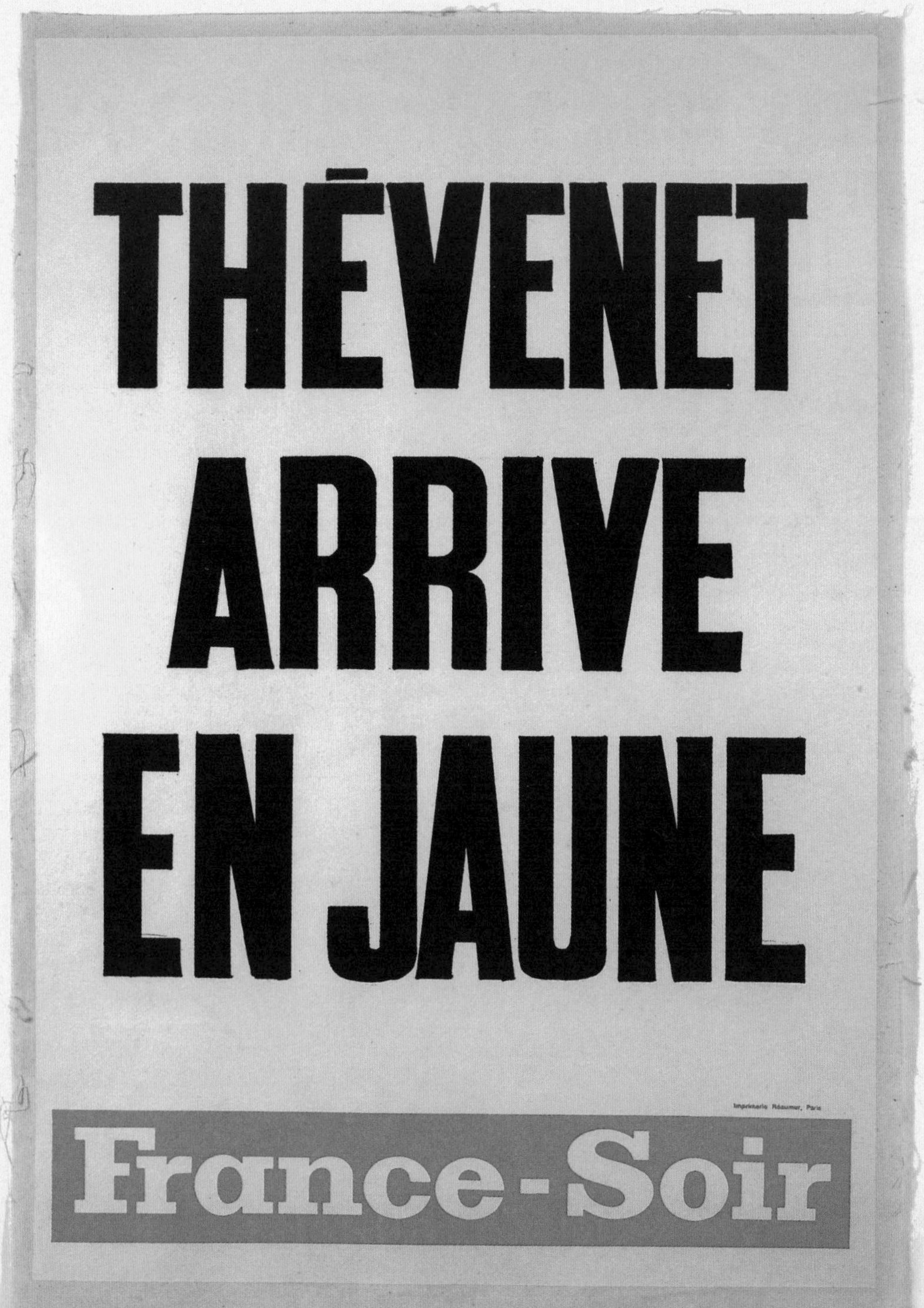

THÉVENET
ARRIVE
EN JAUNE
France-Soir

Eddy Merckx after being beaten in 1975 by Bernard Thévenet: 'There are no such things as miracles in sport. The strongest man wins and Thévenet is the strongest. There's nothing that can be done or said about that. You have to see things as they are. During my five previous Tours de France, everyone was watching for any moment of weakness in me. But there wasn't ever one. For 10 years I've been the man to beat and it was inevitable that I would be beaten one day. This year, I came up against a transcendent Thévenet, a rider too strong for me. I'm not under any illusions.'

Illustration by Red, 'The Tourmalet and Izoard together', 1939. Nicknamed "King René" for his sacrifice to Antonin Magne in the 1934 Tour, Provençal climber René Vietto never won the yellow jersey that seemed to be his destiny. Leader for 11 days in 1939, he yielded to Belgian Sylvère Maes, as depicted in Red's illustration from that year, and lost his best years to the Second World War. During the 1947 Tour, the first following the conflict, he led the race for 15 days, but cracked in the brutal 139-kilometre Vannes–Saint Brieuc time trial, eventually finishing fifth overall

nursery for the nation's bike racers and the most devoted of the sport's supporters. Yet, there was a significant difference between them. The Anquetil family owned the land they worked in Normandy and the income they derived from it enabled them to support the young Jacques in his passion for cycle sport. He did an apprenticeship at sixteen, then won the Grand Prix des Nations at nineteen, when still an amateur, a success that revealed him to the sporting public and opened his path into the pro ranks, where his style and power on the bike became quickly apparent. 'Behind this fluidity and the appearance of ease, he was identified with the image of a winning France and of those willing to take risks,' say Jean-Luc Boeuf and Yves Léonard in *La République du Tour de France*.

Poulidor, on the other hand, hailed from a very poor family of sharecroppers. He left school at fourteen to work in the fields and later spent more than two years on national service in Algeria. He was twenty-four when he started his pro career in earnest. 'Humble people recognised themselves in Raymond Poulidor, whose face – weathered by effort – reminded those who came from the land that the work is both relentless and offers no chance for rest,' explain Boeuf and Léonard. 'Raymond Poulidor reassured those French people who felt the continuous advances during the Glorious Thirty [post-war] years had passed them by.'

In a very similar way to Fausto Coppi and Gino Bartali, the two riders depended on each other as rivals. The 1961 Tour had shown Anquetil's domination but obscured his all-round brilliance in winning it because there was no one in the rest of the field of his stature. From his debut in the race in 1962, Poulidor changed that dynamic. Over the next five seasons, the Norman's objective was straightforward: beat his principal opponent, either through his own efforts or by helping proxies or teammates. At the same time, 'Poupou', as he was dubbed from that season when he achieved the first of eight podium finishes at the Tour, used the rivalry to boost his status and, most importantly, earnings. Although he liked winning, he wasn't driven by the desire to subdue in the way that Anquetil was. 'He was without a doubt the most complete rival, the most capable of winning, and yet he lacked the terrible soul and true complexity of a champion,' says Fournel. Poulidor, the everyman who wasn't driven to excel and for whom financial security and happiness were paramount, cannily played on his reputation as the plucky and unlucky loser to achieve these intrinsic goals.

Fournel beautifully captures the essence of the attitude towards the pair during this period, which can be summed up as Anquetil amassing garlands on the road and Poulidor winning hearts off it. 'Without meaning to, Poupou has become, in the eyes of the public, a kind of positive opposite to Anquetil, and his eternal victim. By contrast, he makes the Norman rider look disdainful, arrogant – in a way Anquetil had never imagined, because he was too busy simply trying to race faster than everyone else... He is somebody it's so easy to admire, but so hard to love...' That final line could equally well be applied to Eddy Merckx, Bernard Hinault, Miguel Indurain or Chris Froome.

Although Anquetil didn't have to withstand jeers as he added three more Tour crowns from

1962, his rival's status as the fans' favourite continued to increase, particularly in 1964, a race remembered mostly for the pair's near-to-slow-motion duel on the slopes of the long-extinct volcano of the Puy de Dôme. In the final kilometres they rode elbow to elbow for some distance. Ultimately, Anquetil, inevitably in yellow, was unable to respond his rival's belated surge, but clung on with trademark tenacity to retain the lead by fourteen seconds. This pivotal moment was as close as Poulidor ever got to winning the Tour, his performance beset, as they frequently were, by ill fortune and poor tactics. If he'd attacked lower down the mountain, the title would surely have been his.

But, as he has repeated many times over the decades since, never winning and failing to spend even a single day in the yellow jersey cemented his reputation and fortune.

'If I'd worn the yellow jersey even for a single day I wouldn't have been remembered in the same way'

he said at the 2018 Tour, where he was working for the eighteenth year in succession as the ambassador for *maillot jaune* sponsors Crédit Lyonnais, decked out for three weeks in a yellow polo shirt. There's also irony in the fact that so many fans ended up identifying with a rider who symbolised misfortune and was dubbed 'the eternal second', but whose palmarès featured victories in many of the greatest races on the calendar.

Merckx's decimation of the field in 1969, when Poulidor was one of the few to emerge with some credit as he finished third, heralded another shift in attitude towards the yellow jersey. Of all the Sun Kings, none has been more dazzling or intimidating. The Belgian was the nonpareil of *rouleur-grimpeurs*, each of his Tour victories founded on the desire to dominate as completely as Anquetil had in 1961. On a very few occasions, most obviously the comprehensive drubbing handed to him by Luis Ocaña at Orcières Merlette in 1971, Merckx was made to look mortal, but for the most part he was other-worldly, a supreme monarch determined to conquer and impose himself whenever the opportunity arose, his presence so intimidating some of his most able opponents that they were content to sit on his coat-tails, happy to scrap for any morsels he might toss them.

Like Rafael Nadal in his pomp at the French Open, Merckx's domination of the Tour became so complete that it began to squeeze the unpredictability out of the race and, as a consequence, reduced interest in it. By 1972 he had won four consecutive titles by a distance, and a fifth looked pre-destined. Fearing the impact this might have on audience figures and, as a result, advertising revenue and newspaper sales, the organisers encouraged him to seek out other territories to conquer. This mirrored the situation at the Giro in the late 1920s, when the organisers paid Alfredo Binda the equivalent of the prize money for first place to stay away after he had won four editions in five years. The Belgian used the opportunity to become the first rider to complete the Vuelta–Giro double, which then ran with just a few days between them.

Looking back in an interview with *Procycling* to that season, Merckx confessed, 'I made a mistake by not riding the Tour in 1973. There were many reasons why I chose not to ride it. On the one hand, it's true, after four victories in a row at the Tour, the organisers made me understand that perhaps it would be better if I concentrated on the Tours of Italy and Spain instead. On the other hand, I'd noticed that in the previous years the French public at the side of the road had begun to react badly to my winning all the time. I was a bit worried about the reaction of some people.' Rather than being influenced by this 'anti-Merckxism', he felt he should have attempted to become the first to win five consecutive Tour crowns, especially as, he admitted in another interview, 'keeping me out of the Tour didn't pay off. I still had as many detractors the following year.'

In 1974, despite undergoing an operation on a saddle sore five days before the Tour got under way, Merckx was as untouchable as ever, winning a record-equalling eight stages. But clear signs of dissent emerged both within and outside the peloton. In *Eddy Merckx: The Cannibal*, Daniel Friebe depicts the Belgian's Molteni team as wilting, the years taking a toll on domestiques such as Vic Van Schil, Jos Huysmans and Joseph Spruyt, who were seen as being increasingly dependent

'after four victories in a row at the Tour, the organisers made me understand that perhaps it would be better if I concentrated on the Tours of Italy and Spain instead'

on underhand and intimidatory tactics to control their leader's rivals, of imposing a 'sporting dictatorship'. When, on the stage to Pla d'Adet, Spruyt launched a tirade of abuse at Cyrille Guimard after the Frenchman attempted to break the unspoken ceasefire early on in the day, the encounter degenerated. After the Frenchman attacked a second time, Spruyt used his fists to bring him back into line. Following the stage, won with immense acclaim by the thirty-eight-year-old Poulidor, his first Tour success for nine seasons, Guimard spoke on TV of a 'mafia' controlling the race, in which, says Friebe, 'Merckx was naturally cast as its boss.' On the following stage, the whistles of discontent from within the peloton that always signalled Molteni's intention to ramp up the pace and pain at the front of the race were accompanied by similar abuse from the roadside.

Libération's Pierre Carrey suggests that there's a trace of France's anti-monarchist past in this response. 'There is an evident regal aspect to the *maillot jaune* and, of course, France was a monarchy for a long time until it was eventually brought down by the people. If you look back at all

*Merckx holds his stomach, having been punched
by a 'fan' in the 1975 Tour*

the great names who have worn the yellow jersey, most of them have had to deal with some degree of unpopularity. Winning it shows that you are the best, but you're unlikely to be the most popular,' he says.

In 1975, the antipathy towards the yellow-clad Belgian took a more direct and violent turn as the race headed for the top of the Puy de Dôme. Although Merckx had been in yellow for nine days, his domination was far from being as absolute as it had been. His lead was a comparatively slim ninety-two seconds and his closest challenger a home rider, Bernard Thévenet. With a couple of kilometres to the line, the Frenchman slipped clear of the yellow jersey with Lucien Van Impe, who kicked away on his own to win the stage. But the little climber's victory was a sideshow. When Thévenet crossed the line fifteen seconds later, the grimacing Merckx was still a couple of hundred

metres behind, swaying from side to side with effort, the seething crowds greeting his passage with a mixture of cheers and whistles. A man sprang forward to give him a push, then another jumped out, his fist clenched. He threw it into Merckx's flank. The Belgian's instinctively flicked his hand back to the impact point over his right kidney, then pushed on towards the line, crossing it thirty-four seconds after Thévenet, his lead reduced to less than a minute. Pictures taken in the changing room at the finish show him clutching his midriff. Contemporary reports describe him telling French rider Jean-Pierre Danguillaume that, 'I've just encountered a madman.' Within a few minutes, he made his way back down to identify his assailant, a fifty-five-year-old local, Nello Breton, who had been restrained by other fans, but insisted when he spoke to the Belgian and the police accompanying him that he had been pushed.

Merckx has always insisted that the punch cost him the title. 'Receiving a punch when you're making an effort like that is quite something,' he told Manuel Caillaud from Clermont-Ferrand newspaper La Montagne in 2016. 'The doctor gave me medicine to thin my blood. I didn't react well to that, notably on the stage to Pra-Loup.' Following a rest day, Merckx appeared to have recovered well as the race headed for the resort in the southern Alps. He was alone at the front going onto the final 6.5-kilometre climb, but cracked in the final two thousand metres, *L'Équipe*'s Pierre Chany describing as moving 'at the speed of a country postman'. Thévenet took full advantage, exchanging a fifty-eight-second deficit for a lead of the same margin. The next day, he pushed it out beyond three minutes. The title was his.

A few weeks after the race, Merckx launched a legal suit against Breton, who was assigned a young Clermont lawyer to defend him – Daniel Thévenet. Interviewed by Caillaud, he revealed that the decision to appoint him had been taken deliberately because of the surname he shared with the Belgian's conqueror. Initially, the lawyer was confident he would get his client off because none of the witnesses were able to state that Breton had thrown the punch. In a court encounter, the defendant even told Merckx he liked him. A few days later, the judge contacted Thévenet to tell him the assault had been filmed and Breton's punch was clearly visible. His client claimed in pre-trial hearings, though, that he had been trying to push Merckx. When the judge said this clearly hadn't been the case, he denied being the person pictured.

'Was he in denial?' Thévenet recalled asking himself, admitting that it would have been easier for Breton to accept the charge. 'I remember that at that time Eddy Merckx was very unpopular. Firstly, because he used to win all the time, he was Belgian, and he also had a certain arrogance, he was quite cold, quite distant. I could have said that my client had been influenced by the crowd, by the atmosphere at that time.' In the end, Breton, who had no previous criminal record, received a two-year suspended sentence and had to pay Merckx symbolic damages of one franc. 'It was a quite exceptional moment,' Thévenet said of the incident. 'I think it was the first time we'd seen a spectator hit a cyclist.'

'It was the first time there had been hooli-

'since the 1960s, the French media and public have tended to prefer a noble loser to a dominant winner'

gans on the Tour. Brainless types. I was the first rider who could have won six Tours. But I was a foreigner and there was animosity,' Merckx told Caillaud. The carried-along-by-the-crowd defence that Thévenet had initially planned justifies the Belgian's perspective on the episode. But, as the whistling of Anquetil had shown, French riders did come under fire as well. When Bernard Hinault succeeded Merckx as the Tour's patron and started to dominate the race in much the same way, he also had to put up with similar treatment.

There is a tendency to look back on his reign as a golden era in the Tour's history, but the middle three of his five victories were far from gripping. They did include moments of extraordinary ability that compared with Merckx at his best, but the inevitability of Hinault's ultimate success diminished them as sporting contests. Their routes were skewed ridiculously towards his main strength, with 200–300 kilometres of individual and team time trialling, while his opponents simply weren't of his calibre. Uncompromising, sometimes belligerent and largely indifferent to his popular standing, Hinault did care enough to produce performances of memorable panache. During the 1981 Tour when the Breton won five stages – including all four individual time trials – and finished almost quarter of an hour ahead of runner-up Lucien Van Impe, there were whistles among the cheers when he was presented with the yellow jersey. Hinault answered them by whistling back.

How could French fans react in this way to their most outstanding Tour champion? Partly because they wanted him to be less cocksure and seem a little more fallible and human, but also for the simple reason that they figured that another home champion to whom they could transfer their affection and support would quickly emerge. They had become blasé about winning and wanted their stars to behave in a particular way, to triumph despite the odds stacked up against them, rather than scornfully trampling their opponents to dust. When, in 1984, Hinault came up against a rider in Laurent Fignon who was stronger than him in every domain, his popularity soared. Throughout the race, he persisted in harrying his former team-mate and defending champion, only to be defeated with the same contemptuous ease that he'd previously displayed himself. According to William Fotheringham, 'since the 1960s, the French media and public have tended to prefer a noble loser to a dominant winner', and here was the proof of it. When Hinault rebounded to regain the title in 1985, the press eulogised and the fans were in raptures. Very few yellow jerseys since have savoured a comparable reception, and not only because there hasn't been a Frenchman among them.

During his period of yellow jersey hegemony in the early 1990s, Miguel Indurain tranquilised the Tour audience by serving up the same predictable performance for five consecutive seasons. Although affable, courteous and very popular within the peloton and his homeland, the enigmatic Spaniard neutralised any obvious display of discontent through his lack of engagement. With nothing to react against, fans endured rather than revolted.

From Indurain's wake, Lance Armstrong eventually arose as the Tour's new ruler. Brash, despotic, paranoid and uncompromising, he was an easy champion to despise and ultimately was more responsible than any other for tarnishing the yellow jersey and, above all, the standing of the rider in it. By 2004, as the American closed in on the sixth of the seven victories that he would later be stripped of for doping, the atmosphere around the *maillot jaune* became so febrile that the race organisation was receiving threats against him. As a consequence of these, in addition to the bodyguard that always shadowed him, he raced that year's Alpe d'Huez mountain time trial with security staff employed as outriders and another sitting alongside US Postal DS Johan Bruyneel in the team car behind. Given the exceptionally tense atmosphere on the famous climb, packed like never before for the short time trial, it was almost surprising that, catcalls and insults apart, the most unsavoury incident was Tour director Jean-Marie Leblanc witnessing two 'idiots' spitting at Armstrong as he raced past.

There has been a plethora of incidents since. In the cases of Michael Rasmussen and Alberto Contador, the anger directed at them was fuelled by the impression fanned in the media that they were breaking anti-doping regulations, which was later confirmed. The rancour aimed at Team Sky has stemmed from a perception that they too have engaged in unethical or even prohibited practices, although the British squad has never had a rider test positive. This has been bolstered by criticism of their approach to racing and of an astronomical budget that enables them to have the best of everything required to win the Tour. Speaking to *Libération* in 2016, journalist Pierre Ballester suggested that this 'financial doping', as it has been described, was at the root of Sky's lack of popularity. 'In the French imagination, the Tour is full of dreams that hark back to past exploits. Whereas Sky is a machine with a budget of well above 20 million euros,' he said. 'They are here to win the Tour, to run a business. The French vision of the Tour, poetic, full of heritage, is outdated. Sky has no consideration for this history, for the legacy of the Tour.'

But does this 'French imagination' tally with reality? When Bradley Wiggins won the title in 2012 and Chris Froome succeeded him as champion, Sky's method of racing up strategically important climbs with a line of very talented domestiques in order to prevent their opponents attacking and to put them under physical pressure was clinical, especially when backed up by their use of power data to monitor their rivals. Yet, this was essentially a retune of the extremely effective tactic used by Coppi, Anquetil, Merckx, Hinault and many others, but cloaked beneath talk of marginal gains. It may have been lacking in the poetic sense, but no less so than the French team's suffocation of their competition in the 1961 Tour.

Fundamentally, it was a way to achieve success in a race where the overall level of competition and ability is higher than ever, with margins between the contenders amounting to a few dozen seconds over 3,500 kilometres of racing. There is little room for harking back and nods to heritage when these margins are so fine.

As this development was taking place, the response from fans to the Tour riders and particularly the yellow jersey was also changing. While most roadside critics did no more than heckle Sky's line of riders as they passed, an increasing number went further. There were more reports of spitting, while one unidentified assailant threw urine in Froome's face in the 2015 race. This kind of aggressive antagonism worsened in the aftermath of the 'Jiffy-bag' scandal that embroiled Wiggins and Sky boss Dave Brailsford at the end of 2016, which included the claim from the House of Commons' Digital, Culture, Media and Sport Committee that a powerful corticosteroid had been used to prepare the 2012 Tour winner and its suggestion that the team had entered a grey area in its usage of therapeutic use exemption certificates (TUEs) to administer it.

It was further exacerbated by the leaking of news about Froome's adverse analytical finding for salbutamol in 2017. The affair resulting from this dragged on so long that the Briton's attempt to defend his title in 2018 race was only confirmed days before the race got under way when he was cleared of any wrongdoing. His absolution didn't, though, remove the feeling among many fans, and not just those in France, that Sky had been up to no good, an impression fuelled by ASO's attempt to ban the Briton from defending his title the day before the UCI announced the case had been resolved to prevent damage to the Tour's image. Coming after Hinault had insisted that rather than recording an abnormal control Froome had 'tested positive' and had called on the Tour peloton to strike if he started the race, it encouraged the opinion that Froome was bringing the race into disrepute. Predictably, he was booed when he appeared at the Tour presentation. That treatment continued when racing began, spectators brandishing signs labelling him a doper and telling him and his team to go home.

'It's a shame that the Tour has started in this kind of atmosphere, hostile rather than festive,' lamented LottoNL-Jumbo team manager Richard Plugge. 'The French have to an extent provoked this kind of behaviour. We've had eight months of killing Chris Froome in interviews and stories in the media, which hasn't helped because the fans don't really understand what is happening, what this case involved, so they have ended up taking sides against Froome for the wrong reasons and that's impacting heavily on him.' Although the barracking eased over the first week, it returned when Geraint Thomas took the yellow jersey at La Rosière.

The antipathy towards the pair and their teammates became so threatening that rival team managers advised their riders to avoid following Froome's wheel because they feared a domino effect if the defending champion was knocked from his bike. Unfortunately, this concern proved justified. On the following stage to Alpe d'Huez, where a heavy security presence dampened the traditional raucousness, a fan knocked Vincenzo Nibali to the ground as smoke from a flare billowed around the yellow jersey group. Although the Italian managed to remount and finish, an X-ray revealed a fractured vertebra that forced him to abandon the race. In an echo of the Merckx incident on the Puy de Dôme, the Italian subsequently launched a legal action against his alleged aggressor for damages.

As Thomas closed in on Sky's sixth *maillot jaune* in seven seasons, Froome made the point that Sky don't receive this kind of hostility at any other event on the calendar. 'When we race in Spain, in Italy or anywhere else, we don't get the same kind of reception,' he said. There was none either when Thomas won the week-long Critérium du Dauphiné in the French Alps five weeks before the Tour. Protest is confined almost exclusively to the contest for the yellow jersey, the single race all season that is important to every fan, no matter how casual. Featuring the biggest audience all year, the best line-up of riders and the greatest prize in cycling, it inevitably polarises fans, and increasingly so as teams take on what is almost national status, transforming the race into cycling's World Cup, where everyone has their favourites and, for most, the dominant team are the villains, especially when they are perceived as being anti-heroic, of suppressing the *maillot jaune*'s poetic aspect. 'When you think what it means to this sport, what the Tour ought to be, a festival, a celebration, and people come to boo and protest... I don't know, but it isn't my concept of what a festival is,' said Froome.

Introduced to make the Tour leader stand out,

the yellow jersey has become a beacon in many different ways, not only picking out the man in it from the rest of the pack, but also for praise and abuse. 'It was the case with Jacques Anquetil, it was the same with Eddy Merckx, and it's being repeated now,' said race director Christian Prudhomme of the evident dislike for the Tour leader. The concern is that running the gauntlet of those threats is becoming more perilous than ever.

BERNARD THÉVENET
TOUR DE FRANCE
1964

13

TOUR À LA WALKOWIAK

Le Maillot Jaune

Chris Froome 2017

SPONSORED BY LCL, WHOSE OWNERS CRÉDIT AGRICOLE
ALSO BACKED A PRO TEAM FOR A DECADE

The Best Racer Always Wins

It's the morning of the team time trial at the Critérium du Dauphiné. Yet, rather than trying to cadge quotes and insight from the great and good of the World-Tour peloton gathering in the little town of Pont-de-Vaux, I'm seventy kilometres further down the Saône valley, sitting in the back of a bike shop in the equally small municipality of Jassans-Riottier, talking to Antonin Rolland. His name might not mean much, but the Frenchman sits high

on the ranking of days spent in the yellow jersey thanks to a twelve-day spell in the lead at the 1955 Tour, which puts him alongside Tour winners Lucien Van Impe and Ferdi Kübler and one ahead of Alberto Contador. He is also, as he approaches his ninety-fourth birthday, the oldest living rider to have worn the *maillot jaune*.

Along with the one remaining yellow jersey he has of the dozen he received, the shop, now run by

his grandson Cyril, who is in the workshop next door servicing a Lapierre bike, is the most tangible evidence of Rolland's success in that Tour and across a seventeen-year career during which he raced with Fausto Coppi, Louison Bobet and Jacques Anquetil, made a best friend of Brian Robinson, Britain's first Tour stage winner, and almost won the greatest title in the sport. Sprightly, engaging and still blessed with a clear memory of racing in what was arguably cycling's golden age, Rolland established what was then a petrol station as well as a bike shop in the early 1960s with the money he'd saved from racing.

'There weren't as many buildings around here then, this one was about the last before you reached the bridge over the river to Villefranche,' he says. 'It was a good location for a petrol station, but that side of it came to an end because of competition from the big supermarkets. My son kept it going, but when my grandson took over he said that there were aspects of the petrol station that didn't fulfil regulatory requirements and a lot of major work needed to be undertaken. It wasn't worth it, especially as running a petrol station is not one of those businesses that you do on your own any more. It doesn't provide a good enough salary.'

Born on 3 September 1924 in Sainte-Euphémie, just half a dozen kilometres west of where we're talking, Rolland had a passion for cycling from an early age. At the local primary school that now bears his name in tribute to his exploits on the road, he would act out bike races with his friends using toy cyclists fashioned from lead. 'Each one of us had to defend his rider. One was Charles Pélissier, another André Leducq, another Maurice Archambaud, and I was Antonin Magne, because of the shared Christian name of course, but also because Magne was a great rider. He'd won the Tour twice and even then, for a kid, the Tour was the yellow jersey,' he says. 'I was fascinated by the Tour. I can remember coming in from cutting hay in the fields and listening to the finish of the stage on the radio, waiting to hear the result. It's funny because Magne later became my directeur sportif.

I told him about my childhood games with a lead figure of him painted yellow and he thought it was very funny.' He made his Tour debut in 1949, the year Coppi took his first victory. 'In my era there is no doubt that Coppi was the best. He was also a really nice man, very easy to talk to,' says Rolland, who finished 45th that year in the violet-and-white colours of the Sud-Est team led by Pierre Brambilla, who had been denied victory by Jean Robic in the 1947 race on the final stage into Paris. The next season, Rolland made a breakthrough, winning the Midi Libre stage race, finishing third in the illustrious Grand Prix des Nations time trial and taking the Challenge Sédis as the most consistent French rider. He also finished runner-up to Bobet in the French championship, a race that he remembers with regret.

'It took place on the circuit at Montlhéry, and on the final lap I was away with Bobet and Camille Danguillaume. We were about ten kilometres from the finish when two motorbikes that were following the race collided with each and knocked Danguillaume and me to the ground. As Bobet rode on alone to win the title, I was left with a broken wheel and no chance of catching him because in those days we didn't have team cars following us. I ended up having to run for two hundred metres with my bike in order to exchange it for another one. I finished second when I really could have been the French champion, but I was the lucky one because Danguillaume never got up. He had sustained a fracture of the temporal bone and died a few days later.'

In 1952, Rolland was selected for the France's Tour team, racing alongside Jean Robic, Jean

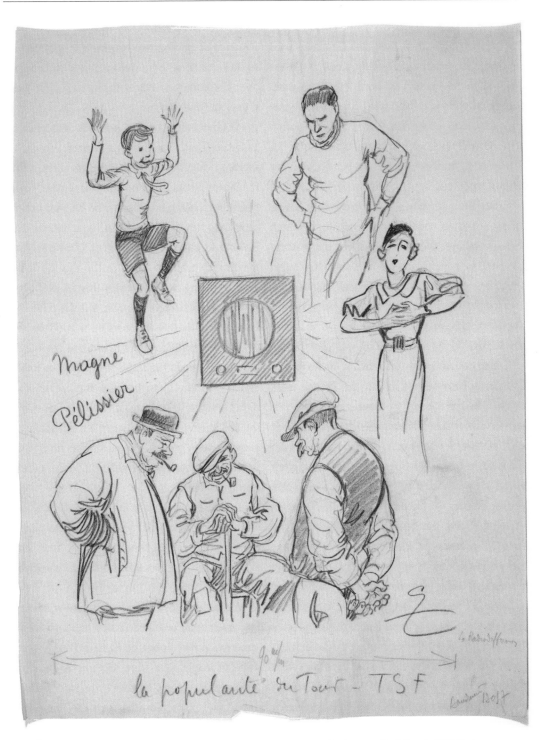

| *Antonin Rolland wasn't the only one tuning in to all the Tour action, as depicted in this 1920s sketch from André Gallard*

Dotto, their best finisher in eighth place behind the untouchable Coppi, Raphaël Geminiani and his close friend Bernard Gauthier, three weeks his junior and now a near neighbour. 'I think my main quality as a rider was that I was better than average on every kind of terrain. I had a good sprint, climbed well and could hold my own on the flat too. I used to finish well placed on just about every kind of stage and could certainly perform well in a sprint, although when it got dangerous I was happy not to get involved. It's terrifying to watch them nowadays, because there are so many riders involved,' he says. 'I won the final stage into Paris, which finished in the Parc des Princes, outsprinting about a dozen riders. The stadium was packed. There must have been 45,000 people in there, which made for an absolutely spine-tingling finale.'

Having missed that 1952 edition due to illness, Louison Bobet returned to lead the French team in 1953, taking the first of three consecutive victories, with Rolland among his domestiques on each occasion. 'I can't complain about the time I spent on the team with Bobet. He was always good to me, always honest with me, and we did get a certain amount of freedom to ride for ourselves when it suited the team's main objective,' he says. 'Nowadays it is a little bit different because the yellow jersey is almost always completely surrounded by his teammates. If a guy wants to get in the break he has to get the OK for it and often just gets told to stay with his leader to set the pace for them, give them shelter, protect them, set them up for the finish. In our era, we did used to protect them but not in the same way. We used to race in a more individually within teams. We were given a little more leeway, the chance to act on their own initiative by getting into breaks. It was important to do so because there were so many of them and even the leading names would try to get into them if they saw the chance.'

Disappointing on his previous appearances, Bobet rode into Tour legend that year, winning by fourteen minutes, the yellow jersey taken with a magnificent solo ride over the Izoard pass, where defending champion Coppi, who had sat out the race, was among the spectators at the summit. Rolland finished seventh, one of four riders from the France team to finish in the top 10. 'I was actually racing better that year than in 1955 when I finished fifth. I was stronger, but the difference back then was that you needed a good number of things to come together in order to get into the right break and in 1953 it just didn't happen for me. When you did get into the break in those days, you didn't see the peloton again until they came over the line behind you, and there often used to be big gaps between groups. The racing was much more interesting than it is now when the riders are so evenly matched.'

A top 20 finisher again in 1954, when Bobet was an even more convincing victor, Rolland jumped from support role to headliner a year later, when Robinson led the first British team to participate. Prior to the start, the 10 members of the French team signed a loyalty pact committing them to help each other when necessary, although they all understood that Bobet, going for a Tour hat-trick, was the leader. 'We were all there to help him, apart perhaps from Geminiani, who was effectively the second protected rider,' says the Frenchman.

That didn't change after Rolland followed France DS Marcel Bidot's order for his riders to infiltrate any breaks and led in a small group on the second stage in Roubaix to move up to fourth overall. 'There were some cobbles on it although not as many as we would do in Paris-Roubaix. We just did the final few sections, the last fifty kilometres of the Paris-Roubaix course. We didn't have the same sections of cobbles they do today. The Arenberg Forest, for example, wasn't introduced until well after I had retired. But we did have Carrefour de l'Arbre and some of the other bits of pavé that still feature.'

When Bobet won the next stage that finished with the steep climb up into the citadel at Namur, Rolland crept up the standings again, to second place behind Dutchman Wout Wagtmans. On the following stage to Metz, he found his way into the right break again. 'We went clear early on in the stage. There were two of us from the French team in the group, François Mahé and me, and seven others. We missed out on the stage win, but that didn't matter. I knew I was going to be presented with the yellow jersey, but I refused to put it on until the bunch had finished almost 12 minutes behind us and the result became official. I didn't want it to be taken away from me if there was some kind of timing error,' he says. 'It was presented to me by Yvette Horner, the famous accordion player and singer who was just about the only woman on the race and used to perform on top of a vehicle in the publicity caravan. The podium was nothing more than a platform and the ceremony was over in a minute. You'd get the jersey, then ride off in it to your hotel as soon as possible. There weren't

'The jersey handed over at the finish had to be used on the following day's stage'

any press conferences. The journalists would do their interviews in the riders' hotel rooms, which wasn't a problem. I do sympathise with the riders now who have to wait around for so long to fulfil protocol commitments.'

In common with many others who haven't been able to take in the enormity of their achievement straight away, Rolland hung the jersey on a chair at the end of his bed. 'Like today, taking the yellow jersey was a big event, especially if you were a French rider. I know that when I was a kid and used to dream of racing the Tour de France, the idea of having the yellow jersey was quite magical. I wouldn't say it changed my life, but it certainly put something extra in my legs,' he says, cutting away briefly from his account to greet a long-standing customer who has come in to collect a bike that's been repaired. 'Having the yellow jersey did change your status within the bunch. It's like becoming the king of this little planet that is the Tour de France. You do find yourself with a little bit more space in the bunch because the riders have such great respect for it.'

Manufactured then as it is in the modern era by Le Coq Sportif, it was a mix of synthetic fibres and wool, with a collar and pockets on the front, which was the trend at the time, and Henri Desgrange's initials embroidered on the chest. 'It wasn't a fake jersey like those they present on podiums today. The jersey handed over at the finish had to be used on the following day's stage. You had to take care of it. The race organisation used to wash it every evening, which saved you a bit of time as it was one less thing the race leader needed to do.'

More than nine minutes ahead of second-placed Wagtmans on GC, a massive lead by modern standards, Rolland held the jersey for three days before losing it to another Dutch rider, Wim van Est, who was in a nine-man group that breezed in a colossal seventeen minutes ahead of the peloton. But the Frenchman was confident the loss would be fleeting. 'The next stage took us from Thonon-les-Bains to Briançon over the Aravis, Télégraphe and Galibier. I was definitely a lot better as a climber than Van Est and was pretty sure that I was going to take back the jersey, as long as I didn't have any accidents. Charly Gaul had one of those days when no one could get near him, and even though I was more than quarter of an hour behind him, Van Est was even further back and I finished the day seven minutes ahead of him. Bobet was in sixth place on GC, more eleven

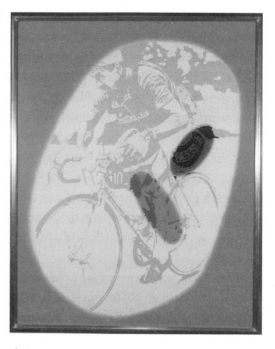

| *Ivan Messac, Le Ravitaillement, 1974, featuring Rolland*

minutes behind me, but as you can see, gaps like that could be turned around quite quickly then. He was happy for me. It suited him just fine to have me in the yellow jersey because it meant that it kept the pressure off him.'

Fourth with Bobet on his wheel and also teammate Geminiani the winner on another big mountain stage through the southern French Alps to Monaco, Rolland's lead extended to eleven minutes. By that point, his status within the French team had changed. He would be the first to be massaged each evening, unless Bobet insisted on taking precedence, in which case Rolland would fall asleep on his bed and get the soigneur to wake him up when he'd finished with his teammate, then fall asleep again on the massage table.

On the rest day in the principality, Bidot held a

Ferdi Kübler and Rolland battle on the slopes of Mont Ventoux in 1955

meeting with his riders to decide on strategy. With a rider in the lead and the defending champion in third, France were in a strong position, but the two-time winner was struggling with a saddle sore. Bidot, the DS in Bobet's team, got the riders to agree that they would wait to see what happened on the stage to Avignon over Mont Ventoux, then reassess. 'Clearly, Louison was there to win it, and that didn't bother me. That said, as long as I was in the contest, nothing prevented me from winning. Louison had to drop me,' says Rolland with a smile.

He describes Ventoux as the climb that's changed the least since his era, in terms of the road surface and the test it sets the riders. Others, he says, have changed dramatically, notably the Izoard, which he last climbed when he was in his late seventies and was 'like a billiard table'. He adds, though, that he wasn't afraid of what lay ahead, despite soaring temperatures. 'Everyone complains about the Ventoux, about how difficult it is, but I never really found that. I wasn't the kind of climber who could follow Charly Gaul or Federico Bahamontes when they accelerated, because you just had to let them get on with it. I just used to find what was a nice rhythm for me, knowing that I was good on the descents as well. I knew that I could often recuperate any losses going downhill.'

That stage, and specifically the climb of the 'Giant of Provence', is most often remembered for the bizarre behaviour of 1951 champion Ferdi Kübler and for France's Jean Malléjac falling unconscious from his bike and having to be revived by the race doctor, Pierre Dumas. Part of the lead group of three riders going onto the infa-

'Le Désert Jaune', a 1975 painting by Bernard Taverner, Kübler digs deep on Ventoux

mous ascent, Kübler readied himself for an attack, Geminiani warning him as he did so, 'Watch out, Ferdi, the Ventoux isn't a climb like any other.' Kübler shot back: 'Ferdi isn't a rider like any other.' Soon after, the Swiss was weaving back and forth across the road in distress. He managed to finish almost half an hour down, after stopping for a beer, restarting in the wrong direction and falling off several times, but quit that night, his Tour career over, uttering, 'Ferdi, he is too old. He is bad. Ferdi has killed himself! Ferdi has killed himself on the Ventoux!' Fortunately, despite being dosed up on amphetamines, he hadn't quite managed that, but Malléjac almost did succumb for the same reason.

After Bobet had pushed on alone halfway up

the Ventoux, Rolland stuck to a steady pace, with Malléjac at his side. 'Bidot had said that he was going to stay with Bobet and that Malléjac had to stay with me because I had the jersey. We both used the same size of bike so if there was any kind of problem he could have given me his. We were still in the forest below Chalet Reynard when he collapsed. He was lucky because the doctor was in the car right behind us, following me because I was in the yellow jersey, and the doctor certainly saved his life. Although it was incredibly hot that day, I actually got over the climb OK. I managed to get back up to the group containing Charly Gaul and actually finished just ahead of him,' Rolland explains. It was later revealed that Luxembourger had also been badly affected by something he'd been provided by his soigneur, who also worked with Malléjac. Tossed off the race, the soigneur was subsequently the subject of a legal complaint made by the Tour doctor on a charge of poisoning.

That evening, Bobet revealed to his younger brother and teammate Jean Bobet that his saddle sore had worsened so much that he thought he would have to abandon the race, although he decided to continue, hoping that a run of easier stages across the Midi would allow the wound to heal a little. He recovered sufficiently to attack on the Col du Portel during the first stage into the Pyrenees, but eased off when three GC rivals joined him but Rolland failed to. When the race returned to high mountains again three days later, the yellow jersey was struggling again. The French team set a high pace from the start in Toulouse to the Aspin, where Geminiani maintained a rapid tempo. When, on the subsequent climb of the Peyresourde, Bobet flew off in pursuit of lone breakaway Gaul, Rolland began to wilt.

'It was on that stage to Saint-Gaudens that I lost the yellow jersey to Bobet. I simply had a bad day. The next day we climbed the Tourmalet and Aubisque and I was good again going over those bigger climbs. I've got no explanation of what happened really. It was just *un jour sans*, just like Simon Yates suffered on the [2018] Tour of Italy. If you don't have any problems then you can go on and win, but if you do, well it's a different story,' he says with a shrug. 'I had plenty of friends in the bunch and a lot of them tried to help me that day. I was getting pushed by the Belgians and the Italians, but the French riders couldn't because they would have been penalised. For some reason, the foreign riders seemed to get away with it.' Despite this show of support, he slipped to second, three minutes behind Bobet. 'The podium didn't count for much, like it does now. Only winning meant something.'

Fighting the effects of a fever, he held second place until the final time trial on the penultimate day, which he rode against doctor's orders. He conceded another nine minutes and dropped to fifth. He was, he confesses, disappointed with the way he had been treated. 'I didn't get any presents from the French team and said as much to Bobet and "Gem". If they had really ridden in support of me I could have won the Tour, despite that day of weakness. But in order to have got that support would have required Bobet not being part of the team, and, as I've already said, Bobet had been clear on his intentions right from the start. On the other hand, if someone had said to me before the start that I would wear the yellow jersey for twelve days and finish fifth, I would have signed for it with both hands! After all I was a good rider, but not a star.'

A year later, the Tour provided an extraordinary counterpoint to Rolland's tale of the little guy flirting with victory in sport's greatest race but eventually being reminded of his place within the competitive hierarchy. Bobet had declared after he secured his hat-trick of wins that he wouldn't defend the title, confessing that his powers were on the wane. His runner-up, Belgium's Jean Brankart, was touted as a possible successor, as were Gaul and Bahamontes, the two outstanding climbers of the era. Geminiani got the nod as France's leader,

with Rolland, Malléjac, Gilbert Bauvin and Jean Fores-
tier as wild card options. However, although the title
was claimed by a home rider, it went not to a member
of the national team, but to Roger Walkowiak, a late
call-up for Nord-Est-Centre and indisputably the most
unexpected and underappreciated winner of the
yellow jersey.

He secured it without winning a single stage,
giving rise to the designation '*un Tour à la Walkowiak*'
to describe a race lacking panache and the stardust
of big names. Humble, fragile and one of the least
talented of Tour's winners, Walkowiak never came to
terms with his success, with the suggestion that he was
a usurper. When he died in February 2017, *L'Équipe*'s
Philippe Brunel wrote in a beautifully contemplative
and respectful obituary that, 'unfortunately his life
was nothing less than a long misunderstanding, of
suffering aggravated by an acute feeling of persecu-
tion, by a tendency towards sentimentality, by tearful
outbursts. Because Walko often used to be reduced
to tears, his mind lost in his memories or in the folds
of his beautiful yellow jersey, the trophy he was most
proud of, that weighed so heavily on him and which he
was sometimes ashamed of.' Describing Walkowiak as
'history's condemned man', Brunel asked, 'How can
the enigmatic winner of the 1956 Tour de France... be
restored to legendary status, above all controversy?'

For most of Walkowiak's peers, that status has
always been recognised. For Brian Robinson, the
Frenchman was a brave and talented rider who saw
his chance and seized it, and should be lauded for
that. 'He saw his opportunity, took it and deserved it,'
says the Yorkshireman. Rolland is of the same mind.
He acknowledges that if he had managed to hold on
in 1955, his success might have been dismissed in a

*Roger Walkowiak takes a lap of honour
round Paris' Parc des Princes in 1956*

'Because Walko often used to be reduced to tears, his mind lost in his memories or in the folds of his beautiful yellow jersey, the trophy he was most proud of, that weighed so heavily on him and which he was sometimes ashamed of'

similar fashion. 'I didn't manage to pull off what "Walko" achieved. I was better than him, and I say that honestly, without underestimating him. But he did exactly what was necessary to win the Tour de France. He was a gentle boy, Roger, who received a lot of criticism afterwards. The expression "un Tour à la Walko" is unbefitting,' he asserts.

He was born and raised Montluçon, where his Polish father, who had come to work in steel mill, met and married his French mother. As a teenager, Walkowiak left school to take up an apprenticeship as a lathe operator. Encouraged by a friend, he began to devote his free time to cycle racing. He turned pro in 1949 after finishing his military service, but another two years passed before he began to make an impact. Jean Bidot, elder brother of Marcel and manager of the French team in the early 1950s, was one of the first to notice him, declaring, 'This boy reminds me of a Bobet. The resemblance is striking: the same speed on the bike, the same physical power, even the same style on the climbs.'

A Tour debutant and finisher in 1951, he lacked the leadership qualities of a Bobet and seemed destined for a career as an unassuming domestique. Yet there were occasional signs that he had more quality than that, notably the 1955 edition of the Critérium du Dauphiné Libéré, where he proved a revelation, harrying Bobet through the Alps and on the Ventoux before taking second place behind France's great champion. Released by Gitane at the end of that season, he hawked himself around the other squads, eventually persuading fellow *Auvergnat* Geminiani to offer him a place his Saint-Raphaël team, racing *à la musette* – for a bike, two sets of kit and enough money to cover his social security payments. A stage win at the Vuelta riding for the French national team earned him selection, at the very last moment, for a fourth Tour appearance with the Nord-Est-Centre managed by Sauveur Ducazeaux, a Tour stage-winner twenty years before.

Robinson, too, had a late call-up to the Tour for the Luxembourg-Mixed team led by pre-race favourite Gaul and managed by Nicolas Frantz, a two-time champion in the inter-war years. On the opening stage, from Reims to Liège, the Yorkshireman and Walkowiak featured in the break, Robinson staying with the pace to finish third on the line behind French sprinter André Darrigade, while 'Walko' was dropped and fell back to the bunch. Both riders continued to feature over the next few days, the Englishman holding his place well up in the top ten, the Frenchman a few places behind in a race conducted at a frantic pace because no one could impose any control. Most were looking to Gaul to provide this, but his British teammate could see that the Luxembourger wasn't capable of doing so. 'Quiet and shy by nature, I think he became unnerved by the unceasing attention from reporters, photographers and radio men, and this must undoubtedly have affected his form,' Robinson wrote in his race diary, serialised in the magazine *Coureur*.

Most days, Gaul could be found sitting at the rear of the peloton, unconcerned about what was happening at the other end of it, which was plenty. Breakaways were dominating to the extent that even sprinters such as Darrigade and Miguel Poblet were looking to get into them. The day after Robinson had written that diary entry in Lorient, the Tour took a significant twist when a group of thirty-one riders, featuring only Bauvin from the among likely GC contenders, escaped, gaining eighteen minutes on the bunch on the line in Angers. As the highest placed of the breakaway riders, Walkowiak inherited the yellow jersey from Darrigade.

Looking back to that day, Rolland draws a comparison with World Championship races where riders have allegiances to national and trade teams, the latter more covert perhaps, but significant because they pay salaries throughout the year. 'Geminiani had teammates scattered through lots of different squads, and that had an influence on the way the race panned out,' explains the Frenchman, then on Bobet's BP-Hutchinson roster. 'I was in the French team with Geminiani when the break that featured Walkowiak went clear. I can remember saying to Gem, "Should I try to get into that break?" But he was like, "No no, no, no, it's fine." The thing was that there were plenty of riders in it from Geminiani's team including Walkowiak, Bauvin, Louis Caput and Jean Dotto.

'I did make an effort to bridge across and got to within 200 metres of the break before my legs gave up on me. What a shame that was, but that's the way it goes. I just lacked a little bit of juice and made my move a little bit too late. I should have asked Geminiani about it earlier because he really knew what was going to happen every day, and by the time I did ask him it was a little bit too late.'

Nord-Est-Centre DS Ducazeaux quickly realised that the timid Walkowiak, who preferred to avoid taking responsibility, could claim the title in the right circumstances. 'I believe that Roger has a good chance of winning the Tour,' *L'Équipe*'s Pierre Chany reported him saying to his confidants. 'But

we mustn't tell him that, because it will scare him. We have to make him realise that he is the strongest. When he becomes aware of the possibility that's presenting itself, the job will be all but done.'

The action continued in the same frenzied manner. The only certainty each day was the speed would be high, often averaging more than forty kilometres per hour, and a breakaway would go the distance. 'You had to be very attentive. You had to watch all the time who was going clear, what was going on, whether you could let somebody escape and if you did how much time to allow them,' says Rolland. 'We always used to have a guy who was in the break at the front and would be watching who was up there with him. Sometimes you would have the numbers of key riders marked on your arm in pen or on your bars, just to keep a check on those riders who you couldn't allow to escape and you had to watch.'

Walkowiak and his teammates certainly weren't strong enough to enforce any discipline in such frenetic circumstances. He held the lead for three stages and was then happy to relinquish it, his spell in the spotlight seemingly over. However, as Dutchman Gerrit Voorting, France's Darrigade for the third time in the race, Belgium's Jan Adriaensens and Wout Wagtmans took turns in yellow, 'Walko' continued to hover in the top ten, moving up to second on the first day in the Alps over the Izoard, Montgenèvre and Sestriere passes to Turin.

Ducazeaux's canny strategy of letting others carry the burden of the yellow jersey while at the same time quietly persuading his leader that he could still win the race received its dividend when the Tour returned to France. After crossing

Mont Cenis, next up was the long ascent of the Croix de Fer. 'It was not the gradient so much as the surface which made it tough; at home such a road would certainly be marked "unsuitable for motors",' Robinson noted in his diary, adding that his seventh place on the stage was the best day of racing of his whole career, further gloss provided by Gaul winning in Grenoble.

Wagtmans lost ground on the Croix de Fer and his grip on the yellow jersey on the short but viciously steep Col du Luitel. 'Walkowiak must have ridden magnificently, for he had hardly left Gaul all day and only succumbed to the "Angel" on the Luitel,' Robinson wrote of the new leader, whose fifth place finishes on the two hardest days in the Alps were his best of the race. 'Any other year, and the Tour would have been written off to the man wearing the *maillot jaune* at the end of the last big mountain stage. Not this year, however!' added the Briton of the next stage to Saint-Étienne. It began easily enough, the Yorkshireman having time at one point to stop at a roadside fruit stall and grab a basket of peaches. 'Among my customers (who still haven't paid the bill!) were [Stan] Ockers, Charly (he took two) and Wagtmans.'

The picnic ended when Walkowiak got caught up in a crash and second-placed Gilbert Bauvin immediately accelerated. The unwritten rule of not attacking the yellow jersey when he's on the ground had yet to be dreamed up, so Walkowiak had to depend instead on his own strength to reel in his rival. Thwarted on that occasion by the yellow jersey, Bauvin did gain significant ground the next day in a seventy-three-kilometre time trial, but Walkowiak hung to win the title, one minute twenty-five seconds ahead of his Saint-Raphaël

teammate.

The Frenchman's wasn't a swashbuckling victory, remarkable for outstanding solo victories or demonstrations of crushing power, but it was well deserved and, initially, highly praised. Double Tour champion André Leducq declared simply, 'There's never been a Tour as exciting as this one.' In *L'Équipe*, Jacques Marchard, stated, 'Walkowiak might have taken advantage of internal rivalries among the national teams, but knowing how to exploit that was a good tactic. Little "Walko" ended up beating the big boys, therefore he was one of the big boys himself. He might have been the winner of a Tour without great stars, but he was the winner of a great Tour, which, in our eyes, is even better.' In the same paper, Antoine Blondin declared simply, 'Walko was the bravest, the most constant, the most consistent.' Tour director Jacques Goddet, who later described the 1956 Tour as his favourite, also paid homage to him, writing, 'Walko's case highlights what human society needs to see more of, the expansion of the right to accession.'

Yet, all too quickly, Walkowiak's star fell. A far from charismatic personality who failed to make a connection with bike fans, he secured comparatively few contracts for the post-Tour criteriums. Promoted to the French national team in 1957, his position as leader was assumed by Jacques Anquetil, stylish, popular, brilliant and, significantly, unquestionably French. 'For everyone, I was nothing more than a factory worker, a Pole during a period when there weren't that many foreigners in the peloton,' Walkowiak said after his career had petered out with barely another result of note, his two final Tour appearances finishing with an abandon in 1957 and seventy-fifth place

WINNING THE TOUR WITHOUT WINNING A STAGE

YEAR	WINNER		MARGIN
1922	Firmin Lambot	( )	+ 1hr 42' 54"
1956	Roger Walkowiak*	( )	+ 1' 25"
1960	Gastone Nencini	( )	+ 5' 02"
1966	Lucien Aimar	( )	+ 1' 07"
1990	Greg LeMond		+ 2' 16"
2006	Óscar Pereiro		+ 32"
2017	Chris Froome		+ 54"

*Of these, Roger Walkowiak is the only rider to have never won a stage of the Tour de France in his career.

a year later. In his obituary of the 1956 Tour winner, Brunel suggests that some of the blame for Walkowiak's dismissal as a Tour legend lay with his directeur sportif, Sauveur Ducazeaux, who was widely lauded for his tactical genius and pulled attention away from his rider, encouraging the injustice and misunderstanding.

This perspective persisted. Reflecting on his first Tour win in 1983, when he inherited the lead after Pascal Simon finally yielded to a broken shoulder blade, Laurent Fignon said he took umbrage in the final days because 'a few commentators had begun to talk about "a Tour of second-raters", a "Tour à la Walkowiak" – a reference to the 1956 winner Roger Walkowiak, who owed his victory to a lucky early break. I didn't like that in the slightest, but I kept my head.' Praising Fignon's convincing victory in that edition's final time trial, L'Équipe's Chany suggested that, 'An average performance in this contre la montre would have revived memories of recent events – Hinault's

withdrawal, Simon's crash – and the temptation to draw parallels with flukish wins of the past would have been too strong. Laurent Fignon's image would have suffered.' The allusion to Walkowiak is unmistakeable.

Embittered by his treatment, Walkowiak returned to Montluçon following his retirement in 1960. He ran a café, then returned to manual work in a factory, torn between pride and loathing for his yellow jersey. In an era when France produced so many winners, his success was, says Brunel, characterised disparagingly as 'un Tour à la Walko', a triumph lacking heroic feats and decided by 'une échappée bidon', a breakaway on the sly. 'Journalists have tended to talk down the quality of his success and, as a result, the public has picked up the idea that Walko wasn't a proper winner,' 1966 champion Lucien Aimar told Brunel. 'Often what was said about Roger Walkowiak lacked elegance and those from his generation always tried to re-establish the truth.'

Amid all that sniping, there is one certainty about the Tour winner that didn't get properly applied to Walkowiak, perhaps because so much credit was given to Ducazeaux's string-pulling. Ask any Tour man who will take the yellow jersey and the same mantra-like response is all but guaranteed: the strongest rider always wins. Yet there is a tendency, both within but particularly outside the peloton, to associate 'strength' solely with physical prowess, to forget the necessity for mental fortitude and tactical insight that every champion has also depended on. As Brian Robinson witnessed and Antonin Rolland confirms, during his moment of grace that July Walkowiak saw an opportunity and seized it. Gilbert Bauvin and Charly Gaul may have been stronger in the leg, but 'Walko' outwitted them.

Thomas Voeckler, another racer whose potency came more from his head than from his legs, makes precisely this point when talking about his own career in *Secrets de Maillots Jaunes*. 'In this milieu, we all listen to the guys who win. I used to win, of course, but that was largely down to the mental aspect and strategy. I very rarely triumphed because I was evidently the strongest, and that upsets people,' says the Frenchman who wore the yellow jersey for ten days on two occasions and almost served up his own '*Tour à la Walko*' in 2011.

Partly as a result of that race, another where no one rider or team was able to subdue the rest of the pack and an underdog nearly triumphed, the perception of Walkowiak's victory is changing, although unfortunately too late for him to be able to appreciate this. Back in 1956, two-time Tour champion André Leducq declared, 'There's never been a Tour as exciting as this one,' and Tour director Christian Prudhomme clearly agrees, regularly

evoking his desire for a *un Tour à la Walko*, a race that is open and packed with twists and turns, where the winner could emerge from anywhere. He talks of upsetting the established scenarios and tinkers with the route in order to bring this about.

'Everything is so precisely calculated nowadays,' says Rolland, who remains an avid fan of racing. 'They let a break go clear, let them have an advantage of one, two, maybe three minutes and that's enough, then leave them hanging out there until the point whether want to reel them back in. That's how it is with the earpieces these days. It's no longer the riders who are in control but the team directors in the cars behind them.' Although many riders and directors would argue this isn't the case, Rolland's contention that the Tour has become predictable is legitimate and widely held. There is a clear danger that a race that lasts for six hours but is often almost without incident until the final one will ultimately lose its audience.

Prudhomme has been endeavouring to change this, but the first week of the 2018 race, when line-ups had been cut from nine to eight riders, supported Rolland's complaint that the racing has become too predictable. Romain Bardet has suggested cutting the teams further still to six riders and including more racing on gravel roads. Some insist that reducing the riders' access to the technology of earpieces and power meters is the answer, others that 'financial doping' needs to be addressed.

As that debate continues, it is worth reflecting on Brian Robinson's words towards the end of his 1956 Tour diary. 'I certainly hope the 1957 Tour will be as lively a race as it was this time, for I much prefer to be "on the move" the whole time, rather than have periods of promenade sandwiched between flat-out sprints. And the public and the promoters – and even the journalists! – prefer it that way too.'

Vive le Tour à la Walkowiak!

CHRIS FROOME
TOUR DE FRANCE
2015

14

BLEU, BLANC, JAUNE

Le Maillot Jaune

Louison Bobet 1950

THE FRENCH CHAMPION'S JERSEY THAT BOBET WON
AHEAD OF ANTONIN ROLLAND, BOTH OF THEM
FUTURE YELLOW JERSEYS

LE TOUR DE FRANCE 57

Jacques Anquetil fera dans le Tour des débuts attendus,
et déjà il a disputé (en souriant) le maillot jaune à Louis Bobet.

Dans ce numéro :

LA CARTE
DU TOUR

Anquetil and Bobet fight over a yellow jersey;
they finished their careers with eighty-four between them

France & the Yellow Jersey

'**The first time I saw** the Tour de France, I was standing at the side of the road with my parents, my brothers and my sister in 1970. I was 10 years old and we were on the Col de Cou in Haute-Savoie. I remember very clearly the fact that I didn't see Raymond Poulidor pass but I did see the yellow jersey, Eddy Merckx. I can still remember that day clearly.'

The words are Tour director Christian Prudhomme's, but the majority of France's sixty-seven million people will have a similar tale of the day they were first taken to watch the Tour pass, the thrill of seeing the publicity caravan, the glimpse they got of the *maillot jaune*. It is an indelible part of French sporting and cultural life, the yellow evoking unforgettable memories. 'It is colour of France in the summer, of the sun, the beaches, the sunflowers, the warmth,' says

The wait for another French champion continues

LCL director-general Michel Mathieu. 'It's associated with holidays, with children enjoying themselves, with families being together and having a good time. It's luminous.'

The Tour has mattered immensely to the French public since its very first edition in 1903, when the race journeyed around a country where the bicycle was becoming an instrument of liberation and mass transportation. From the off, it was a popular sporting sensation, but it quickly gained a significance beyond mere entertainment, initially as a unifying force within a nation that had suffered a humbling defeat in the Franco-Prussian War three decades earlier. It had been described by Henri Desgrange that first year as 'a ring that

goes right around France', and became exactly that in 1906 when the Tour ventured into the Prussian-held Moselle region around Metz 'in order to symbolically re-appropriate the "lost provinces"', as the race director put it. In 1919, just weeks after Alsace and Lorraine had been ceded back to France by the Treaty of Versailles, Desgrange celebrated this restoration of *L'Hexagone*, the six-sided shape of continental France, by including Alsace and its capital Strasbourg on the route, yellow jersey Eugène Christophe and the other survivors of that race receiving a huge ovation as they entered the province for the first time.

By the 1920s, the Tour had found a place in France's national mythology, becoming an event

| *Adulation for Anquetil, the five-time winner*

that marked the passing of the year and that was followed closely even by those who had no interest in sport. Offering what historian Richard Holt described as 'a mobile spectacle for a widely scattered rural population unable to support other forms of professional spectator sport', it generated huge interest and coverage. When, in 1930, the race director pulled off what he described as his '*trois glorieuses*' – the introduction of national teams, the publicity caravan and radio reporting from the race – the combination of a run of yellow jersey success for home riders and more immediate reporting of the action meant that, 'Henri Desgrange had finally managed to paint France "blue, white and yellow" every summer during the

inter-war years,' according to Jean-Luc Boeuf and Yves Léonard in *La République du Tour de France*.

The election in 1936 of the Popular Front government and the subsequent introduction of paid holidays further cemented the race's status. Spectator numbers each July rose considerably, an increasing quantity travelling from one part of the country to another to see the action, the mountain stages becoming a favourite destination. Speaking in 1938 following his retirement, Desgrange reflected on what he had achieved, telling *Paris-Soir*, 'The Tour de France offers a lesson into precious things, not because of the qualities it demands of its competitors, but because it is, more than anything, a wonderful occasion to travel across, to get to know and therefore to love France, a magnificent, welcoming, vibrant, adorable country… Our racers are the little missionaries for this annual crusade.'

Beyond the touristic, it also retained its place as a unifying force, helping to shape public opinion, contributing to what Desgrange had described as 'patriotic pacifism', a concept that was widely held during the inter-war years, especially among those like him who had fought in the First World War. The Tour director offered a clear example of this in 1932 when Kurt Stöpel became the first German rider to wear the yellow jersey. The Tour director praised him as a 'brave boy… who is the beautiful kind of roadman,' and said that when he saw him battling with André Leducq, 'I thought back to those nights in the war when, in an unstable trench, I submitted to the disciplined assaults of the enemy troops. And that was truly what we call war! But if we'd done a little bit of sport together, we would undoubtedly have understood, admired and loved each other more.'

Bearing in mind the turn political life was taking place in Germany at that point, this attitude might seem naïve, but it captured the general desire within France to avoid another conflagration and the huge loss of life likely to be result of it. The sentiment was reiterated by Jacques Goddet on the eve of the first post-Second World War race in 1947. 'Although our country, broken by so many tough years… dealing with the convulsions that beset it, the Tour de France, this great popular celebration, is regaining its place. The Tour is a message of joy and confidence. Its existence evokes the idea of peace in intense fashion,' he wrote in *L'Équipe*.

During the *Les Trentes Glorieuses*, the thirty years following the war when the French economy and living standards grew rapidly, the Tour enjoyed its golden age. Largely unconcerned and unaffected by doping, cycling's position as the country's national sport was highlighted by the fervour generated over the battle for the yellow jersey each summer. Its champions were mythical, beginning with Gino Bartali and Fausto Coppi and continuing with Louison Bobet, Jacques Anquetil and Eddy Merckx. Filling the midsummer gap in the sports calendar, its association with family holidays, sun and celebration broadened as it sought out popular destinations.

Compared to these legendary multiple Tour winners, Bobet may not have the same stellar reputation among foreign fans, but he had particular resonance in France, where, thanks to the spread and popularity of television broadcasts, he replaced Marcel Cerdan as the favourite of the masses after the boxer was killed in a plane crash in 1949. According to Boeuf and Léonard, the Breton was 'the incarnation of a France that is being rebuilt, methodical and laborious, borne by the dynamic of the Glorious Thirty.' When television coverage extended to daily transmission of the Tour action in the late 1950s, Anquetil took over Bobet's mantle, his handsome looks and elegance on the bike encapsulated the nation's sense of progression and success.

Yet, even as the Norman became the pre-eminent Tour racer of his generation, the French were adopting a more nuanced attitude towards the yellow jersey and its wearer, as a consequence of television's more complex perspective into racing

France teammates Louison Bobet and Jacques Anquetil in discussion during the 1958 Tour

and its kings of the road. The preference for a plucky loser and the idea of a glorious defeat had long been apparent. Eugène Christophe encapsulated this idea wholly, as did René Vietto to much the same extent. But it became unmistakeably apparent in the adoration of Raymond Poulidor. His standing with the French public became so high that rival riders both resented him for it and made him pay for it, attacking when he was out of position or had fallen. 'Poulidor is not loved by his peers because he is loved too much by the public,' Jean Bobet wrote in *Le Monde* when 'Poupou' crashed in the 1968 Tour. But these setbacks only fed his popularity. While Anquetil represented a France that was advancing, his rival was the face of those who had been left behind during the Glorious Thirty, often in the depths of the countryside, where there was stagnation in the small towns and villages who had lost their young generation to the cities. Although Poulidor enjoyed a highly successful career, his performances at the Tour and especially his unconsummated flirtation with the yellow jersey chimed with those who felt forgotten or that they had been the victim of some fate that was beyond their means to control.

The term 'poulidorien' emerged from this, describing people, teams, companies or even countries that struggle as others waltz away with the major prizes and rewards. Since the oil crisis of the mid-1970s, France has been affected in this way, the economic dynamism of the Glorious Thirty gradually eroded in the face of the advance of new and more competitive commercial powers. At the same time, it has struggled to define its political place in a more fragmented and globalised world. It became, said former French president Valéry Giscard d'Estaing, 'a middling power'. In 2002, *Le Monde* claimed, 'The country is suffering from a Poulidor complex', the story suggesting that French companies were less disciplined than those in Japan. 'It's a permanent lament of a protectionist France that doesn't know how to sell, withdrawing into itself and not knowing how to evolve, threatened by globalisation, relying on a cultural exemption that is threatened, always behind someone like the cyclist Raymond Poulidor used to be.'

Strikingly, the cycling analogy also reflects the country's relationship with cycling and particularly the Tour de France since Bernard Hinault

completed France's last success in 1985. The sport has globalised, bringing in riders and teams from North and South America, Australia, Asia and Africa, as well as from new two-wheeled powers

'**They would love to wear the *maillot jaune* but they're scared of it at the same time. In French we would say it's *une attraction-répulsion*'**

across Europe, including Great Britain and, following the isolationism and introspection of the Franco era, Spain. At the same time, French cycling hasn't evolved. Doping scandals have affected the sport's popularity, cutting the influx of riders at the grassroots and reducing the talent pool.

It's become increasingly evident, too, that producing a rider capable of winning the Tour is, to a large degree, the result of good luck. There aren't that many Hinaults and Fignons around, especially given growing competition for young talent from other sports. Football has long usurped cycling's place as France's national game, while rugby, tennis, basketball and even more niche sports also exert a strong pull on budding athletes. It would have been interesting, for instance, to have seen how Martin Fourcade might have fared on two wheels in light of his multiple Olympic and world titles in an endurance sport like biathlon. At the same time, though, France's failure to produce a single rider with the ability to contend for the yellow jersey indicates systemic flaws as well. 'We haven't had an athlete since Fignon and Hinault with the right qualities to win the Tour,' Jean-François Bernard underlined in William Fotheringham's *The Badger*. 'For many years, we've had no riders who are capable of winning time trials in the Tour. We have super climbers, no problem there, but no time triallists. Who's the last French rider to win a long time trial in the Tour? It's me... beyond belief!'

There is also additional pressure on the home riders, above all those with credible Grand Tour credentials, to end this 'Tour complex'. From Bernard onwards, several have been anointed 'the next Hinault', from Luc Leblanc and Jean-Philippe Dojwa through to Jérôme Coppel and Pierre Rolland. But it's a heavy label to carry. The generation that has emerged in the current decade has borne it most adeptly, but each has had the same deficit in his skillset when it comes to time trialling and has been to some extent affected by the psychological baggage that Hinault always dealt with so comfortably. 'It's the focus for all of the riders' fears, obsessions and neuroses,' says *Libération*'s Pierre Carrey. 'If you speak about the yellow jersey to Romain Bardet or Thibaut Pinot, for instance, it is terrifying for them. They talk about the Tour de France being too big, about it crushing them. They would love to wear the *maillot jaune* but they're scared of it at the same time. In French we would say it's une attraction-répulsion.'

A stage winner on his debut in 2012 and a very distant third overall at the 2014 Tour, Pinot has looked particularly burdened by the expectations placed on him, acknowledging at one point that he found it difficult to deal with that pressure and that the Tour had become '*un passage obligé*' for him, a race in which he's obliged to participate. In 2016, fresh from victory in the national time trial championship that appeared to signal his arrival as a very credible contender for the yellow jersey, he crumbled on the first high-mountain stage and quit halfway through the race, debilitated by a virus. 'For the public, the Tour is the only race that counts,' he said the following season, as he prepared to go against that flow by making his debut at the Giro d'Italia. 'I don't ascribe to the logic that has it: "I'm French, so I have to do the Tour,"' he stated. More content in relative anonymity than in the direct glare of the public eye, he's looked happier when racing in Italy or Spain, where his performances attract far less attention, even when they have been very worthy of note.

Bardet, too, has toyed with the Giro as a

competitive distraction, acknowledging that its route often suits his qualities as a climber far better than the Tour. However, as the undisputed leader of a French team, he has found it harder to escape the Tour's magnetic pull, especially since finishing runner-up in 2016 and third a year later. He's acknowledged that his relationship with the race has a love-hate aspect. It has made him popular, given him huge confidence in his ability, and is essentially what motivates him. 'Battling for the yellow jersey is what drives me on, I've been working for that for years,' he said at the end of 2018. But the race does, he acknowledges, always takes so much from him physically and, above all, mentally. 'The feeling of oppression is the hardest thing to deal with. I find it hard to get a moment to myself. Everything always reminds you of the Tour. In the morning, you can't take a step without someone talking to you about the stage the day before and the one just ahead, you're constantly connected. You open your phone and you're delighted to have a message from the mates that you've not seen for ages, but what do they talk to you about? The Tour. Not the barbecue you'll be having with them in two weeks' time,' he said during the 2016 race.

The spearhead of the French challenge, Bardet admits he can't devote much thought to what the yellow jersey and overall victory might mean, that it would only become a distraction if he did dwell on it. Naturally, foreign riders are getting this same question regularly too, but not usually until they become genuine contenders for the *maillot jaune*. Few have to deal with the urgency edging towards desperation that means that any French rider has to deal with when their performances suggest even the slightest possibility of Tour-winning potential, Julian Alaphilippe, Pierre Latour and David Gaudu emerging as the latest in the firing line. 'It does have more impact on French riders, because the whole country is looking to see a performance from one

'People from outside France are drawn to the Tour because of its quintessentially French qualities, and having French cyclists performing well is part of that picture'

of its own,' says Cofidis team manager Cédric Vasseur. 'The fans are hoping and expecting that a French rider will be in yellow. They desperately want it to happen, for that rider to emerge.'

Thomas Voeckler, who, like Vasseur, savoured being in yellow and got everything he could from the experience to the point where it seemed he might even end the French drought, his performance producing hysteria on roadsides and in the French media, insists there is no way that riders like Bardet and Pinot can escape the inescapable pull of the Tour, that they are caught within that schematic and should embrace it rather than considering ways to get out of it. 'Their career path is set and hinges on the Tour. They have the ability to do it, the opportunity and the public are waiting for them to do so,' he said following his retirement from racing at the end of 2016. 'The public hasn't fallen out of love but there isn't the same passion there was when [Richard] Virenque was monopolising the polka-dot jersey. But, if a French rider were to take the yellow jersey on a mountain stage and defend it into Paris, raising his profile in the process, it would unblock all kinds of things. It would be like the great era of French cycling once again, Hinault's era. And it is achievable.'

While not as convinced as Voeckler that France has as yet unearthed a Tour de France champion, *Libération*'s Pierre Carrey agrees that this scenario is long overdue and much needed. 'I think there'll be a huge shock within France when a home rider wins the Tour again. It is something that has become quite foreign to French people, almost alien to them because no French rider has worn it into Paris for such a long while, becoming something that the French people don't associate with their own riders, almost something that they don't think the home riders should have,' he suggests. 'Maybe when it does happen the perception of the yellow jersey being associated with cheating, with doping, will change, as would the whole of French cycle sport. I just hope that the roots between the

top of the sport and its foundations haven't been broken too much already for it to happen.'

Although the return of those glory days primarily concerns fans and racers in France, it also matters beyond *L'Hexagone* because French success in the sport's showcase event is a key part of the race's plot and crucial to its ongoing vitality. As William Fotheringham highlights, 'Because the Tour is rooted permanently in France, French success enhances it, bringing out fans, bringing in sponsors, oiling the wheels of officialdom.'

Given the extent by which the Tour dwarfs every other event on the calendar in terms of its audience and significance, any dimming of that picture could have repercussions throughout cycle sport.

Unfortunately, there are signs that the Tour's lustre has been fading despite the pep the new generation of home riders have supplied. 'This Tour was a rough ride,' race director Christian Prudhomme confessed at the end of the 2018 race, citing the salbutamol affair that beset defending champion Chris Froome until just days before the start and resulted in the Briton being heckled and booed as the race criss-crossed the country, a protest by farmers in the Pyrenees that blocked the road and resulted in the peloton being inadvertently tear-gassed, and the 'idiot on Alpe d'Huez' who knocked 2014 winner Vincenzo Nibali off his bike and out of the race. As the Tour lurched from one ugly incident to the next, the racing failed to offer much of a distraction thanks a soporific opening week followed by two more where Sky's stranglehold on their rivals was as tight as ever.

With the sporting world, and especially

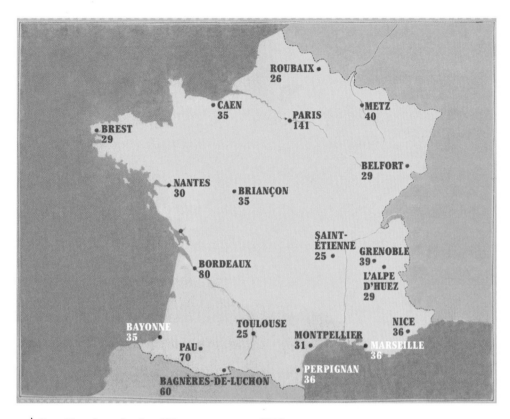

| Some cities and towns have hosted 25 or more stage starts and finishes

champions France, in the grip of a post-World Cup hangover and fears of terrorist attack very apparent, spectator numbers at the roadside looked smaller. On Alpe d'Huez, they were noticeably lower, most evidently at 'Dutch Corner', where heavy security completely neutered the traditional mayhem and numbers were in the hundreds rather than the thousands. Heavily armed police were very visible at starts and finishes and elite unites ready to respond to potential threat were hidden away in side streets. Bag searches, sniffer dogs and the deployment of concrete road blocks added to the sense of an event under siege and detracted from the festival atmosphere for which the Tour has always been renowned. TV viewing figures were down too, and not only France where the victorious exploits of *Les Bleus* in Russia were an obvious distraction. In Italy they collapsed with Nibali's downfall, and even in Britain they dropped a surprising 15 per cent despite Geraint Thomas's success.

It didn't help that at the end of a World Cup lauded as one of the most open and exciting in recent memory, the battle for the yellow jersey went the other way. Prudhomme and his route director Thierry Gouvenou have endeavoured to be innovative in an attempt to shake up established scenarios, but Sky have always found the

UNE ÉTAPE DU TOUR DE FRANCE

Cette année, les départs sont donnés aux heures qui permettent au public de nos provinces d'y assister. Scènes pittoresques. Avant l'étape, les coureurs se rafraîchissent. Antonin Magne signe la carte que lui tend une admiratrice. Leducq est à ses côtés. Les équipes sont prêtes. Tous vont s'élancer à la conquête du "Tour".

The front cover of *L'Illustré du Petit Journal* shows 'A Stage of the Tour de France'.

The caption explains: *'This year the stage starts are taking place at times that allow the public in our provinces to attend them, producing some eye-catching scenes. Before the stage, the riders are having a little refreshment. Antonin Magne is signing a card that an admirer has handed to him. Leducq is beside him. The teams are ready. They are all set for the conquest of the "Tour".'*

André Leducq won the Tour in 1930 and in 1932. Here, he is part of the Alcyon-Dunlop team but his two Tour victories came wearing the tricolor jersey of the national team

*Andre Leducq's bib from the 1932 Tour. He took six stage wins
and spent a total of nineteen days in yellow*

NATIONAL PRIDE: RANKING COUNTRIES BY THEIR RIDERS' YELLOW JERSEYS

RANK	COUNTRY	YELLOW JERSEYS	TOUR WINS	MOST RECENT RIDER	MOST RECENT	DIFFERENT HOLDERS
1	**France**	709	36	**Tony Gallopin**	**2014, Stage 9**	94
2	Belgium	434	18	Greg Van Avermaet	2018, Stage 10	60
3	**Italy**	210	10	**Fabio Aru**	**2017, Stage 13**	29
4	Spain	135	12	Alberto Contador	2009, Stage 21	12
5	**Great Britain**	101	6	**Geraint Thomas**	**2018, Stage 21**	8
6	Luxembourg	96	5	Andy Schleck	2011, Stage 19	10
7	**Germany**	75	1	**Tony Martin**	**2015, Stage 6**	15
8	Switzerland	74	2	Fabian Cancellara	2015, Stage 2	9
9	**Netherlands**	72	2	**Erik Breukink**	**1989, prologue**	17
10	Denmark	43	1	Michael Rasmussen	2007, Stage 16	6
11	**Australia**	33	1	**Rohan Dennis**	**2015, Stage 1**	7
12	United States	26	3	George Hincapie	2006, Stage 1	3
13	**Canada**	15	0	**Steve Bauer**	**1990, Stage 9**	2
14	Norway	10	0	Thor Hushovd	2011, Stage 8	1
15	**Ireland**	7	1	**Stephen Roche**	**1987, Stage 25**	3
16	Estonia	6	0	Jaan Kirsipuu	1999, Stage 7	1
=17	**Colombia**	4	0	**Fernando Gaviria**	**2018, Stage 1**	2
=17	Portugal	4	0	Acácio da Silva	1989, Stage 4	1
=17	**Slovakia**	4	0	**Peter Sagan**	**2018, Stage 2**	1
20	Ukraine	3	0	Serhiy Honchar	2006, Stage 9	1
=21	**Poland**	2	0	**Lech Piasecki**	**1987, Stage 2**	1
=21	Russia	2	0	Eugeni Berzin	1996, Stage 8	1
=21	**South Africa**	2	0	**Daryl Impey**	**2013, Stage 7**	1
24	Austria	1	0	Max Bulla	1931, Stage 2	1

key to negotiate these obstacles. 'It's a shame that the teams only think about defending what they have,' lamented Prudhomme. 'No one seems willing to risk in order to win. We want more fight, more suspense.' With the performance difference between riders so narrow, and especially so at the Tour, which showcases the cream at the top of the sport, changing the route is not a panacea. Even if Sky are vanquished or disappear, their conquerors are likely to be no more than a variation or upgrade to the British team's model, which had already been moulded over previous decades by other super strong squads.

'How many people are captivated?' wondered UCI president Davd Lappartient at the end of the 2018 race. 'In football, you get these extraordinary comebacks, but we don't have much of that on the Tour France.' To bring that about, cycling's major stakeholders need to agree fundamental modifications to racing, or at least to its premier event, to restore that vital element of unpredictability. Banning race radios, power meters and cutting team sizes more drastically have all been cited as possible cures, but each of them has been knocked down in one quarter or another as gimmicks and short-term fixes that will inflict harm rather than unlocking the way towards Tours that are more often à *la Walkowiak*.

While this is a debate for the whole sport, France has a fundamental issue of its own to tackle too – ensuring that future generations of racers continue to emerge. 'The sport is dying at its base,' says Pierre Carrey. 'Society is very different nowadays. It's not rural any more, and that's where cycling's roots in France used to be. Cycling in France is in the midst of a huge crisis.' The prevailing impression within France is that road racing is an old man's sport. Its adherents not only know who Raymond Poulidor is, but may well have seen him race. Although the total membership of the French Cycling Federation reached 119,218 in 2017, a rise of more than 20 per cent since 2009, almost all of that growth has been in mountain biking and BMX. The resurgence of French competitiveness for the yellow jersey hasn't resulted in a significant lift in road racing, and half of the increase that has occurred has been among racers who are male and more than fifty years old, where the numbers are three times bigger than that for racers between seventeen and twenty-four.

As Carrey indicates, the sport has not followed the population shift into the cities, nor has it embraced the first- and second-generation children within them in the same way that it did the likes of Roger Walkowiak, Jean Stablinski and Nello Lauredi in the post-war years. There's no cycling equivalent of Kylian Mbappé, Paul Pogba or N'Golo Kanté, members of France's World Cup-winning football team whose parents hailed from West, Central or North Africa. As a result, there is a danger of the race becoming anachronistic, no longer representing what France is but what traditionalists and foreign lovers of the Tour believe it should be, with its starts and finishes in stunning locations, its marketing of the country as a destination increasingly pre-eminent, its distance from large sections of the French population continuing to widen.

The route of the 2019 Tour offered a significant sign that ASO is not only aware of this issue but is ready to halt this drift away from what should be one of the sport's key constituencies. After years of discussion, the twelfth stage running between Toulouse and Bagnères-de-Bigorre was set to start not in Place de la Capitole, the huge square with its magnificent town hall in the centre of '*la ville rose*', the pink city, but in Bagatelle, a disadvantaged neighbourhood to the west.

The association behind the initiative, Média Pitchounes, was established in that area in 2005 with the objective of running projects based around sport and journalism for local children aged between ten and eighteen – *pitchounes* is the Occitan word for kids. Every year it sends a small group to the Tour to produce written and televised reports on the race, working as a fully accredited part of the media corps. In 2010, the children initiated the 'Le Tour au pied des Tours' project (the Tour at the foot of the towers) with the aim lobbying ASO and politicians in Toulouse for a stage start or finish in the shadow of the tower blocks where they live in the kind of inner city area that the race has always skirted past.

'I want to say thanks to Média Pitchounes for its ten years of work, of hope, of conviction. Next to the traditional postcard of the landscapes of France, there will be one of these neighbourhoods. We're proud of that,' said Toulouse mayor Jean-Luc Moudenc when news of the Bagatelle start was confirmed in the official route launch in Paris in October 2018. Laurent Girard, founder of Média Pitchounes, admitted his hope is that the Tour will continue with the initiative every year.

'These neighbourhoods are part of the cities, we shouldn't exclude them,' he said, emphasising that it would allow cycling to establish itself in areas where it is still a marginal sport. 'In ten or twenty years, it'll be a guy from one of these neighbourhoods who will win the Tour de France.'

Perhaps this is the great yellow jersey story that the race is saving up for home fans and, just as importantly, for a sport that depends so much on its greatest event, although many, and not least Christian Prudhomme, will be hoping that the Tour complex and the long wait that has resulted from it doesn't extend that far. Yet, whether it's one year, ten or even fifty before a Frenchman rides into Paris in the *maillot jaune*, the Tour must continue to adapt, reacting to the perception that the race is not exciting enough, to the dangers facing both participants and spectators, to ensure that it remains embedded in the childhood of the French and 'part of their common secular and republican heritage,' as Richard Holt described it.

'It's funny to think that the yellow jersey is not really a victory, it's something much more important than that. It's a symbol, highlighting what this incredible event is all about,' says Thomas Voeckler. 'The Tour is part of the country's history. After the two world wars, it offered the French people a way of escaping thoughts of those great conflicts and the devastation they caused. It still has that ability to transform. When you're on the Tour, everyone smiles all the time, everyone is happy. It's a good moment for the country, something that's quite magical.'

LOUISON BOBET
TOUR DE FRANCE
1954

15

THE FUTURE FOR THE YELLOW JERSEY
Le Maillot Jaune

Joop Zoetemelk 1980

A YELLOW SKINSUIT, LYCRA JERSEY
AND SHORTS STITCHED TOGETHER FOR
AERODYNAMIC EFFECT

An Andre Gallard watercolour from the 1920s highlighting reverence for the yellow jersey

Forever the one to win

It was 1990, but I remember my first sight of the Tour de France and the yellow jersey with more clarity than most races that I've covered in the three decades since.

Travelling with my best friend Andy, our journey began with an odyssey, first by train from London to Plymouth, then by ferry to Santander. Our plan was vague, but focused around two objectives: to see the race in the Pyrenees and then ride north to return to England by boat from Cherbourg. After weaving our way into the rugged Cantabrian countryside to the south of the port city, we turned south-east and set a meandering course for the Col d'Aubisque.

Riding twelve-speed bikes fitted with creaking racks piled with tents, food and, it quickly became apparent, not enough water, we rode through the heat of the day, climbing one big pass to reach a town in the saddle between it and the next. It was the middle of the day, oppressively hot, and nothing was open. We rode on, climbing again, our bottles close to empty, until I had to stop. Then again, and again. Finally, I lay down and slept. Not enough water and too much sun had resulted in heat stroke. I've never been careless enough to forget its impact, how it left me in a zombie-like state, wondering how I'd ever turn my pedals again. But the next day, loaded with pasta and sloshing with water, I was revived, and on we went, across the high plateau through Rioja, Navarra and into the Pyrenees to reach France via the Larrau pass.

Checking the map, the Aubisque was too distant to reach before dark, so we set sights instead on the close and significantly smaller Col de Marie-Blanque, completely unaware of the final horror that lay in store for us on its western flank, with four kilometres of climbing at an average of 10 per cent. From there we swept down two or three kilometres to an area where the mountain flattens and broadens and pitched our tents in the roadside meadow, where we slugged down cheap red wine and watched as an encampment formed around us. After a night disrupted by headlights burning through the canvas, we woke to find ourselves in a mini-Glastonbury, marquees set up right at the edge of the roads within which Basque fans were getting very quickly sozzled, the entertainment initially provided by jittery livestock trampling empty tents that had been unknowingly erected where they grazed.

Once the publicity caravan had swept past, causing the cattle to stampede, there was a long wait until the first helicopters signalled the arrival of the riders. A group of thirteen led the way, including Johan Bruyneel, Pascal Simon, Steve Bauer, Davide Cassani and Dmitri Konyshev, who would end the day as the Tour's first Russian stage winner. Five minutes later, the peloton sped by, yellow jersey Claudio Chiappucci well protected by his Carrera teammates, Greg LeMond in the rainbow stripes of the world champion tracking him closely, Miguel Indurain and Sean Kelly among the easier faces to pick out in the pack. Several minutes later, two more groups passed, moving more slowly, and, finally, the back marker, Basque climber Javier Lukin, who would abandon before the finish in Pau. When he'd gone through the meadow started to empty, and we packed up too, starting our long ride north, tracking the race through the pages of *L'Équipe*, elated to read that LeMond had won.

'The single constant in each case is the presence of the yellow jersey'

Talk to any rider, team manager, Tour staff member, journalist or fan, and each will have a similar tale of the day that they first went to see the race or that it went through their town or village. The single constant in each case is the presence of the yellow jersey. Within a pack that's, for most, a blur of colour, its luminescence draws the eye and the loudest yells of encouragement. 'You are the reference for everyone, the focus of everyone's attention, whether that's other riders, or when you're in the bunch or when you're at the podium,' says Charly Mottet, *maillot jaune* for six days in 1987. 'That is especially the case for the public because all they're looking out for is the yellow jersey. He is the main reference point for them. When they see him pass, they say to themselves, "There goes the yellow jersey, that's what I've come for, I feel happy now." In essence, the role of the yellow jersey is to make everybody happy.'

From its muddled inception in 1919 and throughout most of the remainder of that century, the yellow jersey achieved that almost unquestionably. Initially disregarded by riders and the race organisation, its popularity and fame emerged from the fans at the roadside, for whom it delivered clarity of the competitors. Within a handful of years, the Tour and the *maillot jaune* became incontestably interlinked, the jersey the instantly recognisable symbol of a race that was a popular phenomenon, watched by millions at the roadside and followed by millions more in the press, comic books, box-office hits at the movies and, from the 1930s, on the radio, its wearers and, particularly, its winner lauded and royally rewarded for their exploits.

In the post-war years, the Tour's status and with it that of the yellow jersey climbed even higher as France enjoyed a sustained economic boom. Louison Bobet, Jacques Anquetil and, thanks to his relentless but vain pursuit of the *maillot jaune*, Raymond Poulidor, were national icons, as celebrated then as the players on the country's 2018

World Cup-winning football team have become. That momentum was sustained through the 1970s and 1980s as the race became more international in its reach, both within and beyond the peloton. However, this could only be maintained by keeping a lid down on the Pandora's box of doping. Once the charade of respectability was exposed and the extent of the deception was revealed, first by the Festina Affair and subsequently by a long string of scandals, the respect and adulation for the race's star performers gave way to suspicion and cynicism. While the Tour continued to thrill and delight, it had been tarnished, but not indelibly.

In spite of initial reticence, professional cycling has turned around and taken a lead in what is the necessary but inevitably vain quest for clean sport. More and better targeted anti-doping initiatives, combined with a gradual but very marked change of attitude within the peloton suggest that professional cycling has genuinely embraced a new, more ethically focused dynamic. Understandably, doubts remain, largely because fans refuse to – or simply cannot see – the impact of these changes, their scepticism confirmed by, for instance, the storm whipped up around Chris Froome's salbutamol case in the run-up to the 2018 Tour. But most would agree that bike racing is in a much healthier state than it was when I first strained to catch a sight of Claudio Chiappucci racing by in the yellow jersey in 1990.

Having covered most Tours since that edition, many of them plagued by scandal, what has stood out above all has been the race's resilience, the fact that it still delivers that same sense of wonder that was felt when it first ventured onto France's roads in the early years of the twentieth century. Sometimes that's been hard to sense from the cocoon of the pressroom, but it is impossible to miss when you're at the roadside, fans waving joyously at every race vehicle that passes, the anticipation steadily rising until the riders appear, the yellow jersey pointed out, cheered, his image captured on millions of smartphones as he breezes by, the experience highlighting the Tour's continuing popularity and how it remains synonymous with France.

Yet the race is at a crossroads. The way ahead should lead towards the ideal that Charly Mottet describes, to the perpetuation of the all-round feel-good factor the Tour generates. But there are concerns about security within and around the race, the predictability and even monotony of much of the action, and also the impression that the Tour is an institution that needs to modernise to stay relevant and appeal to more than just its diehard fans.

Of these, the first is the most difficult to deal with because the race's most defining facets, that France is its arena and that it is free and open to everyone, make it fundamentally vulnerable, although in this the Tour is far from unique because it is a reality that now affects so many aspects of society. As a consequence, a heavy security presence has become very visible. While this runs counter to the race's festival feel, it is indisputably necessary and, unfortunately, has become expected and accepted in so many parts of public life. ASO believe they found the right balance between security and maintaining the openness of the Tour.

Concurrently, security within the race has become a more complicated issue to resolve, in spite of appeals from the riders and race organisers for fans to give their support but refrain from becoming actors on the Tour stage. While not a new phenomenon, the behaviour of some spectators is presenting ASO with a dilemma – how to maintain the Tour's unique spirit but ensure that the riders aren't limited in their ability to perform. For the most part, the danger to them is essentially accidental, resulting from brainless acts like running alongside them or by fans turning their backs on the action to get a selfie with the yellow jersey as he passes. Putting out more barriers is a solution, but one that threatens the tradition of fans being able to get close to the riders. What's more, it is only practical at specific points given the Tour's scope. Investing fans with a greater role by following the vogue in Britain for 'Tour makers', volunteers who provide information at key points with the objective of ensuring spectator and rider security, would appear a better solution. ASO and the French police have also been quicker to take advantage of judicial and legislative options when dealing with more threatening conduct, such as the use of flares or in cases of assault. Essentially, though, the solution lies with fans themselves, in better awareness of what is acceptable.

As far as the race action goes, the question of how to unlock the grip that a team like Sky has on its rivals is perplexing and has no obvious answer – although the broadcasting company's withdrawal at the end of the 2019 might provide it if it results in the dispersal of its racing and backroom talent. Having got his wish with a reduction in team sizes

Steven Kruijswijk battles both l'Alpe d'Huez and the exuberant crowds in 2018

from nine to eight in 2018, Christian Prudhomme has continued to push for the suppression of earpieces and power meters as a further solution. The first of these proposals, although with the caveat that one-way communication from Radio Tour to the riders should be permitted in order to ensure security issues are relayed, appears more likely to succeed because it would augment the onus on tactical skill within the peloton, theoretically adding a dynamising, enlivening element of unpredictability.

Yet, as Chris Froome and other Grand Tour specialists have pointed out, the Tour director also needs to reflect on the organisation's route-planning strategy, which is built around a philosophy of keeping the contest for the yellow jersey bubbling for as long as possible, and often in recent years to the penultimate day. This sounds dramatic, but has had the opposite effect, ensuring that the contenders adopt a defensive mindset and are unwilling to take the kind of risks that they would at the Giro d'Italia or Vuelta a España, where there is less at stake. As a result of this, when it comes to the amount and quality of the action, it has lost ground on both of these races. With five summit finishes, the 2019 Tour marks a welcome shift away from this policy, assuming the riders respond to this shift in policy by being more aggressive and don't simply continue to stalk each incessantly.

As already noted, the route will also break new

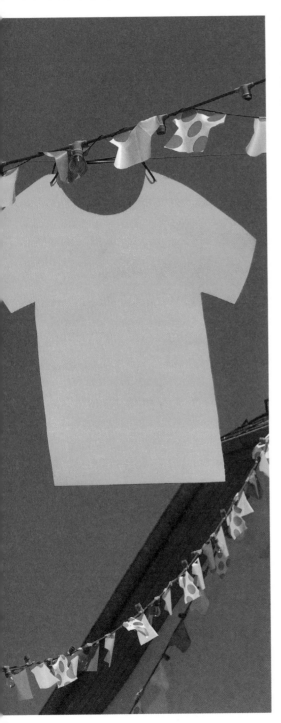

ground in France's inner cities. In time, this may prove to be an inspired move by a race that has, like a lot of institutions viewed with affection and sentimentality, failed to adapt to changes in the world around it and ends up losing its former attachments and relevance. Talking to many influential personalities associated with the Tour for this book, it was interesting, but in all honesty not totally surprising, to hear how many evoked memories of Raymond Poulidor when talking about the yellow jersey. 'To someone like me who was born in 1960, the yellow jersey is something that Raymond Poulidor never had,' Prudhomme, for instance, told me. Poupou's place in Tour legend is undisputable, but the tendency to hark back four, five and six decades is like looking through binoculars the wrong way, the distant past coming into focus rather than the future.

The Tour's attempt to reach a new generation of fans by going off-grid in Toulouse is a sign that this backward-looking perspective is changing, but nothing would do more to make the race look progressive than the re-introduction of the Tour Féminin. There may be economic and logistical reasons against it, but here too the Tour has to adopt the pioneering approach that initially characterised it as a ground-breaking sporting event. It needs to modernise, to be inclusive, to reach out to the widest audience, for the yellow jersey to become a shining light for equality. This is the way to re-establishing bike racing as a sport that is cherished rather than distrusted.

France needs it too, because it would provide two opportunities to win the yellow jersey. Home success is crucial because no matter how successful the Tour's foreign escapades are and how many fans it brings in from outside *l'Hexagone*, the race depends fundamentally on enthusiastic engagement by the French public, which has dwindled after so many doping affairs, the competition and distraction provided by other sports and, most importantly, the yellow jersey drought, which is now extraordinarily long given the regularity with which French riders claimed the prize up to the mid-1980s.

Writing about the *maillot jaune* soon after that, Jacques Goddet implored, 'Let's always love and respect this emblem that personifies man's strength of action within our times, just as it symbolises the champion's effort within our Tour.' By then the former Tour director, he had been affected profoundly by the unsavouriness that clouded the final days of Pedro Delgado's Tour success in 1988 and wanted to remind the cycling world that the yellow jersey designates the race's winner, but also stands apart, the iconic symbol of the Tour de France, belonging to no one, but to everyone at the same time, making and evoking memories. Over the decades since, its lustre has been tarnished again and again by scandals and lies, but it has endured because the Tour de France is so exceptional among the great sporting events on the international calendar, so unique in its setting and cultural significance, its demise as unthinkable as its leader's jersey changing colour.

Over the course of a year spent talking, reading, watching and writing about the *maillot jaune* and the Tour de France, I've realised that my strongest and favourite memories stem almost entirely from occasions when I've encountered it as a fan – spectating in a Pyrenean mountain meadow packed with visitors from across the world, standing on a kerb in Yorkshire as the peloton, cheered on by staggeringly huge crowds, whooshed by just centimetres away, taking my kids onto the Col de Menté and sharing their shock and delight as Garde Républicaine motorcyclists screeched past, announcing the arrival of the peloton lined out behind them. The prospect of new memories has also arrived with the announcement that the 2019 edition will race up the mountainside that dominates the view across the valley from where I now live in the Pyrenees. Tour fever is growing, conjuring thoughts of an unforgettable day, one that I, like millions of others will spend picnicking at the roadside with my family, friends and neighbours, still not quite believing that some of the world's best athletes will be racing past our homes, eagerly awaiting the peloton, its arrival inevitably leading to the question so preciently foreseen by Alphonse Baugé in 1919: 'Did you see the yellow jersey?'

JOOP ZOETEMELK
TOUR DE FRANCE
1979

INDEX – Page references in *italics* indicate images.

LIST OF ILLUSTRATIONS

BIBLIOGRAPHY

Bacon, Ellis, and Birinie, Lionel, *The Cycling Anthology* (Yellow Jersey, London)

Baugé, Alphonse, *Messieurs les Coureurs* (Librairie Garnier Frères, Paris, 1925)

Carrey, Pierre and Endrizzi, Luca, eds, *Secrets de Maillots Jaunes* (Hugo Sport, Paris, 2018)

Chany, Pierre, *La Fabuleuse Histoire du Cyclisme* (Éditions ODIL, Paris, 1975)

—— *La Fabuleuse Histoire du Tour de France* (Éditions de la Martinière, Paris, 1995)

De Mondenard, Jean-Pierre, *Les Grandes Premières du Tour de France* (Hugo Sport, Paris, 2013)

Diamant-Berger, Marcel, *Histoire du Tour de France* (Librairie Gedalge, Paris, 1959)

Droussent, Claude, *1000 Maillots du Tour de France* (Éditions de la Martinière, Paris, 2016)

—— *Maillots Jaunes* (Gründ, 2017)

Fignon, Laurent, *We Were Young and Carefree* (Yellow Jersey, London, 2010)

Fotheringham, William, *Merckx: Half Man, Half Bike*, (Yellow Jersey, London, 2012)

—— *Fallen Angel*, (Yellow Jersey, London, 2010)

—— *The Badger*, (Yellow Jersey, London, 2015)

Gault, Olivier, *1919, Le Tour le Plus Long* (Textes et Prétextes, 2002)

Guimard, Cyrille, *Dans Les Secrets du Tour de France* (Éditions J'ai Lu, Paris, 2012)

Laget, Serge, *100 Ans de Maillot Jaune* (Hugo Sport, Paris, 2018)

Laget, Serge, and Maignan, Claude, *Le Compte-Tours* (Ccommunication, Dreux, 2018)

Laget, Françoise & Serge, *Jours de Fête* (Éditions Chronique, Paris, 2012)

Moore, Richard, *Étape* (Harper Sport, London, 2014)

—— *Sky's the Limit* (Harper Sport, London, 2011)

—— *Slaying the Badger* (Yellow Jersey, London, 2011)

Pickering, Edward, *The Yellow Jersey Club* (Bantam Press, London, 2015)

Reed, Eric, *Selling the Yellow Jersey* (University of Chicago Press, Chicago, 2015)

Rey, Jean-Paul, *Eugène Christophe: Le Damné de la Route* (Éditions Cairn, Pau, 2013)

Wiggins, Bradley, *My Time*, (Yellow Jersey, London, 2013)

I also drew heavily on back issues of *L'Auto*, *L'Echo des Sports*, *Le Miroir des Sports*, *La Vie au Grand Air*, at the Bibliothèque Nationale de France in Paris, and of *Sporting Cyclist Coureur* held by the Veteran Cycle Club.

ACKNOWLEDGEMENTS

This book is dedicated to those who have worn and won the yellow jersey, and I would particularly like to thank those within this exclusive club who granted me their time and insight while researching this book, namely Steve Bauer, Chris Froome, Fernando Gaviria, Simon Gerrans, Thor Hushovd, Daryl Impey, Michelle Martin, Charly Mottet, Stuart O'Grady, Michael Rasmussen, Antonin Rolland, Peter Sagan, Andy Schleck, Geraint Thomas, Greg Van Avermaet, Cédric Vasseur, Richard Virenque and Thomas Voeckler.

I would like to express my gratitude to those who offered insight into specific issues relating to the yellow jersey, including Anna Barrero at Donnons des Elles au Vélo; activist, film-maker, racer and Trek's equality ambassador Kathryn Bertine; Team Sky manager Dave Brailsford; *Libération* correspondent Pierre Carrey; journalist and broadcaster Orla Chennaoui; Tour de France route director Thierry Gouvenou; UCI president David Lappartient; LCL director-general Michel Mathieu and directeur de réseau Guy Gnemmi; CCC team manager Jim Ochowicz; LottoNL-Visma team manager Richard Plugge; Team Sky directeur sportif Nicolas Portal; Tour de France director Christian Prudhomme; former Welcome To Yorkshire CEO Gary Verity, and Mitchelton-Scott directeur sportif Matt White.

I am also indebted to the press officers who managed to accommodate my interview requests, with particular thanks to Phoebe Haymes (CCC), Ian Taylor and George Solomon (Team Sky), and Fabrice Tiano (ASO). My appreciation also goes to Cyril Rolland Cycles Antonin Rolland in Jassans-Riottier for setting up my interview with his grandfather.

The design and photography add considerably to this book, and my thanks goes to Art Director Matt Broughton at Random House and snapper Seamus Masters for their immense contributions. The three of us also received considerable assistance from the staff at the Musée National du Sport in Nice, with special mention to Claire Vasdeboncoeur and Claude Boli. The staff at the Archives Départmentales in Tarbes were also immensely helpful in sourcing material from the Eugène Christophe collection that is held there.

Right from the start, Tim Broughton, my editor at Yellow Jersey Press, has been hugely supportive and enthusiastic about this book, guiding it in a pictorial direction which I hadn't envisaged and which enhances it hugely. My thanks also go to the rest of the team at Yellow Jersey – Anna Redman for directing the publicity side, production editor Phil Brown, Rowena Skelton-Wallace, Graeme Hall, Maddy Hartley, copyeditor Justine Taylor, and to proofreader Kati Nicholl.

Once again, I owe a large debt to my literary agent David Luxton and Rebecca Winfield at David Luxton Associates. A special word of thanks too for Ed and Evie Slateford, who have helped me through this period in a way for which I will be forever grateful.

Finally, my love and gratitude goes to my wife, Elaine, and my children, Lewis and Eleanor, who have given advice, support and, above all, much-needed distraction. *Bisous!*